WOW - Words of Wisdom

An insightful and pragmatic pearl of wisdom each day to keep your mind sharp and your heart focused on our loving God, Yahweh.

Copyright © 2018 by Apply Wisdom.com

Edition 1

All rights reserved. No part of this publication may be reproduced, distributed or transmitted in any form or by any means, without prior written permission.

Apply Wisdom.com

Words of Wisdom / Paperback -- 1st ed.
ISBN: 978-1-946373-08-3
$10.99 everywhere

Words of Wisdom / Daily Email
Free at www.Apply Wisdom.com

January 1st Apply Wisdom

"By wisdom a household will be built up, and by discernment it will prove firmly established. And by knowledge will the interior rooms be filled with all precious and pleasant things of value" (Proverbs 24:3-4).

Greetings from Apply Wisdom.com. We hope and pray that you will build up your house (family) with wisdom from above.

The bible is the ultimate source of wisdom and we hope that you read it, study it, and live in accordance with it. Our goal is that someday soon you will stop reading what we at ApplyWisdom.com have to say and only seek wisdom directly from the bible. But until then, we are happy to keep pointing you towards God and to help you to apply His loving and life-changing wisdom.

The Daily Words of Wisdom (WOW) series is designed to give you a daily, consumable, dose of Biblical Wisdom to help you be disciplined, discern the more important spiritual matters of the world, gain understanding, insight, righteousness, shrewdness, knowledge, and the ability to think for yourself.

January 2nd God's Name is Yahweh

"I am YHWH, and there is no one else. With the exception of me there is no God" (Isaiah 45:5).

God has a name. His name is יהוה. These four Hebrew letters are called the Tetragrammaton (which means "four letters") and are pronounced as Yahweh. Hebrew is read backwards so you can see for yourself that the first and third letters are different and the second and forth letters are the same. All scholars spell the Tetragrammaton YHWH but there is discussion between pronouncing YHWH as Yahweh, Jahweh, or Jehovah. Most languages in the world incorrectly pronounce YHWH as Jehovah, with three syllables, while YHWH in Hebrew is pronounced Yahweh, with only two syllables. It is rational to pronounce God's name the way His people pronounce it. Furthermore, it is not rational to add another syllable to anyone's name.

The best and most simple proof of the proper pronunciation of YHWH as Yahweh is the word Halleluiah. When you say or sing this word, which means "praise YHWH," you pronounce the last syllable as "Yah," using a "Y" as in the word "yellow" or "yesterday." The oral tradition of this word has carried on for centuries that the first syllable of YHWH is pronounced as "Yah."

Knowing and using God's name is essential. And for the rest of this devotional we are going to write God's name as Yahweh or YHWH.

January 3rd There is only One God and Yahweh is His Name

"That people may know that you, whose name is Yahweh, You alone are the Most High over all the earth" (Psalms 38:18).

There is only one God and Yahweh is His name. Yahweh, alone, is God Most High.

Jesus is not God, he is God's son. Buddha is not God, but was just a man. Satan is not God, but is a fallen angel. Allah is not God, but is a demon pretending to be God.... There is only one God and Yahweh is His name.

As true Christians, we are supposed to be motivated and inspired by love. But we can't be so loving that we accommodate or tolerate others and their false gods. This would be disloyal to the only true God, Yahweh. So be nice to others and love you neighbor. But don't forget that they serve and worship false and powerless pagan gods.

January 4th Glorify the Name of Yahweh

"Our Father which art in heaven, Hallowed be thy name. Thy kingdom come. Thy will be done in earth, as it is in heaven" Matthew 6:9-10.

It is very important to know and glorify the name of God. Today's scripture is the beginning of the example prayer which Jesus teaches his disciples to pray. Jesus states in one of the most memorized scriptures of all times the importance of the divine name.

Original text and manuscripts of the bible write YWHW (Yahweh) around 7000 times. Yet, to misdirect the prestige and honor of YHWH or to sell more bibles, many translations have written out the divine name. Likely you will find in the introduction of your bible an explanation that the editors replaced the original YHWH with "LORD" (all caps). What a shame that they have the audacity to write out the name of YHWH over seven thousand times.

It is impossible to glorify the name of God if you don't know it. Just think how ironic the above scripture is because of the millions and millions of faker Christians who daily or weekly say **"hallowed be thy name"** (King James Version) and yet don't even know that His name is Yahweh. Jesus said in the model prayer that His Father's name (Yahweh) must be glorified.

If you did not know that our Heavenly Father has a name, then congratulations on learning one of the first and most important facts of life. Your church leaders should have shown you this important fact years ago.

January 5th Don't misuse the name of Yahweh

"You must not take up the name of Yahweh your God in a worthless way, for YHWH will not leave the one unpunished who takes up his name in a worthless way" (Exodus 20:7).

Most faker Christians don't know that the 10 commandments are listed in two places in the bible: Exodus 20 and Deuteronomy 5. Most think that interpreting this commandment about misusing Yahweh's name means we should never say things like "oh my god," or in a moment of anger say "Jesus Christ!" Sure this is bad, and depending on the exact phrase, absolutely disrespectful. But the greater sin is when you profess to be a Christian but live a hypocritical and sinful life identical to the atheist next door. That is how you truly blaspheme the name of Yahweh.

Approximately 7000 times in our scriptures Yahweh is used. There is only one true God and Yahweh is his name. And this is a truth that every single human being who has ever lived will come to know (the hard way or the easy way). My prayer and hope is that you will accept this truth now and work to glorify the name of Yahweh from now on.

January 6th Love for Yahweh means Obedience

"For this is what the love of God means, that we observe his commandments; and yet his commandments are not burdensome" (1 John 5:3).

I can't stress obedience enough. The bible is so clear on this point. You must be obedient to what Yahweh says through the scriptures. You can't be a Christian and in a right standing with Yahweh if you are disobedient. Are you obedient to the bible?

January 7th Please Pay Attention to what God Commands

"This is what Yahweh has said, your Repurchaser, the Holy One of Israel: "I, YHWH, am your God, the One teaching you to benefit [yourself], the One causing you to tread in the way in which you should walk. O if only you would actually pay attention to my commandments! Then your peace would become just like a river, and your righteousness like the waves of the sea." (Isaiah 48:17-18)

The most amazing part of this scripture is the tone that our loving God Yahweh uses to implore us to be obedient. As the creator of life, it certainly would be His right to be forceful and command us into obedience. Yet His approach is loving and kind. The scripture basically says "the answers are all there. All you must do is read the bible and be obedient. If you were obedient then you would be protected from so many of the stresses and pain you currently are suffering. Don't be so self-righteous and think you are smarter than God. Pay attention to what He say. Please. Be obedient. Yahweh's ways are best. Yahweh is as close to you as you want Him to be."

January 8th Do you follow the Churches Hypocrisy or do you follow Biblical Truth

"In reply he [Jesus] said to them: "Why is it YOU also overstep the commandment of God because of YOUR tradition" (Matthew 15:3)?

People should follow Biblical truth, not the hypocrisy and traditions of their church. But even before and during the times of Jesus, people were more obedient to their priests than to their Creator. How sad.

We owe our life to the one true God, Yahweh. Lovingly, He has made Himself very known to us through His Scriptures. It is our duty and pleasure to read, study, and live our lives in accordance with the truths and principles of these scriptures.

Sadly, the ancient church ignored many Biblical truths and continues today to teach goodhearted people to follow their man-made traditions. What is worse is that so many of these man-made traditions are in direct violation of scripture.

Knowing and being obedient to Biblical truth is a matter of life and death, everlasting life or judgment. You should be more concerned with gaining the approval of God than your minister or priest.

Do you follow the Church's Hypocrisy, False Traditions or Lies…….or do you follow Biblical Truth?

January 9th Once Saved not Always Saved

"Consequently, my beloved ones, in the way that YOU have always obeyed, not during my presence only, but now much more readily during my absence, keep working out YOUR own salvation with fear and trembling" (Philippians 2:12).

The last words of today's scripture **"keep working out your salvation with fear and trembling"** blow out of the water any argument an immature Christian may use to try to tell you that once you are saved you are always saved. In this context, "saved" is an ambiguous and misused word. It would be much better to describe yourself with words like obedient and loving. Because if we are obedient and loving, will be afraid to sin, afraid to let Yahweh down. It is possible for anyone who once loved God to fall into sin and not make it into the Kingdom of God. This should make us afraid and encourage us to work harder. Jesus even says in Matthew 7:21 that **"not everyone saying to me, 'Lord, Lord,' will enter into the kingdom of the heavens."** So keep on working out your salvation with a fear of letting Yahweh down and a determination to be more righteous and holy.

January 10th Fear God, not Man

"The conclusion of the matter, everything having been heard, is: Fear the [true] God and keep his commandments. For this is the whole [obligation] of man" (Ecclesiastes 12:13).

As true Christians, we are supposed to fear God. This fear for God is more like respect… a respect for who He is and how powerful and loving He is. Ultimately, we love Him so much that we fear ever letting Him down. And so this fear of letting Him down leads us towards obedience, obedience to His bible.

The second implication of "Fearing God" is that we don't fear man. Jesus says in John 5:41 that **"I don't accept praise from man."** This is because men are selfish and change opinions like the wind. A perfect example is when the same people who were singing "hosanna in the highest"[1] when Jesus arrived to Jerusalem during what the church calls "Psalm Sunday" were a week later yelling "crucify him."[2] Few men are good,

---

[1] Matthew 21:9
[2] Matthew 27:22

but most are selfish and could care less about God. So don't accept their praise or approval.

Do you fear letting Yahweh down? And does this fear inspire you to be obedient to what He says?

January 11th Don't Drift Away from God

"That is why it is necessary for us to pay more than the usual attention to the things we have heard, so that we never drift away" (Hebrews 2:1).

It is too easy to drift away from biblical teachings. If you follow the people on your left and right at church then you will quickly drift. If you follow your spiritual leaders, you will quickly drift. If you follow the leaders of the world, the movie and music stars, the sports heroes, the "role models," or the lifestyle trends of this world then you are going to drift.

Obedience to Biblical principles helps you drift towards God. Please don't drift away from our loving God. Yahweh is always as near to you as you want Him to be.

January 12th You Can't be Friends with God and Friends with the World

"Adulteresses, do YOU not know that the friendship with the world is enmity with God? Whoever, therefore, wants to be a friend of the world constitutes himself an enemy of God" (James 4:4).

Today's scripture is very profound. Being friends with the world means being an enemy of God. Wow. We would never want to be an enemy of God. So what does this mean on a practical level? It means that we should not treasure the things of this world like wealth, money, power, fame. We must treasure love, specifically love for Yahweh God. We must love people and use things, not love things and use people. What do you treasure? Value? Love? Seek?

January 13th Don't forget that there is a War going on

"Put on the complete suit of armor from God that YOU may be able to stand firm against the [methods] of the Devil; because we have a wrestling, not against blood and flesh, but against the governments, against the authorities, against the world rulers of this darkness, against the wicked spirit forces in the heavenly places" Ephesians 6:11-12.

It is easy to forget that there are many wars raging all over the world when your neighborhood is safe and quiet. But even though your neighborhood may be safe and quiet, free from a physical war, there is always a spiritual war rampant in the background. This spiritual war is between Yahweh God and His followers and Satan and the forces of evil. We are warned in Ephesians that our real struggle is against wicked spirit forces. So please wake up to the spiritual warfare being wages against your faith in God and love for Yahweh.

In a war zone, you must be deliberate about everything you do. You must always maintain security. You can never become complacent. You should approach your spiritual life in the same manner: deliberately, maintaining spiritual security, never becoming complacent. Never forget that Satan wants to pull you away from Yahweh and he will use any direct or indirect tactics available.

January 14th The world is controlled by Satan

"We know we originate with God, but the whole world is lying in the [power of the] wicked one" (1 John 5:19).

This world is lying in the power of the evil one. This truth is one which many do not want to accept. Of course, YHWH is in charge and sovereign and all capable. But Satan runs the world right now. It only takes a minute to see that human governments have failed man, and that starvation, death, sin, and selfishness abound. Is that a reflection of our holy God of love? No way.

The deceiver is described as the one misleading the entire earth. Revelations 12:9 **So down the great dragon was hurled, the original serpent, the one called Devil and Satan, who is misleading the entire inhabited earth; he was hurled down to the earth, and his angels were hurled down with him.**

The only answer to the problems of this world is God's Kingdom, which will set it all straight again. This is why Jesus said in Matthew 9: 9-10 **"YOU must pray, then, this way: 'Our Father in the heavens, let your name be sanctified. Let your kingdom come. Let**

your will take place, as in heaven, also upon earth." Nothing short of YHWH's kingdom coming will end the evil effects of Satan upon the current system of things.

January 15th Satan kills men, is a liar and rejoices in suffering

"YOU are from YOUR father the Devil, and YOU wish to do the desires of YOUR father. That one was a manslayer when he began, and he did not stand fast in the truth, because truth is not in him. When he speaks the lie, he speaks according to his own disposition, because he is a liar and the father of [the lie]" (John 8:44).

Satan is a man killer and the father of the lie. We see this truth when Jesus is righteously shredding to pieces the hypocritical religious leaders of his time. There is nothing cool about evil. There is nothing fun about evil. Satan loves to pull people away from Yahweh and will use any tactic available.

Satan loves to kill men, literally and spiritually. As Christians we should never kill or want to kill. That is why a Christian shouldn't and couldn't waste his time playing violent video games or participating in a war to support a secular government.

Satan's favorite technique is to lie. He loves teaching lies to the world. As Christians we never want to be like the devil by lying. When you lie, you are honoring the father of lies rather than your loving God, Yahweh.

Be careful out there, Satan hates man and wants to kill us and teach us lies.

January 16th   Don't be Surprised by Satan's Methods

"that we may not be overreached by Satan, for we are not ignorant of his designs" (2 Corinthians 2:11).

The Bible encourages us to not be ignorant of Satan's methods. Satan uses as many methods for pulling people away from worshiping Yahweh God as he can. Satan has many followers (also fallen angels who ignored their assigned role in heaven) and we usually call them demons. Satan frequently uses these subordinate followers (demons) to torment, mislead, and pull people away from Yahweh. In Genesis 6:1-5 we read about angels who came down to earth right before the time of the flood to take wives from the daughter of men. Jesus casts out demons in several places in the gospels (Matthew 8:16, Matthew 12:22, Matthew 17:18.) In the bible, we read many stories about Satan hurting people through demon possession.

Satan has it easier these days to mislead people because sin is everywhere. Let us just take two simple examples: Pornography and Materialism. Not long ago, it was difficult to get pornography. Today, people are just a click away from pornographic material via the internet. Not long ago, to purchase something expensive you had to save for a long time then pay it in cash or in trade. Today, the world tells you: "buy today and pay tomorrow." Credits and credit cards are the most used payment methods in this materialistic world and we do not need to tell you that materialism is a dangerous trap.

Are you aware of the methods Satan uses to pull you away from God?

January 17th Ministers, priest, and prophets are under Satan's influence.

"And no wonder, for Satan himself keeps transforming himself into an angel of light. It is therefore nothing great if his ministers also keep transforming themselves into ministers of righteousness. But their end shall be according to their works" (2 Corinthians 11:14-15).

Satan and his demons are very successful when they transform themselves into false angels and ministers. This is an essential scripture for understanding the lies that your church has been telling you throughout your entire life.

Satan and his subordinate demons have pretended to be ministers and priests to integrate false and unbiblical traditions and doctrine into the church. Because 2 Corinthians 11:14-15 predicts and warns us of this deception, you should not be surprised that your church teaches unbiblical traditions and doctrine.

Satan and his subordinate demons have also pretended to be ministers and priests to start false religions and pull others away from the only True God. Because 2

Corinthians 11:14-15 predicts and warns us of this deception, you should not be surprised to see that there are so many false religions which worship false gods.

Satan and his subordinate demons have also pretended to be ministers and priests to <u>mislead and hurt people</u>. Because 2 Corinthians 11:14-15 predicts and warns us of this deception, you should not be surprised when priests and ministers do and teach evil things.

Do you see the pattern? Never forget: the deceiver hates Yahweh God and wants to steal kill and destroy: John 10:10 **"The thief does not come unless it is to steal and slay and destroy. I [Jesus] have come that they might have life and might have it in abundance."**

<u>January 18th Satan will Tickle Your Ears and tell you the Lies You Want to Hear</u>

"For there will be a period of time when they will not put up with the healthful teaching, but, in accord with their own desires, they will accumulate teachers for themselves to have their ears tickled; and they will turn their ears away from the truth, whereas they will be turned aside to false stories" (2 Timothy 4:3-4).

Satan has bombarded the world with many false religions and denominations which tell people what they want to hear:

- God has many forms (No he doesn't. There is only one God and Yahweh is His name)

- We are all going to heaven (Wrong. Only a very few are going to heaven. Most aren't even going to make it into the Kingdom of God. Most don't even know what the Kingdom of God actually is)
- There are many paths to the same destination (There are two destinations: Everlasting Life or Destruction. And sadly, the road to destruction is very large)
- Just be a good person and you will make it (This is wishful thinking. Jesus will say to many that he never knew them)
- Homosexual marriage is OK (Homosexuality is forbidden: Leviticus 20:13. Marriage is between a man and woman.)

Sadly, we could list hundreds of ways that most Ministers and Priests "tickle the ears" of the people who attend their church and pay their salaries.

The reason so many don't see the truth is that they follow the lies and false teachings of their ministers who are misled by satan and his demons. Satan and his demons love to mislead Ministers and Priest and get them to teach false traditions and doctrine.

Do you follow Biblical Truth or do you go to "church" at a place which tickles your ears?

January 19th Good -vs- Bad

"He that is not on my side is against me, and he that does not gather with me scatters" (Matthew 12:30).

There are only two sides: The Good Side or the Bad Side.

On the "Good Side" you have Yahweh, His angels, and His worshipers. Yahweh has given us life, purpose, and direction through His scriptures. His worshipers are recognized by obedience to the Bible and are known for their love.

On the "Bad Side" you have the devil, demons, and those they have deceived. Satan is misleading the entire world to pull people away from Yahweh. Those who worship Satan or are deceived by him are atheists, agonistics, followers of false gods and false religions, or believers of doctrines which violate biblical truth.

Whose side are you on? Are you sure about that?

January 20th All Men have Sinned, but most keep Sinning

"For all have sinned and fall short of the glory of God (Romans 3:23).

All humans have sinned and fallen short of the glory of God. Yes, this scripture applies to all, men and woman. But for the next week we are going to discuss the sinfulness of men and how this sinfulness has come to affect the modern family and the world.

Despite all men having sinned, some men do their best to honor YHWH with every aspect of their lives. These men are the rare exceptions, because the overwhelming majority of men on this planet are silly, selfish, knuckle-headed boys who continue to hurt loved ones and make this world more evil.

Although women are not perfect either, they are mostly the victims. Men and their sinfulness have caused billions to suffer. This should not be.

January 21st Lack of Male Leadership has Destroyed the Family

"But I want YOU to know that the head of every man is the Christ; in turn the head of a woman is the man; in turn the head of the Christ is God (1 Corinthians 11:3).

Yahweh designed the family before He designed the church and worship. Yahweh designed men to be the head of the household and to be the leaders of the family.

A man is the head of the family. Yahweh holds men responsible for their role as leaders. Sadly, men have become lethargic and have let women usurp their God given leadership role. This makes a disharmony in the family, a reverse leadership disharmony. Rather than providing Godly leadership under which the wife is free to flourish, men let their wives lead, men let their wives work, and men let their wives provide. All of this has consequences:

1. Wives want to or must work outside the home.
2. Kids are raised by strangers at schools or daycare.

3. Families drift away from Yahweh.

January 22nd Men must Provide for their Families

"Certainly if anyone does not provide for those who are his own, and especially for those who are members of his household, he has disowned the faith and is worse than a person without faith" (1 Timothy 5:8).

Yahweh requires men to provide for their families. What this means is that all the dead-beat husbands out there who do not work to provide for their families or who make their wives work to provide for the families are worse than unbelievers. Yahweh places great importance upon accepting your role in life and the woman's role is not to be the provider. Sadly, this "weak husband" dysfunction is so normal that men who act like boys have become the standard, not the exception. As a result of sinful men and their pathetic leadership, the biblical family rarely exists.

Men, do you provide for your family in physical, fiscal, and spiritual ways?

January 23rd   Husbands, are your prayers hindered?

"YOU husbands, continue dwelling in like manner with them according to knowledge, assigning them honor as to a weaker vessel, the feminine one, since YOU are also heirs with them of the undeserved favor of life, in order for YOUR prayers not to be hindered" (1 Peter 3: 7).

Men, if you don't love your fragile wives well you will not have the approval of Yahweh and your prayers will be hindered.

Rather than providing Godly leadership under which the wife is free to flourish, men have neglected their "beloved" wives and lost the favor and attention of God Almighty.

This scripture is great because it reminds all of us that Yahweh's love is undeserved (grace). Yet, it further reminds men that if they want their prayers not to be hindered, they need to treat their wives well.

Men, do you honor your wife?

Women, does your husband honor you?

January 24th Consequences of Sexual Sin

"You heard that it was said: 'You must not commit adultery.' But I say to you that everyone who keeps on looking at a woman so as to have a passion for her has already committed adultery with her in his heart" (Matthew 5:27-28).

Evil men and their sexual sin cause so much pain:

1. Evil men and their sexual sin destroy the family. Statistics about divorce get worse and worse every year. Stupid and disloyal men seek pleasure through an immoral affair. Evil men who love themselves more than Yahweh or their spouse or children want to "upgrade" their wives for a younger woman and in doing so kill the spirit of

their wives and family. Single mothers now have to get a job to pay the bills since their idiot husbands no longer provide for them. Rather than serving, loving, and raising children, the single mother must work for the rest of her life to survive.

2. Evil men and their sexual sin destroy women: When a selfish man treats a woman terribly it leaves a life-long scar. Men and their evil lusts for skinnier, younger woman has caused millions of women to hurt themselves and be completely unnatural in their efforts to be skinnier and look younger.

3. Evil men and their sexual sin destroy peoples' sense of right and wrong. Because men are evil, sex sells. Men love to look at sinfulness which has caused women to do unladylike things and wear unladylike clothes to get men's attention. Sex is now a part of every advertisement, movie, magazine and commercial. Most people have become so familiar with this sinful sexuality that they don't even notice that their TV commercial is as perverted as pornography.

Jesus reminds us that we are not even to keep on looking at a woman who is not your wife. Sadly, Satan has succeeded at making men sexually perverted and adulterers.

January 25th You can't serve Two Masters.

"No one can slave for two masters; for either he will hate the one and love the other, or he will stick to the one and despise the other. YOUcannot slave for God and for Riches" (Matthew 6:24).

Financial Sin has destroyed the world. Because sinful men love things and use people, rather than love people and use things, they spend all their lives worshiping money.

Because men worship money, not Yahweh, they have drifted away from YHWH, destroyed the family, and ruined the earth.

1. Worshiping money makes silly men drift away from Yahweh: Because sinful men love themselves and want to be happy, they spend their time pursuing and worshiping things, possessions, and temporary happiness, rather than Yahweh the author of life and source of eternal happiness.

2. Worshiping money destroys the family: Because men are selfish, they believe the family should make them happy. Rather than investing in the family, they suck the life and joy out of their family. And when they realize that they are not happy, they leave their family in pursuit of freedom or of another family, which they think will make them happy. This sinful mindset destroys the biblical institution of the family and leaves so many devastated children and women in its wake.

3. Worshiping money ruins the earth. If someone loves Yahweh with their all and loves their neighbor as themselves then they are not going to pollute the earth. Factories, power plants, ozone destroyers, vehicle smog, and oil spills are because men want to be rich more than they want to enjoy the earth forever. Global warming is nothing more than a symptom of man worshiping his real god, money.

Do you worship money or Yahweh? Do you spend more time seeking money or Yahweh?

January 26th Keep your Heart Pure

"More than all else that is to be guarded, safeguard your heart, for out of it are the sources of life" (Proverbs 4:23).

Guard your heart by staying pure. One of the ways to stay pure is to not be influences by the entertainment of this world. During the next week we are going to discuss worldly entertainment and how it can push us towards or pull us away from our Heavenly Father. Let's start today with what we read....

Almost all major magazines out there are trash. Let me clarify: in America, many are evil, most are trash. They are full of gossip, sex, lies, materialism. The women and men who pose half naked on the covers of your magazines are no better than prostitutes. They will wear anything or endorse anything for money. Fashion magazines sold to millions of women each month are an amazingly effective tool of the devil to cause lust of the eyes, physical insecurity, pervert YHWH's plan for marriage and sexuality, smash consciousness, and ruin marriages. Trashy tabloids and gossip and humanistic feel good magazines encourage you to love the world more than God and steer you off course. Guard your conscious by not wasting your time with that trash.

Books: What we read is just as important as what we see. Don't think for a second that a 300 page book which has sold millions of copies is any less an instrument of Satan than a trashy magazine. Reading anything which pulls you away from the living God is not good.

Wasting our precious time reading things which glamorize materialism and the rich and famous (who are 100% all faker Christians or not Christians at all) is not good. Honoring God with what we see and read is good.

Junk **in** will mean junk **out**. But good **in** can mean good **out**.

<u>January 27th Don't Watch Stupid TV or Movies</u>

"Jesus said to them: "If YOU were blind, YOU would have no sin. But now YOU say, 'We see.' YOUR sin remains" (John 9:41).

It is so easy to sin with your eyes…

Movies: The entertainment of this world is mostly ugly and defiled and has led so many people off the path of biblical cleanliness. Wake Up. If you watch R rated (R=Restricted for adults only) movies then you are a faker Christian. Shame on you. The sex and violence of

R rated movies burn your consciousness and rip you away from your Holy Father. What about PG-13 (Parental Guidance required for kids under 13) movies? Do you think that 50% less violence or sex or inappropriate innuendos make it OK for you to watch? Your conscious is already burned and you are already ripped away from your Holy Father in heaven.

PG and G (Parental Guidance and General) rated movies can be just as bad and once you have a YHWH trained conscious, you will have a hard time watching any movies or TV shows available through Satan's film and TV industry.

What you probably don't see, because your eyes are not trained to see the truth, is that a constantly increasing number of kid's movies teach you that witchcraft and spiritualism is cool. These practices are strictly forbidden in the scriptures. Friendly ghosts and vampires and materialism and gossip and homosexuality have become cool.

Scary movies no longer scare people because their hearts are so calloused. Most of the Romance movies now a day contain fornication (premarital or extramarital sex) which the scriptures forbid and you think it was a sweet and romantic movie.

Not all movies are bad. Many movies are wonderfully fun or educational or entertaining. A true Christian has to be very deliberate about guarding their heart and eyes and conscious when watching movies.

<u>Television</u> is an amazing source of filth and evil. Faker Christians love to watch Satan's television. Even if you

are watching something good and clean it won't surprise anyone if the first commercial is for condoms, beer, herpes medicine, a sexually explicit soap opera, or a shampoo brand demonstrating their product with half naked models. How sad it is that men are so sinful and so easily distracted by skin. The effects of men and their sexual sin is evident the second you turn on the television. Satan wants to place before you anything he can to pull you away from Yahweh. A real Christian has to be very deliberate about guarding their heart and eyes and conscious when watching TV.

True Christians want to honor God, even at the expense of not being "cool" or "in." True Christians want to honor God by rejecting all kind of unwholesome entertainment, abhorring what is wicked and consistently turning away from what is bad.

January 28th   What you do on the Internet is a Reflection of Your Heart

"Make my eyes pass on from seeing what is worthless; Preserve me alive in your own way" Psalm 119:37.

Consider the internet a reflection of your heart. If you have a pure heart, you use it for shopping, learning, research, coordinating directions, weather, e-mail. If you have no conscious, then you look at evil things. If you have no peace in life and are empty inside, you use the internet for distraction by using your social networking site every hour, playing video games, checking your e-mail 10 times a day, and catching up on gossip. If your existence is more exciting online than in reality you have a sad life and really need make changes so as to live it in accordance with biblical principles.

January 29th Pornography is Evil

"But I say to YOU that everyone that keeps on looking at a woman so as to have a passion for her has already committed adultery with her in his heart" (Matthew 5:28).

Pornography is another very popular form of entertainment, one which comes directly from Satan himself. Many faker Christian leaders love porn. When you look at the statistics about porn there is no difference between the number of atheists who look at porn and the number of ministers or regular church attenders who also look at porn. "63% of pastors surveyed confirm that they are struggling with sexual addiction or sexual compulsion including, but not limited to, the use of pornography, compulsive masturbation, or other secret sexual activity."[3] What a shame.

- Men are 543% *more* likely to look at porn than females.
- Regular church attenders are 26% *less* likely to look at porn than non-attenders, but those self-identified as "fundamentalists" are 91% *more* likely to look at porn.[4]

---

[3] http://www.expastors.com/how-many-pastors-are-addicted-to-porn-the-stats-are-surprising/
[4] http://www.covenanteyes.com/2013/02/19/pornography-statistics/

What a slap in God's face. The Bible challenges us in Proverbs 6:27 to not be burned by the fire of immorality: **can a man rake together fire into his bosom and yet his very garments not be burned?** If you harden your heart to sexual images then you are going to miss the real love and real intimacy that you already have or that Yahweh already has planned for you. Flee from sexual immorality. If you play with fire, you are going to get burned. If you look at porn then you can't be a Christian. A Christian loves Yahweh. Yahweh hates detestable things like pornography. The reason you can't stop looking at pornography is that you don't love YHWH enough. You are a faker.

<u>January 30th   Unbiblical and Abnormal Sexual Relationships</u>

Faker Christians tolerate <u>homosexuality</u> and other <u>abnormal, unbiblical sexual relationships</u>. Faker Christians tell others that living against biblical standards is acceptable. Some leaders in your church are blatant fornicators or tolerate other Christians who are living in sin, fornicating, or practicing adultery. Some even go so far as to say that homosexuals can have the same rights and privileges in marriages.

Homosexuality is detestable to Yahweh. (Leviticus 20:13) **And when a man lies down with a male the same as one lies down with a woman, both of them have done a detestable thing. They should be put to death without fail. Their own blood is upon them.** Yahweh states several times in the Bible that homosexuality is a sin. Leviticus 18:22 and 1 Corinthians 6:9 are scriptures which say that homosexuality is detestable and that practicing homosexuals will not inherit the kingdom of God.

We cannot follow the second commandment at the expense of the first commandment. Jesus tells us in Mark 12:31 that the second most important commandment is **"Love your neighbor as yourself."** So love is always in order. But a sentence before that Jesus gives us the greatest commandment: **"you must love Yahweh your God with your whole heart and with your whole soul and with your whole mind and with your whole strength."** We are told to put God first. That means we need to honor God and follow His rules. His rules, as outlined in His word, clearly state that sexual misconduct is a sin. Yes, we need to love others. But Yahweh's standards must be kept. Yahweh must always be first.

90% of homosexual behavior is learned. This is because it is cool to be homosexual these days. Women don't scream and gawk and chatter and use their hands and wrists as much as gay men. This overly flamboyant and stupid behavior is learned, and is not a result of excessive estrogen. They flaunt their sinfulness in your face and are obsessed with sex and carnal desires, making those who genuinely have biological hormone disorders look bad.

Our hearts need to go out to those with genuine biological problems who, from birth, have always been attracted to those of the same sex. This is not part of God's plan just as being born with a disease or a handicap is not part of His plan. But sexuality is 1% of who we are, not 99% of who we are. So get over it. Homosexuality is a sin. A homosexual should never have sex. But guess what? Heterosexual sex outside of marriage is also a sin. So a heterosexual also has to conquer his sexual desires… or at least until the day he or she is married and able to express these desires within the confines of a biblical marriage. Many have to wait 30 or 40 years to find their wife or husband. Some never do. Straight or homosexual, you simply can't have sex until you are married. That means never for Homosexuals and perhaps after decades of waiting for a Heterosexual.

Honor God with your body and be obedient to biblical rules for sexuality.

January 31st   Those who Love God must Hate Evilness

"O YOU lovers of Yahweh, hate what is bad" (Psalm 97:10).

True Christians must hate what is evil….to include evil entertainment. If you love movies and books and magazines which don't honor Yahweh, innuendos, coarse joking, magic, and sorcery then your choice of entertainment clearly shows that you are a part of this world and therefore aren't a real Christian.

If you hate evil, you will avoid evil. If you don't hate evil, you will play with it.

If you claim to be a Christian but keep seeking comfort from the evil forms of worldly entertainment, you are no better than a dog returning to his vomit (2 Peter 2: 22): **The saying of the true proverb has happened to** them: "**The dog has returned to its own vomit, and the sow that was bathed to rolling in the mire.**"

Do you love Yahweh and hate what is evil? Or do you love bad things and dishonor Yahweh?

February 1st Wasting too much Time

"**That YOU may make sure of the more important things, so that YOU may be flawless and not be stumbling others up to the day of Christ**" (Philippians 1:10).

Too often people waste time and have bad priorities. How long you spend being entertainment is also as important as how you are entertained.

A good thing, in excess, can quickly turn into a bad thing. For example, e-mail and sharing pictures and staying connected with family is good up to the point when you go crazy if you don't have a WIFI connection and can't get onto your social networking site 10 times a day. Helping your kids develop hobbies is important up to the point when parents run themselves crazy. Video games can be fun and diverting. But violent video games are absolutely against Yahweh's principles of (1) guarding one's heart and (2) sacrificially loving one another. Some do fitness for hours every day just to get that perfect physique to get attention or maintain self-esteem. This is wrong. Yes, our bodies do require physical strength and health. But we must spend a few hours a week, not each day, doing physical activities. In and of themselves, sports aren't bad. But it is such a shame that most men in Europe and the Americas know every statistic for their favorite football player or golfer but they don't have 3 scriptures memorized. Sports clothing is now tighter and more revealing than ever. What happened to Christian modesty and embarrassment? Go to a professional sports event and you can feel the collective energy of ignorant men worshiping the heroes of their soon to be forgotten lives. If only they would direct 10% of the passion they have for their favorite team towards learning more about and honoring their Grand Creator.

What do you spend your time doing and what does that say about your relationship with God?

Feb. 2nd God hates You if You Love Violence

"Yahweh himself examines the righteous one as well as the wicked one, and anyone loving violence His soul certainly hates" (Psalm 11:5).

Wow. What a strong scripture. It is not good if you love violence, violent movies, violent hobbies, or violent video games. Please think about this and make changes if necessary. It would be terrible to keep loving violence and separate yourself from the love of Yahweh.

February 3rd Don't Misuse Beverages, Chemicals & Food

"What! Do YOU not know that the body of YOU people is [the] temple of the holy spirit within YOU,

which YOU have from God? Also, YOU do not belong to yourselves, for YOU were bought with a price. By all means, glorify God in the body of YOU people" (1 Corinthians 6:19-20)

Our bodies are temples of holy spirit and we must honor and glorify God with our bodies. Inappropriate use of beverages, chemicals, and food are common forms of recreation which do not honor Yahweh and hurt the temples of our bodies.

Furthermore, we are told to offer our bodies as living sacrifices: **"Consequently I entreat YOU by the compassions of God, brothers, to present YOUR bodies a sacrifice living, holy, acceptable to God, a sacred service with YOUR power of reason. And quit being fashioned after this system of things, but be transformed by making YOUR mind over, that YOU may prove to yourselves the good and acceptable and perfect will of God"** (Romans 12:1-2). Being a living sacrifice means that we offer ourselves, our lives, our bodies, and our health to God. If we are unhealthy and mistreat our bodies then we can't properly worship and love Yahweh and are less effective or useless in His service.

Do you honor and take care of your body?

February 4th Drink, but don't Misuse Alcohol

All my Baptists associates imply that drinking alcohol is a reprehensible sin despite the fact that the bible makes countless references to the blessings of drinking wine. Jesus was called **"gluttonous"** and **"given to**

drinking wine" (Matthew 11:19) so we can assume that he drank. We know that Jesus was sinless so drinking wine is not a sin. Self-righteous religious people were only trying to slander Jesus. In John 2: 1-11 we see at the marriage feast that Jesus did not just change water into wine, he changed it into **"fine wine."** This means Jesus knew the difference between quality and worthless wine.

Drunkenness is a sin. This is obvious. Let's look at the beginning of Isaiah for some strong scriptures about how YHWH sees drunkenness. YHWH warns us not to become drunks. (Isaiah 5:11) **Woe to those who are getting up early in the morning that they may seek just intoxicating liquor, who are lingering till late in the evening darkness so that wine itself inflames them!**

YHWH warns us not to take pride in drinking too much. (Isaiah 5:22) **Woe to those who are mighty in drinking wine, and to the men with vital energy for mixing intoxicating liquor.** It is interesting how YHWH uses the expression men with vital energy for mixing intoxicating liquor. That, among many things, is a reference to bar tenders. And of course that makes sense, because no true Christian would waste his life with a job where he served liquor to people (sad drunks at the local pub or glamorous movie stars at the en-vogue club) for money. Shame on you if you are a bar tender or drink too much or are a drunk or brag about your drinking tolerance or your ability to mix liquors. Those jobs and characteristics do not honor Yahweh.

February 5th Smoking is a Sin

Smoking is a sin and if you smoke you are a faker Christian. Period. Don't roll your eyes. How gross it is to be walking through the doors of your church right before it starts and all the smokers are getting their last hit of nicotine before they go inside. You can't smoke a cigarette, which we all know kills you, and claim to be honoring the Holy Spirit within your body. Jesus tells us that the second most important commandment is to love our neighbor. (Mark 12:31) **The second is this, 'You must love your neighbor as yourself.' There is no other commandment greater than these."** Second hand smoke is proven to be worse than first hand smoke because it doesn't have a filter. How can you love your neighbor if you don't care about his lungs? What about parents who smoke in front of their kids and subject them to second hand smoke all day long?

To the faker Christian who smokes and pretends to follow the bible, please stop making Christians look bad. Please honor your body, a gift from God, by not polluting it. Find something better to take your attention away from the worries of the day. Matthew 6:33-34 reminds us to **Keep on, then, seeking first the kingdom and his righteousness, and all these [other] things will be added to YOU. So, never be anxious about the next day, for the next day will have its own anxieties. Sufficient for each day is its own badness.**

February 6th Eating Disorders

"But pay attention to yourselves that your hearts never become weighed down with overeating and heavy drinking and anxieties of life…" (Luke 21:34).

If our bodies are temples of YHWH's power and we want to honor Him with our bodies, then we must properly use food. YHWH loves food. Look at his generous creation. We are so blessed with yummy fruits and vegetables, and herbs, and meats. YHWH's imagination and generosity is unending. Psalm 34:8 implores us to **"taste and see that YHWH is good."** Jesus loved food. He always talked about figs, and wine, mustard seeds, fish. After his resurrection, Jesus even made barbeque fish for his disciples (John 21:9). Yet, too much or too little of anything can quickly become bad. And so now we must talk about obesity and eating disorders.

If you are so overweight that your health is in danger because you uncontrollably consume unhealthy food and beverages, then you are hurting your temple of your body. You are not investing your talents like a good servant but are wasting the investment that Yahweh has made in you. Think of the millions of people with real handicaps who would love to have a healthy body with working limbs. And here you are with a normal, healthy body that has been so polluted that you are now dysfunctional. This is a sin. It is also possible that you feel bad about being overweight, and so you relieve your guilt by eating a lot of food, which feels good, only to make the problem worse. Food and guilt becomes a downward spiraling circle. You must prayerfully break this downward circle and let your body heal and become healthy. Don't squander the gift Yahweh has given you.

Not-eating is just as sinful. Being so worried about being skinny or fit has made so many people hurt their own bodies. Throwing up food or starving yourself or taking water pills or laxatives in order to become or remain skinny is a sin. Don't hurt your bodies like that. What a shock it would be if when you looked into the mirror what you saw was a reflection of your heart, not what the world sees. Your heart is the part of your body you need to make and keep beautiful. So please make your heart beautiful.

Do you honor Yahweh by taking good care of your body?

February 7th Don't be Yoked with an Unbeliever

"Do not become unevenly yoked with unbelievers. For what fellowship do righteousness and lawlessness have" (2 Corinthians 6:14)?

When you spend time with someone, you are going to be influenced by them. The bible clearly says not to become yoked together with unbelievers and not to mix with people of other beliefs because they will influence you and tear you away from true worship of Yahweh.

For example… you start a business with an atheist you met at the University. You have invited him to church about 10 times but he refuses because he doesn't believe in God. Why in the world would you want to be financially linked with someone who slaps Yahweh in the face every day by refusing to believe in Him? There is no excuse for being an atheist and there is no excuse for becoming yoked together with someone who doesn't love Yahweh. Romans 1:20 reminds us that God's signature on the glorious art of His creation is so obvious that man is excuseless. Romans 1:18 reminds us that YHWH's wrath will be revealed against people like your atheist "colleague" who doesn't believe in Him. (Romans 1:18-20) **For God's wrath is being revealed from heaven against all ungodliness and unrighteousness of men who are suppressing the truth in an unrighteous way, because what may be known about God is manifest among them, for God made it manifest to them. For his invisible [qualities] are clearly seen from the world's creation onward, because they are perceived by the things made, even his eternal power and Godship, so that they are inexcusable.**

February 8th Bad Company Corrupts Good Habits

"Do not be misled. Bad associations spoil useful habits" (1 Corinthians 15:33).

Bad company corrupts good character. What a clear scripture, so easy to understand. If you hang out with bad associates, all of your useful habits or character will be spoiled.

All people in your life should fall into 2 categories:

1) Those <u>who</u> encourage you to be more like Jesus and glorify Yahweh in accordance with biblical principles and
2) Those <u>who do not</u> encourage you to be more like Jesus and glorify Yahweh in accordance with biblical principles.

Let's simplify this dichotomy by labeling them good associates and bad associates.

It is good for you to become friends with good associates. It is foolish to become friends with bad associates. The bible makes it clear that good associates can become friends and bad associates must be ministry opportunities.

So the question becomes how should I interact with bad associates? The answer is to be **"salt"** and **"light"** (Matthew 5:13 & 14). But being salt and light doesn't mean tolerating their sinful behavior. You must do ministry, not hint at or give approval to their unbiblical lives.

Perhaps there is wisdom in the non-scriptural proverb "show me who your friends are and I will show you who you are."

<u>February 9th You will regret having Stupid Friends</u>

"He that is walking with wise persons will become wise, but he that is having dealings with the stupid ones will fare badly" (Proverbs 13:20).

If you spend time with unwise people you will regret it. I know so many faker Christians who are friends with bad associates and call it "being a good example" to them. The problem is that being a good example is not enough. Ministry includes honest, but loving, words of truth.

Many faker Christians justify the fact that their friends are bad associates by saying that Jesus also spent time with sinners. First of all, they are not Jesus. Secondly, Jesus did not spend his time with sinners. Jesus spent his time with repentant sinners who were seeking the truth and the Kingdom of God.

Saving those who are lost means bringing them out of danger. If you want to save a person from falling off a cliff you have to show them the cliff and pull them away from the cliff. If you don't point out what the cliff is and how it is dangerous, they will just go back to the cliff and fall off it once you leave. Similarly, if you want to save someone from death and destruction you have to let them know the sins they are committing and how they need to avoid that sin. It is loving to ask if you can help someone change their life for the glory of Yahweh... but they will likely never change if you don't remind them that their behavior is unacceptable in the eyes of YHWH. This is why it is important to do ministry to, not become friends with those whose actions slap God in the face every day.

Having the wrong kind of "friends" can be dangerous. Let's say for example that you have a friend from work who is a homosexual. You like to spend time together playing sports. You eventually become good friends. One day you ask this man to babysit your little boy and this man molests him. Of course molesting children is evil. But make no mistake about it, the guilty one is the father who let a homosexual be alone with his son. A practicing homosexual is already outside of the will of God. A practicing homosexual has demonstrated that he practices abnormal sexual perversions. The father should never have become friends with a sexual deviant and let the homosexual be home alone with his child.

Today's scripture warns us that we will regret having unchristian friends. So please choose your friends wisely.

February 10th Don't Be Friends with the World

"Adulteresses, do YOU not know that the friendship with the world is enmity with God? Whoever, therefore, wants to be a friend of the world constitutes himself an enemy of God" (James 4:4).

Life is wonderful and an amazing gift from our heavenly Creator, Yahweh. We are encouraged to enjoy life, to live well, and be obedient to biblical principles. Yet, we are also warned against loving the "popular" systems of this world. This means we should not be lusting after the privileges and the riches and power and sin of this world.

Friendship with the world is enmity with God. This is a very strong scripture. We are not supposed to be friends with the world. We should not enjoy the fleeting and dying temporary joys of the world. We must love and enjoy what is good but hate and flee from what is bad.

In what ways are you friends with the world and what can you do to end this friendship and more deliberately seek Yahweh?

February 11th Don't look like the world

"Consequently I entreat YOU by the compassions of God, brothers, to present YOUR bodies a sacrifice living, holy, acceptable to God, a sacred service with YOUR power of reason. And <u>quit being fashioned after this system of things</u>, but be transformed by making YOUR mind over, that YOU may prove to yourselves the good and acceptable and perfect will of God" (Romans 12:1-2).

A real Christian is not fashioned after the world. We are encouraged not to look (figuratively and literally) like the world.

For example… your teenage daughter or son comes home with a group of disrespectful kids who smell like marijuana, curse, dress like slobs or gangster rappers or prostitutes, and have their faces hidden behind their smart cell phones like antisocial misfits. But your child tells you they are the "popular kids" at school. Are you going to let them into your house and let them influence your family? You are not wise if you do.

Worse yet, why are you, full grown adults who claim to be Christians, chasing after the "popular people" of this evil world in an attempt to be like them, look like them, and be their friends. Think about it. Are you any better than a dumb teenage boy who just wants to be popular? A godly child knows she is loved by the creator of the Universe and only wants to glorify Him. A godly child doesn't want to be liked by the "popular people" who are stars in Satan's world. A godly child wants to be friends with like-minded people who love and honor God.

February 12th You only need to make Yahweh Happy

"I do not accept glory from men" (John 5:41).

We should not accept or require praise from our fellow man. We should only seek Yahweh's approval. Many faker Christians are just as bad as the people of the world in that they are lonely and insecure and will put up with anyone as long as they get attention. This is why girls have boyfriends who beat them. This is why peer pressure gets kids to have premarital sex, smoke, use drugs. If you only cared about making YHWH happy, then you wouldn't put up with the ridiculous behavior of people of this world. Jesus sets us straight in today's scripture by reminding us that we should not accept glory from men.

February 13th Jesus was not a part of This World

"They are no part of the world, just as I am no part of the world" (John 17:16).

Jesus was not part of this world and said in his famous John 17 prayer that his followers would also not be a part of this world.

When they tried to make Jesus a political leader, a king from the line of David, Jesus left them. His kingdom is not of this world. Jesus was not political. (John 6:15) **Therefore Jesus, knowing they were about to come and seize him to make him king, withdrew again into the mountain all alone.**

The men in leadership positions in worldly organizations are ambitious and care nothing (they are fakers) for the will of Yahweh. Christian chaplains and many catholic priests forget their "calling" and that their purpose is to love and serve GOD ALMIGHTY, not get promoted and make money. Political leaders are inundated with sex scandals and lies and controversies. Look at how incompetent our military senior leaders are. Look at how evil and selfish CEOs are who ruin companies or banks, costing tax payers billions of dollars, crashing economies as a result. If you want to be a friend of the world then you are not a friend of God.

Only a few times in all of bible history did YHWH raise up a "believing insider" from a worldly government. Joseph became a leader in Egypt to help the Israelites find food and safety. Moses was trained by Pharaoh but eventually help the Israelites escape. Based off of Jesus' example to flee from those who want him to be political, we can see that for 99.9999999% of all men (which means the exception is not you) any one serving God Almighty should be apolitical.

February 14th A Christian Can't serve God and Worldly Governments

"No one can slave for two masters; for either he will hate the one and love the other, or he will stick to the one and despise the other..." (Matthew 6:24).

You can serve only one master so it better be Yahweh.

Let's see an example of how this applies to modern day life. A faker Christian wants to make a difference in the world so he joins the military of one of the corrupt governments of this world and serves as a chaplain. He prays for soldiers who go off to war in support of their national security objectives. This faker chaplain would never have the courage to give "tough-love" and to speak the words of God. He would likely do his best to be politically correct. This faker chaplain is likely as ambitious and as concerned about advancing in rank as the average atheist infantry officer to whom he volunteered to minister. This faker chaplain knows stories of the bible like a well-educated child but doesn't live in accordance with biblical truths. This faker Christian supports his nation at the cost of watering down the truth of the scriptures.

This faker Christian chaplain feels like he is bold when he says "and I pray this in Jesus' name" and yet is such a faker that he doesn't even know or use or try to glorify the name of Yahweh. And if he does know the name of YHWH, he is way too afraid to ever say it in public. That would be a career ender for sure. Do you see how working for a government is impossible if you truly love YHWH and want to live in accordance with His principles?

Now let's imagine a civil war, one like the US Civil War. Just think about hypocritical Baptist chaplains in New York who prayed for God to bless their soldiers as they went off to kill their literal brothers from Virginia. Just think about hypocritical Baptist chaplains in Virginia who prayed for God to bless their soldiers as they went off to kill their literal brothers from New York.

How about an international example? Just think of Lutheran chaplains in Germany praying for God to bless their soldiers as they went off to kill Americans. Or just think of Lutheran chaplains in the USA praying for God to bless their soldiers as they went off to kill Germans. In the last 200 years the only Christian denomination which has never taken up arms against their brothers is Jehovah's Witnesses. Every other denomination presumes to be fighting on God's side and takes up weapons against other Christian brothers who also wrongly assume they are on God's side. Who decides which side has God's blessing?

February 15th Yahweh's Kigndom, not worldly governments, is the only Solution to the World's Problems

"YOU must pray, then, this way: "Our Father in the heavens, let your name be sanctified. Let your kingdom come. Let your will take place, as in heaven, also upon earth" (Matthew 6:9-10).

Jesus was perfect and obviously could have been the greatest king to ever rule in Israel. Yet he didn't want to be a part of the systems of this world. He knew the world was passing away. Jesus knew that the only solution is God's Kingdom. That is why Jesus prayed for YHWH's kingdom to come in His model prayer.

A real Christian should be like Jesus and wait for God's Kingdom to come. We should not serve human governments which have no chance for success. We should love YHWH with our all and love our neighbor as ourselves. We should make disciples of men and teach them to observe the things that YHWH commanded.

Exiled Israelites did not join the military of their captors and fight to support their causes. Take Jeremiah for example. After the Babylonians destroyed Jerusalem did Jeremiah move to Iraq and volunteer to fight for the Babylonians? Of course not. His identity as a child of the living God, an Israelite, required that he stay loyal to Yahweh, not the king of Babylon, Persia, Greece, or Caesar. Jesus's followers did not join the Roman military to fight for Caesar. They remained politically neutral.

Now let's see what a modern, real Man of God would do. He would be apolitical, he would be neutral. He would be clean and loving and not look like the world. If given an opportunity to speak with someone serving in any military, he would lovingly tell them the good news about the Kingdom of God, and ask if he could help that soldier come into an accurate knowledge of YHWH and live in accordance with biblical principles. A real Man of God would never wear a uniform which has the flag of a nation which kills and aborts over a million babies a year, spends billions of dollars a year waging war or making weapons of war, and continually slaps YHWH in the face by legalizing homosexual marriages and claiming on their money that "In God We Trust."

But what about Christians from another country, say for example China? Collectively, the Chinese are just as evil as any other world power, but in different ways. They don't value life, kill babies, eat dogs, aggressively suppress freedom of speech and religion, worship false oriental gods, and have extreme socio-economic polarity. What about a Muslim country like Turkey, Syria? A Christian in China or Turkey or Syria can't join the military and kill people to support their nation's "evil" way of life. A Christian can't join the Chinese or Turkish or Syrian government and support such a corrupt political system. Regardless of where you live, as a Christian you must remain neutral, mind your own business, pay taxes, obey the speed limit, and be a law abiding citizen. But your loyalty but be to Yahweh. A real Man of God knows that our lying, dishonorable world leaders are absolutely outside the will of YHWH and not worthy of our service.

If you vote or sign a petition it would be as if you were saying that human governments or leadership can solve the world's problems. The only solution to the world's problems is YHWH's Kingdom.

February 16th Give to Caesar what is Caesar's

"Jesus then said: "Pay back Caesar's things to Caesar, but God's things to God" (Mark 12:17).

Because we all live in a country, and every country has rules, we must obey those rules as long as they don't conflict with biblical principles. We must pay taxes, obey the speed limit and so on. But that doesn't mean we have to approve of and participate in wars, political parties, immoral cultural norms. We must give to Caesar what is Caesar's. We must be good tourists, but never forget that our citizenships are in the Kingdom of Yahweh.

February 17th This World is Passing Away

"Do not be loving either the world or the things in the world. If anyone loves the world, the love of the Father is not in him; because everything in the world—the desire of the flesh and the desire of the eyes and the showy display of one's means of life—does not originate with the Father, but originates with the world. Furthermore, the <u>world is passing away</u> and so is its desire, but he that does the will of God remains forever. (1 John 2:15-17)

The world is a sinking ship and it would be a waste of time trying to become the captain of that ship. Spending time rearranging chairs and making your bed on the Titanic was a waste of time. It is the same for the world. Working for governments which are not the solution to man's problems is a waste of time because the world is passing away. What we do and what we spend our time doing must be of lasting value. What we do must make Yahweh happy.

The world is passing away so do the will of YHWH in order to live forever.

February 18th Yahweh Provides

"In turn, my God will fully supply all YOUR need to the extent of his riches in glory by means of Christ Jesus" (Philippians 4:19)

Does God need your money? The answer is "NO." Yet, Yahweh is reasonable and knows that humans these days need provisions (food, clothing, shelter..) for survival. When His servants needed money in the past, YHWH always provided. They never had to have a bake sale, an auction, sell bricks, sell candles, sell forgiveness of sins, pass a plate, or make automatic bank account deductions.

YHWH provides: The Egyptians gave the Israelites gold and valuable when they left Egypt (Exodus 12:36). The gold brought to Mary and Joseph by the astrologers possibly finances their time of refuge in Egypt while Herod was killing all the children in Bethlehem (Matthew 2:11-15).

Chances are that Yahweh has already provided so much for you. If you have a roof over your head, food on your table, and clothes on your body then you are already in the richest 90% of people in this world.

February 19th Prioritizing Riches Leads to Destruction

"However, those who are determined to be rich fall into temptation and a snare and many senseless and hurtful desires, which plunge men into destruction and ruin. For the love of money is a root of all sorts

of injurious things, and by reaching out for this love some have been led astray from the faith and have stabbed themselves all over with many pains" (1 Timothy 6: 9-10).

Pagan and Christian men, alike, have lied, stolen, and killed to gain riches. How sad. Today's scripture reminds us that those who are determined to be rich fall into destruction and ruin. It warns us that the love of money has caused all sorts of injurious things. Both warning apply to people and the church.

Faker Christians and their churches and denominations love to make money, especially to make money off of anything spiritual. This is one reason that modern Christian churches have strayed so far from Biblical truth.

February 20th Shame on Priests who Instruct for a Price

"Her leaders judge for a bribe, Her priests instruct for a price, And her prophets practice divination for money. And yet they lean on YHWH, saying: "Is not YHWH with us No calamity will come upon us" (Micah 3:11).

Micah prophesied about the corruption of faker Christian churches which accept bribes and charge for their services. How much does your priest charge you to conduct a marriage ceremony or funeral? How much did you pay to go to a bible seminar or retreat? Instructing for a price is not biblical.

The Catholic Church used to sell "indulgences" to pay for their luxurious living and grand buildings. A rich man could buy forgiveness. How revolting and satanic and unbiblical. Although the sale of indulgences is no longer practiced formally, modern day church leaders frequently prostitute themselves to the rich and powerful. This is in violation of biblical principles and turns the church into a den of thieves.

February 21st You cannot serve Yahweh and Riches

"No one can slave for two masters; for either he will hate the one and love the other, or he will stick to the one and despise the other. YOU cannot slave for God and for Riches" (Matthew 6:24).

You can't serve two masters.

Faker Christians who say we should pray for riches like Jabez in 1 Chronicles 4:10 ought to read the rest of the bible which says the first will be last, love our neighbor, keep your eye simple, seek first the kingdom, make disciples of all men, love YHWH with your all, and put others first. Shame on you who say and publish these unbiblical lies.

Buying a faker Christian book at the local book store or Christian book store costs as much as buying a secular book. That is because the faker Christian book companies are only interested in making money. They simply use faker Christian book sales as their means of making money.

If you really believe that what you were writing has the hope of changing a person's eternal destiny then you would make it available for free, or in my case, simply cover the cost of printing the book.

Most Christian book authors are hypocrites who do not live in accordance with biblical principles. Disgusting faker Christian ministers flash money around and pervert and twist the scriptures to make you believe that if YHWH loves you, you will be rich. The "prosperity gospel" is a lie from Satan and it doesn't matter if you have a mega church in a football stadium, you are outside the will of YHWH.

February 22nd Don't Store Up your Treasures on Earth

"Stop storing up for yourselves treasures upon the earth, where moth and rust consume, and where thieves break in and steal. Rather, store up for yourselves treasures in heaven, where neither moth nor rust consumes, and where thieves do not break in and steal. For where your treasure is, there your heart will be also" (Matthew 6: 19-21).

Don't store up treasures on earth.

Like many other religious organizations, the Vatican is a den of thieves. In some European nations, if you claim to be catholic, then a certain percentage of your wages are garnished and are electronically transferred each month to the Vatican Bank. This is Nauseating!

How many people know about all the financial investments, properties, and businesses of the Vatican? Jesus and Paul and Peter worked hard until the day they were killed for the sake of the Kingdom of God. How much money does a local priest get for his retirement? Do you know how much money does a retired bishop get for his retirement?

What about the last Pope Benedict who left in shame, after having been caught in a scandal, disgracing the name of God to all who associate Yahweh with this faker Christian organization. Shame on the Vatican? How much money a month is that criminal ex-pope getting for his retirement? The Vatican is not a representative of YHWH. It is a money making machine. No wonder the kings of the earth commit fornication with you (Revelations 18:10). No wonder the merchants of the world will be sad to see your destruction (Revelations 18:11). What you do is in violation of biblical principles and reveals your catholic church to be a den of thieves.

February 23rd Don't Profit from Things of Faith

"Now they came to Jerusalem. There he entered into the temple and started to throw out those selling and buying in the temple, and he overturned the tables of the money changers and the benches of those selling doves; and he would not let anyone carry a utensil through the temple, but he kept teaching and saying: "Is it not written, 'My house will be called a house of prayer for all the nations'? But YOU have made it a cave of robbers" (Mark 11:15-17).

Jesus particularly did not like faker religious leaders who turned things of god into money making ventures.

The angriest account of Jesus recorded in the bible is when he flips the table and accuses the fakers of turning a house or prayer into a den of thieves. This should tell you something. Jesus, who is a perfect reflection of YHWH, gets the most upset at those who take advantage of the people for financial gain.

Some catholic and protestant cathedrals charge entrance fees. This is in violation of biblical principles and turns the cathedral into a den of thieves.

It is impossible to enter into a catholic church in Europe which doesn't have candles for sale. Most cathedrals now have an entire corner where they sell books, post cards, stamped euros or pennies, rosaries and crosses. These gift shops are in violation of biblical principles and turn the church into a den of thieves.

I remember taking my family to the famous cathedral in Canterbury, England. They were charging a $15 per person entrance fee. My teenage daughter and I got a bit grumpy at this hypocrisy. Perhaps that is why we usually write things like "a $15 entrance fee is absurd. Please read Mark 11:17" on the guest registers at churches like this.

February 24th You Received Free, Give Free

"YOU received free, give free" (Matthew 10: 8).

Jesus tells us the standard for Christian ministry: Free

Bible publishers, if you actually believe that the Word of God is living and active you should do your best to provide it for free or at cost. Most of you are satanic publishing companies which only want to make money. Shame on you!

I read Zondervan's New International Version several times. As I began to have my eyes opened to biblical truths it became obvious that Zondervan is run by faker Christians who hide the name of Yahweh and who charge way too much for the precious and life changing word of God. If you have printed millions of copies then the overhead costs must become very, very low. How sad that you keep the rights to your poor translation. Shame on you for charging almost a hundred dollars for a copy of the King James Bible with references to Greek and Hebrew words. The Strong's Concordance was written over a hundred years ago. You should charge six or seven dollars for the paper and leather, not 80 dollars. Meditate on Matthew 10: 8 **"YOU received free, give free."** All people want to do is look up the original Greek or Hebrew word in order to better understand the truth. If you actually believe the word of God is living and active then you should stop focusing on selling the bible to English speakers and would try to help translate the bible into many other languages to reach the lost sheep.

If you actually believe that the word of God is inspired then you must believe that the Catholic Bible is not inspired. Why in the world would a publishing company publish and sell the inspired bible and also publish and sell the uninspired bible? You are fakers and your goal is money, not the Kingdom. Your organization is a den of thieves and shame on you for making money off of the inspired word of God.

February 25th Salaried Ministers don't care out their Sheep

"The hired man, who is no shepherd and to whom the sheep do not belong as his own, beholds the wolf coming and abandons the sheep and flees—and the wolf snatches them and scatters them" (John 10:12).

Salaries: Yahweh's faithful servants work out of love, not for huge salaries. Jesus warns us of shepherds who are paid and only work for money.

Yahweh deserves those who will worship Him in spirit and truth. True Christians do their best to mitigate costs and do everything and give everything for free. They give their lives to the Kingdom of God. True Christians would never force money collections, charge for services, charge for spiritual truths, charge for literature, charge for bibles, and make you pay to attend a spiritual conference. Jesus reminds us that the standard for Christian ministry is "free." (Matthew 10:8) **"YOU received free, give free."**

How sad it is that so many have made millions of dollars off of lies. This is in violation of biblical principles and turns their ministries into a den of thieves.

February 26th Yahweh's Son is Jesus

Look! Also, a voice from the heavens said: "This is my Son, the beloved, whom I have approved" (Matthew 3:17).

Jesus is the son of God, not God. Jesus is Yahweh' son, not Yahweh.

Although this truth is written in black and white all throughout the bible and is obviously logical, millions of so called Christians mistakenly believe in and follow the doctrine of the trinity.

Jesus is wonderful, our loving savior, who gave himself as a ransom for all, set the perfect example, and will be the King of Kings in the Kingdom of Yahweh God. Yet, he is not Yahweh. Only Yahweh is Yahweh.

We will spend the next two weeks discussing qualities of Jesus and then address the unbiblical doctrine of the trinity in greater detail. The take home concept for today's "Word of Wisdom" is simply that Yahweh is the only true God and that Jesus is His Son.

February 27th Jesus is the Firstborn of all Creation

"He is the image of the invisible God, the firstborn of all creation; because by means of him all other things were created in the heavens and on the earth, the things visible and the things invisible, whether they are thrones or lordships or governments or authorities. All other things have been created through him and for him. (Colossians 1:15-16)

Jesus is the firstborn of all creation who helped Yahweh make all things.

Jesus helped create humans and is referred to when Yahweh says of man let <u>us</u> make him in <u>our</u> image. (Genesis 1:26) **Then God said: "Let <u>us</u> make man in our image, according to <u>our</u> likeness, and let them have in subjection the fish of the sea and the flying creatures of the heavens and the domestic animals and all the earth and every creeping animal that is moving on the earth."**

Please read Proverbs 8:22-31 because it is Jesus talking about his life before the Earth was created. It is a fantastic scripture, one which most people overlook.

It is fun to ponder the wonderful imagination of our loving Father YHWH and His firstborn Jesus who helped Him create all the wonderful things we enjoy here on Earth. Just think of a juicy piece of corn. The seeds are so delicious and sweet. Now flip the seeds to the inside, make them red, round, and even sweeter, and you now have a pomegranate. What unique seeds and what variations. Just think of an eagle soaring, or how a humming bird flaps its wings thousands of times a minute. Both are wingers and yet so different. Cocoa and coffee beans are my two favorite vegetables. It is amazing how wonderful and complex the world's design is. Doctors still can't fully understand the human body. NASA can only take pictures of space, let alone build it, define it, regulate it, and name it. Our loving Father and His son truly are master builders.

February 28th Jesus gave us a Perfect Example to Follow

"In fact, to this course you were called, because even Christ suffered for you, leaving a model for you to follow his steps closely (1 Peter 2: 21).

Jesus came to earth to give us a perfect example. This was because men were not living righteously and "religious leaders" were doing it wrongly.

Men not living righteously: If men like Adam and Noah, and their descendants, would have lived more righteously and would have continued to walk with love and integrity with Yahweh, it is possible that Jesus never would have needed to come to earth to show us the way. But our forefathers did not walk in love and integrity with Yahweh, but became sinful. So Jesus had to come to earth to show us the way.

Religious Leaders doing it wrongly: Religious leaders like the Sadducees and Pharisees thought they were doing it correctly and were forcing their traditions on men. So Jesus had to come to earth to prove the Sadducees and Pharisees wrong and to set a perfect example for us to follow. It is sadly no different today. Religious leaders teach traditions of men which violate the word of God. Thankfully, we have access to the Bible and can read truth and see for ourselves the example that Jesus made.

Are you following Jesus' steps closely?

March 1st What you need to know about Sacrifices

"For there is one God, and one mediator between God and men, a man, Christ Jesus, who gave himself a corresponding ransom for all—this is what is to be witnessed to in its own due time (1 Timothy 2: 5-6).

Sin separates us from the perfect and loving God, Yahweh. As creator of life, Yahweh makes the rules. And His rule was that sin is only atoned for through blood sacrifice.

In days of old, when someone sinned, they had to give an animal or pay for an animal, and sacrifice that animal on the altar. A sacrifice offering was expensive, because animals are valuable. And the sacrifice was scary, because seeing an animal die is terrible. Yahweh's provision for forgiveness of sins was to make humans suffer financially and emotionally so that they would not want to sin again and would not sin again.

Jesus came to earth to be our perfect example and to be the final sacrifice. Jesus's death was the final sacrifice for sin and has opened the door for us to have everlasting life. Yahweh's provision through Jesus' death was to make humans suffer emotionally so that we would not want to sin again and would not sin again. Jesus was the last accepted sacrifice. After Jesus' death, Yahweh no longer accepted sacrifices.

March 2nd Jesus is at God's Right Hand

"He is at God's right hand, for he went to heaven, and angels and authorities and powers were made subject to him (1 Peter 3:22).

Jesus is not dead, but is alive and well at the right hand of the Father. This is where we get the expression "my right-hand man." Jesus is the right-hand man of Yahweh.

When the Kingdom of God becomes also the Kingdom of Man, Jesus will return to earth and rule as the King of Kings. This will happen soon, but no one knows the day or the hour.[5] But until then, Yahweh has His firstborn of creation and His only begotten son right next to him in Heaven.

March 3rd Yahweh has Delegated all Authority to Jesus

"Jesus approached and spoke to them, saying: "All authority has been given me in heaven and on the earth" (Matthew 28:18).

Jesus has been delegated all authority….in heaven and on earth.

Heaven: In heaven, we know that Jesus is at the right hand of Yahweh as they prepare for the coming of the Kingdom of God to earth.

---

[5] Matthew 24:36

Earth: 2000 years ago, Jesus demonstrated Yahweh's authority by driving out demons, doing miracles, and speaking and teaching wisely. Jesus was the most courageous person to ever live. Imagine the courage it takes to tell the faker religious hypocrites that they are working for Satan. In John 8:44, Jesus said to them: **"You are from your father the Devil, and you wish to do the desires of your father."** When Jesus returns to earth to rule as King of Kings in the near future, He will exercise His authority is amazing ways.

March 4th Jesus will Judge for Yahweh

"I solemnly charge you before God and Christ Jesus, who is destined to judge the living and the dead, and by his manifestation and his kingdom, preach the word, be at it urgently in favorable season, in troublesome season, reprove, reprimand, exhort, with all long-suffering and [art of] teaching" (2 Timothy 4:1-22).

Jesus will judge the living and the dead. What an amazing responsibility. The good thing is that Jesus can see the heart and not just superficially. He can and will just righteously and perfectly.

As the righteous judge, Jesus will prevent so many people from inheriting everlasting life. This means Jesus will say "No" to billions of people who did not prioritize honoring Yahweh. (Matthew 7:21-23) **"Not everyone saying to me, 'Lord, Lord,' will enter into the kingdom of the heavens, but the one doing the will of my Father who is in the heavens will. Many will say to me in that day, 'Lord, Lord, did we not** prophesy in your name, and expel demons in your name, and perform many powerful works in your name?' And yet then I will confess to them: I never knew YOU! Get away from me, YOU workers of lawlessness."

March 5th Jesus will be King in the Kingdom of Yahweh

"On his outer garment, yes, on his thigh, he has a name written, King of kings and Lord of lords" (Revelation 19:16).

Today's scripture reminds us that Jesus will rule as the King of Kings in the Kingdom of God. The Kingdom of God will come in the near future, but no one knows the day or hour.[6] Yahweh and Jesus will rule in the Kingdom of God. (Revelation 11:15) **And the seventh angel blew his trumpet. And loud voices occurred in heaven, saying: "The kingdom of the world did become the kingdom of our Lord and of his Christ, and he will rule as king forever and ever."**

The only answer to the problems of this world is God's Kingdom, which will set it all straight again. That is why Jesus said in Matthew 9: 9-10 **"YOU must pray, then, this way: 'Our Father in the heavens, let your name be sanctified. Let your kingdom come. Let your will take place, as in heaven, also upon earth."** Nothing short of Yahweh's kingdom coming will end

---

[6] Matthew 24:36

the evil effects of Satan upon the current system of things.

May God's Kingdom come soon.

March 6th You can only get to Yahweh through Jesus

"Jesus said to him: "I am the way and the truth and the life. No one comes to the Father except through me. If you men had known me, you would have known my Father also; from this moment on you know him and have seen him" (John 14:6-7).

As written earlier this week: "Jesus came to earth to be our perfect example and to be the final sacrifice. Jesus's death was the final sacrifice for sin and has opened the door for us to have everlasting life. Yahweh's provision through Jesus' death was to make humans suffer emotionally so that we would not want to sin again and would not sin again. Jesus was the last accepted sacrifice. After Jesus' death, Yahweh no longer accepted sacrifices."

Today's scripture reinforces the fact that in order to get to the Father and into the Kingdom of God, you must go through Jesus. Going through Jesus means that you must acknowledge Jesus sacrifice for your sins and live a life worthy of Jesus' sacrifice. You must not take your salvation for granted but must work out your salvation with fear and trembling.[7] You must resist temptation to

---

[7] Philippians 2:12

the point of spilling your own blood to forsake it.[8] You must live righteously, loving Yahweh with your all and loving your neighbor as yourself.[9]

March 7<u>th</u> God is One, not Three

"Listen, O Israel: Yahweh our God is <u>one</u> Yahweh" (Deuteronomy 6:4).

Yahweh is one, not THREE!

There is no such thing as the trinity.

The term trinity is not even in the bible.

Jesus is not Yahweh, but is Yahweh's first born of creation, His son.

Holy spirit is not Yahweh but is another way of saying "Yahweh's power."

Many pagan cultures had ideas of the three gods. The Egyptians had a "big three" of their false gods. The Greeks also had a top three. It is easy to see in history how the faker catholic church adopted this idea of three in one to appease the pagans and bring them into the church.

Yahweh doesn't like confusion, disorder. (1 Corinthians 14:33) **For God is [a God], not of disorder, but of peace.**

---

[8] Hebrews 12:4
[9] Mark 12:30-31

Being a God of order, He would never want to make himself a "mystery," confusing, or unknowable. It is sad when the church says that the trinity is a "mystery," that father, son, and spirit are all the same substance, three in one, and that sometimes the parts act together and other times they act independently. This is nonsense.

There is only one God and his name is Yahweh, not Jesus. Yahweh is the only God. All else are fake gods and false gods. (Isaiah 45: 5)

I am Yahweh, and there is no one else. With the exception of me there is no God.

March 8th Prayer demonstrates that the Father is above the Son

"YOU must pray, then, this way: "Our Father in the heavens let your name be sanctified" (Matthew 6:9). Jesus taught us to pray to Yahweh.

All the fathers of the faith, all of the priests, and all of the prophets in the Bible prayed to Yahweh and only to Yahweh. No one in the Bible ever prayed to anyone other than Yahweh. This is because Yahweh, alone, is God. Jesus, also, only prayed to Yahweh.

Jesus was not schizophrenic. When he prayed, he did not pray to himself but prayed to Yahweh, his father. (John 17: 1-3) **Jesus spoke these things, and, raising his eyes to heaven, he said: "Father, the hour has come; glorify your son, that your son may glorify you, according as you have given him authority over**

all flesh, that, as regards the whole [number] whom you have given him, he may give them everlasting life. This means everlasting life, their taking in knowledge of you, the only true God, and of the one whom you sent forth, Jesus Christ.

Because prayer is always and only directed to Yahweh, we see that Yahweh, alone, is God and that everyone, even Jesus, is subordinate to Yahweh.

Prayer is yet another proof that the doctrine of the trinity is not biblical.

March 9th Yahweh doesn't share His glory

"I am Yahweh. That is my name; and to no one else shall I give my own glory, neither my praise to graven images" (Isaiah 42:8).

Yahweh shares his glory with no one, not even Jesus.

Solomon tells us that Jesus is different from Yahweh. (Proverbs 30:4) **Who has ascended to heaven and then descended? Who has gathered the wind in the palms of both hands? Who has wrapped up the waters in his garment? Who has established all the ends of the earth? What is his name and the name of his son—if you know?** Here Solomon is referring to Yahweh and Jesus, His son.

Yahweh and Jesus are different beings. They are not a part of a trinity. Yahweh is God, and simply put, Jesus is His son. Yahweh shares His glory with no one.

March 10th God's Power is called Holy Spirit

"And the earth was without form, and void; and darkness was upon the face of the deep. And the Spirit of God moved upon the face of the waters" Genesis 1:2.

Yahweh's power is called Holy Spirit all throughout the bible. Church leaders have created the fake doctrine of the trinity and have said that the holy spirit is 1/3 god. But this is not true. If you substitute "God's Power" for Holy Spirit every time it is printed in the bible then it makes perfect sense that Holy Spirit is nothing other than God's Power.

Yahweh's power is translated as a **"helper"** (John 14:16), or the **"spirit of truth"** (John 16:13). This does not mean that holy spirit has a mind of its own. It simply reveals that Yahweh's power helps people.

Yahweh's power (holy spirit) doesn't have its own personality.

Yahweh's power (holy spirit) has no name. If they were three personalities in one, then the holy spirit would have a name. But the holy spirit doesn't have a name because the holy spirit is not a person but is a way of describing Yahweh's power.

Yahweh's power (holy spirit) isn't a person. Stephen is given a glimpse of the throne room of Yahweh and sees Jesus at his right hand (Acts 7: 55-56). But Stephen never sees a 3rd person of the holy spirit. This is because holy spirit is simply a way of describing YHWH's power.

March 11th God's Hierarchy Disproves the Trinity

"YOU heard that I said to YOU, I am going away and I am coming [back] to YOU. If YOU loved me, YOU would rejoice that I am going my way to the Father, because the Father is greater than I am" (John 14:28).

The Father is greater than Jesus.

Jesus is not part of a false trinity but is subordinate to God. (1 Corinthians 11:3) **But I want YOU to know that the head of every man is the Christ; in turn the head of a woman is the man; in turn the head of the Christ is God.**

Jesus was not eternal like Yahweh but was made by Yahweh. (Colossians 1:15) **He is the image of the invisible God, the firstborn of all creation.** The creator is always above the created.

Not even Jesus knows the hour of the coming of the Son of Man. (Mark 13:32) **Concerning that day or the hour nobody knows, neither the angels in heaven nor the Son, but the Father.** If they were three in one (a trinity) then Jesus would also know.

Jesus and his father were / are distinct. (Matthew 26:39) **And going a little way forward, he fell upon his face, praying and saying: "My Father, if it is possible, let this cup pass away from me. Yet, not as I will, but as you will."** If Jesus was in a trinity then why would he schizophrenically pray to himself? He prayed to his father because his father, Yahweh, is superior.

The trinity doesn't exist because God is one, not three. God is superior to all, including Jesus.

March 12th Jesus was Delgated many Powers but is still not God

"Jesus approached and spoke to them, saying: "All authority has been given me in heaven and on the earth" (Matthew 28:18).

Because Yahweh delegated to Jesus many powers, Jesus was powerful and was described as "a" god in John 1:1 but not "the" God. (John 1:1-2) **In the beginning the Word was, and the Word was with God, and the Word was a god. This one was in the beginning with God.** Many Greek scholars translate John 1:1 as the Word (Jesus) was "a" god, using the definite article "A." About the same amount of Greek scholars translate John 1:1 as the Word was god, without using the indefinite article "A." If you use the term "a god" then it makes sense because we all know the amazing powers Yahweh delegated to Jesus made Jesus "god like."

Jesus was delegated powers which made him "god like." But Jesus never considered himself equal to Yahweh. (Philippians 2:5-8) **Keep this mental attitude in YOU that was also in Christ Jesus, who, although he was existing in God's form, gave no consideration to a seizure, namely, that he should be equal to God. No, but he emptied himself and took a slave's form and came to be in the likeness of men. More than that, when he found himself in fashion as a man, he humbled himself and became obedient as far as death, yes, death on a torture stake.**

There may be those who are "god like" but there is only one God, Yahweh. (1 Corinthians 8:5-6) **For even though there are those who are called "gods," whether in heaven or on earth, just as there are many "gods" and many "lords," there is actually to us one God the Father, out of whom all things are, and we for him; and there is one Lord, Jesus Christ, through whom all things are, and we through him.**

Moses was just a man and yet Yahweh called him "God to Pharaoh". Exodus 7:1 **Consequently YHWH said to Moses: "See, I have made you God to Pharaoh, and Aaron your own brother will become your prophet."** In the eyes of Pharaoh, Moses was a god because of his ability to make miracles happen. Yet, we all know Moses' miracles came from Yahweh's power. In the eyes of many people, Jesus was a god because of his ability to make miracles happen. Yet, we all know Jesus' miracles came from Yahweh's power.

March 13th Yahweh healing a woman, unbeknownst to Jesus, is another example of how the trinity is false

"Immediately Jesus realized in himself that power had gone out of him, and he turned around in the crowd and asked: "Who touched my outer garments" (Mark 5:30)?

The story or YHWH using His power to heal a sick woman, unbeknownst to Jesus, is another proof that the trinity is wrong.

Since his baptism, Jesus, the son of God, was full of the power of God (also known as holy spirit). Of course Jesus's coat did not have any power and was not full of Holy Spirit, it was Jesus who had God's spirit or power within him. But when the woman touched Jesus's coat, God saw her faith and healed her by sending power from Jesus into her.

Many people are so rooted in church traditions that they can't see for themselves that the trinity is not found in the bible, that Jesus is simply Yahweh's son, and that Yahweh's power can be described as "holy spirit." Satan has blinded these people. They are also blinded by their own pride. Please don't be like them. Please open your eyes to a simply, biblical truth. The trinity is not in the bible. Yahweh alone is God and alone is worthy of our prayers and worship.

March 14th Christmas is not in the Bible

"For there has been a child born to us, there has been a son given to us; and the princely rule will come to be upon his shoulder. And his name will be called Wonderful Counselor, Mighty God, Eternal Father, Prince of Peace" (Isaiah 9:6).

Here goes a quick summary of Christmas: Jesus rebuked religious leaders who liked traditions of man more than the word of God. The bible doesn't say WHEN Jesus was born. Jesus was not born on the 25th of December. To a true Christian, every day is a day to celebrate Jesus' sacrifice and to honor him. Being bad tempered and stressed out while buying gifts in December is not a way to honor Jesus' life. Sad, financially stressful times are not biblical. Manger scenes are wrong because the Magi visited Jesus in a "home," not a manger (perhaps up to 2 years after Jesus' birth). No one knows the number of the Magi. (why do you sing that they were 3?) Magi were astrologers (which God strictly forbids) who followed a star. Herod inquired of the magi, which resulted in Herod doing a terrible thing, killing all kids under two years old. Bad associations (even at Christmas parties) corrupt useful habits. Stay away from bad people unless doing ministry on them. Honor God and Jesus by being obedient. Worship Yahweh in spirit and truth.

Christmas is a great example of a seemingly good idea gone bad. The ancient Catholic Church wanted to honor Jesus by celebrating a festival to him. The ancient church attempted Christ's Mass to redeem a favorite pagan celebration day and bring thousands of pagans into the church. They assimilated the winter solstice (the shortest day of the year with the least amount of sun light), which was a pagan celebration, with an unbiblical and erroneous celebration of Jesus's birthday. Over the years this pagan celebration has become perverted to the point that it has nothing to do with honoring Jesus.

Yahweh never told us the exact day of Jesus' birthday. This is because Jews don't and never did celebrate birthdays. Furthermore, Yahweh never said to celebrate birthdays, let alone Jesus' birthday. Birthday celebrations are a pagan tradition.

Jesus was not born on 25 December. The 25th of December was the winter solstice (a pagan holiday) and early Christian church leaders decided to mix the pagan date with a Christian event to redeem the date and gather more support. Who decided this? Was it God? Was it Jesus? No. <u>It was Constantine in 336 A.D. who made this decision, not Yahweh.</u> Why should we follow a date that is not commanded by God?

<u>March 15th Jesus's Exact Birth Location Was Predicted and Written Down 700 Years Before His Birth</u>

"And you, O Bethlehem Ephrata, the one too little to get to be among the thousands of Judah, from you there will come out to me the one who is to become ruler in Israel, whose origin is from early times, from the days of time indefinite" (Micah 5:2).

Jesus was born in Bethlehem Ephrata. There were two Bethlehems during biblical times. One was in Judah outside Jerusalem where Jesus was born and the other was north near Nazareth, where Jesus spend many years. How wonderful is it that the bible predicts years earlier where he would be born.

<u>March 16th The Timeline of Jesus' Birth</u>

"There were also in that same country shepherds living out of doors and keeping watches in the night over their flocks. And suddenly Yahweh's angel stood by them, and Yahweh's glory gleamed around them, and they became very fearful: (Luke 2:8).

Jesus was borne when it was not yet fully winter. Winters in Bethlehem are very cold and require bringing domestic animals inside. Although Jesus was born in a manger, he was born when it was still warm enough outside for local shepherds to still be out in the fields with their flocks.

The bible is full of many gems of knowledge for those who love Yahweh and actually spend time studying it. Below is a perfect example.

Diligent bible study of timelines and mathematical research clearly prooves that Jesus was likely born around the end of September to first week of October. Do your own research of the timeline in the beginning of Luke and the Leviticus priestly service calendar in 1 Chronicles 24 and you will arrive at the same conclusion. Hint: Jesus was born how many months after John the Baptist? John was born 9 months after Zachariah served as High priest during his tribe's designated service time. When was that?

March 17th Astronomy is Good, Astrology is Evil

"This is what Yahweh says: "Do not act like the other nations, who try to read their future in the stars. Do not be afraid of their predictions, even though other nations are terrified by them" (Jeremiah 10:2).

Astronomy is Good, Astrology is evil. Astronomy is studying stars and planets and physics (think NASA). Astrology is human made up interpretation of stars (think omen / fortune tellers). One example is the daily horoscope. This is strictly forbidden by God. **"When you enter the land the Lord your God is giving you,** do not learn to imitate the detestable ways of the nations there. **Let no one be found among you who sacrifices his son or daughter in the fire, who practices divination or sorcery, <u>interprets omens</u>, engages in witchcraft, or casts spells, or who is a medium or spirits or who consults the dead. Anyone who does these things is detestable to the Lord, and because of these detestable practices the Lord your God will drive out those nations before you"** (Deuteronomy 18:9).

The Magi were led by the star. That means they were astrologists. That is a "no go" in the eyes of God.

Good power comes from Holy Spirit. Bad power comes from the devil. Magic is evil. Therefore, the Magi (same word) were evil.

For your edification, the bible doesn't say there were 3 Magi. It just says Magi. (Matthew 2:1) **Now after Jesus was born in Bethlehem of Judea in the days of Herod the king, magi from the east arrived in Jerusalem.**

<u>March 18th Manger Scenes are Inaccurate</u>

"After coming into the <u>house</u> they saw the Child with Mary His mother; and they fell to the ground and worshiped Him. Then, opening their treasures, they presented to Him gifts of gold, frankincense, and myrrh" (Matthew 2:11).

The magi visited a house, not a stable with a manger. The Hebrew and Greek words for house and stable are complete different so there can be no mistake. Mary and Joseph were in a house when the magi visited. This fact alone proves the historical inaccuracy of manger scenes. Yet, millions of people still put them up every December.

The timeline of the Magi's visit is not specifically given so we must assume, based upon Herod's murderous actions, that it was within two years of Jesus birth. (Matthew 2:16) **Then Herod, seeing he had been outwitted by the astrologers, fell into a great rage, and he sent out and had all the boys in Bethlehem and in all its districts done away with, from two years of age and under, according to the time that he had carefully ascertained from the astrologers.**

Sadly this tragedy was predicted 600 years in Jeremiah 31:15: **"This is what YHWH has said, 'In Ramah a voice is being heard, lamentation and bitter weeping; Rachel weeping over her sons. She has refused to be comforted over her sons, because they are no more.'"**

March 19th Worship Yahweh in Truth

"God is a Spirit, and those worshiping him must worship with spirit and truth" (John 4:24).

True Christians must worship in spirit and truth, not out of tradition and error.

Santa Clause is not biblical. There is no such thing in reality as a magic fat guy in red clothes who makes iPhones in the North Pole with elves to give to family members you don't like.

Saint Nicolas is not Biblical because Saints are not biblical. God wants us to only worship Him, not dead and powerless men.

I want to spend a few seconds getting personal with you about Christmas so you can learn from my experience. Like you, I always knew that Jesus was not born on the 25th of December. But because I love Jesus, I thought it was as good of a time as any other to celebrate and honor him.

Also, I didn't want to be the only "weirdo" to not celebrate Christmas. But don't worry, there are millions of true hearted Christians out there who don't celebrate Christmas. You may have to look for them. But there are millions.

When my wife and I told our families that we would not celebrate Christmas for the previously explained reasons they all thought we were crazy. Our kids were the most disappointed. Even though we were doing the right thing, the first year without Christmas was hard. That was the year we threw away all our Christmas decorations and Christmas music. That year our families were the meanest to us. The second year was easier as we knew we could do it and the family got more tolerant of our integrity. And by the third year, it was absolutely pain free, drama free.

So please take courage that it is possible to love Yahweh and Jesus, His son, but to not celebrate Christmas. Expect drama and stupidity from your associates and family when you first take a stand against a tradition of man which violates biblical truth.

March 20th Easter is Not Biblical

"The day of the unfermented cakes now arrived, on which the Passover [victim] must be sacrificed; and he dispatched Peter and John, saying: "Go and get the Passover ready for us to eat" (Luke 22:7-8)

Biblical Truth tells us that Jesus died at Passover, not Easter. Easter doesn't honor Jesus's sacrifice, is celebrated on the incorrect day, is pagan, and certainly not scriptural.

Jesus died during Passover. You can read this for yourself in the gospels. We can see in today's scripture that Jesus had the last supper on the day of the Passover sacrifice.

Because the Jewish day began right after sundown and ended as the sun went down, Jesus had the Passover dinner with his disciples, ordered the tradition of drinking wine and bread in remembrance of him, prayed in Gethsemane, was arrested, tortured and died all during the same day. As we see in the Luke 22 scripture, he did this on the Passover sacrifice day. Jesus was, in fact, our Passover sacrifice, once and for all.

If you were married on Saturday the 14th of a particular month, you would not celebrate your anniversary each year during the second Saturday of that particular month. You would celebrate your anniversary on the

14th, regardless of what day of the week it was. Likewise, Jesus was sacrificed on the 14th of the month of Nissan and so true worshipers should celebrate Jesus' ransom sacrifice during the 14th of Nissan.

False religion celebrates the ransom on the wrong day. They celebrate Jesus' sacrifice not on the 14th of Nissan but in accordance with directions and guidance set forth by faker catholic church leaders on the first Sunday after the third full moon after the winter solstice. It is easy to justify since all the Christendom does it. But just because so many millions do it wrongly, does that make it right? Would you celebrate your wedding anniversary on the wrong date? Would that honor your spouse?

March 21st Easter is Named after a False Goddess

"You must be careful to do all that I have said to you, and you must not mention the names of other gods; they should not be heard on your lips" (Exodus 23:13).

Easter is another good idea turned bad. The Catholic Church many centuries ago decided to incorporate celebrating the memorial of Jesus' death with a pagan harvest celebration to a goddess (again another demon pretending to be a god) whose name is a variation of the word Easter. This celebration brought in thousands of pagans who worshiped this false goddess during harvest time fertility parties. Bunny rabbits, as many know, reproduce rapidly. That is why they were adopted as a symbol of Easter's fertility and harvest celebrations. Eggs are also a symbol of new life so they were adopted into the symbols of Easter to signify the new life of Easter's fertility and harvest celebrations.

The Catholic Encyclopedia even admits that Easter is named after a false god. "The English term, according to the Ven. Bede (De temporum ratione, I, v), relates to Estre, a Teutonic goddess of the rising light of day and spring"[10].

Every time you say Easter you are referring to a false god and violating a direct commandment from Yahweh not to even mention false Gods.

March 22nd Honor Yahweh in Word and Deed

"And Yahweh says: "For the reason that this people have come near with their mouth, and they have glorified me merely with their lips, and they have removed their heart itself far away from me, and their fear toward me becomes men's commandment that is being taught" (Isaiah 29:13)

If you celebrate Easter you are a faker Christian and are outside the will of Yahweh.

Like Christmas, the first year my wife and I did not celebrate Easter all our friends and family thought we were crazy or joining an occult sect. But this holiday tradition is so off from the truth and so obviously not celebrated on the right timeline (meaning not celebrated during Passover) that it was intellectually and

---

[10] Catholic Encyclopedia, New Advent, http://www.newadvent.org/cathen/05224d.htm

emotionally simple to stop celebrating. Please know that there are millions of Yahweh loving Christians out there who don't celebrate Easter.

YOU ARE NOT ALONE!

And more importantly, Yahweh sees that you are trying to worship Him in truth. When your family and faker Christian friends all think you are crazy then you will know for sure that you are doing the right thing.

March 23nd God is Love

"He that does not love has not come to know God, because God is love" (1 John 4:8).

Yahweh is our father and creator. He loves people and wants the best for all of us. He wants us to know and love Him and to be obedient children. As today's scripture proclaims, "God is love."

The modern church misleadingly teaches that sometimes death and pain and suffering come from God or are tests from God. But this is not true.

Biblical truth shows us that Yahweh doesn't cause suffering.

Suffering is a result of (1) human sin, (2) Satan, or (3) chance and unforeseen circumstances. We will study scriptures about each of these causes of suffering later this week.

Life is hard. No matter how rich you are or how isolated you are, you are going to experience pain. You can't hide from suffering. We all eventually get touched by hardship. The problem is that most people don't know the source of their suffering and many faker Christians imply or even say that Yahweh is the cause of this suffering. But this is not so. Yahweh doesn't cause suffering. Yahweh is love.

March 24th God cares about You

"Humble yourselves, therefore, under the mighty hand of God, that he may exalt YOU in due time; while YOU throw all YOUR anxiety upon him, because he cares for YOU" (1 Peter 5:6-7).

Yahweh cares for you. Wow. What a wonderful and humbling realization. The creator of the world, our all-powerful and all-knowing, loving God, Yahweh, actually cares about us.

When you care about someone you don't send them trials, temptations, suffering. You give them love, support, and good advice. That is exactly what Yahweh give us.

Biblical truth shows us that Yahweh is love and that He cares for us. He doesn't cause suffering. Suffering is a result of (1) human sin, (2) Satan, or (3) chance and unforeseen circumstances.

March 25th God Doesn't Tempt People

"When being under trial, let no one say: "I am being tried by God." For with evil things God cannot be

tried nor does he himself try anyone" (James 1:13-14).

God doesn't tempt people. Many faker Christians imply that God is testing them and tempting them to see the strength of their faith. This is bad theology and not true. Satan tempts people. People give into their own desires and sin. Sin then leads to death. Jesus' brother James reminds us in today's scripture that Yahweh doesn't tempt people.

Biblical truth shows us that Yahweh is love and that He cares for us. He doesn't cause trails, temptations, or suffering. Let's not forget that suffering is a result of (1) human sin, (2) Satan, or (3) chance and unforeseen circumstances.

March 26th Human Sin Causes Suffering

"For all have sinned and fall short of the glory of God" (Romans 3:23).

Today's scripture reminds us of the simple fact that we are all sinners.

Jeremiah 10:23 tells us that men, left up to themselves, always mess things up: **I well know, O YHWH, that to earthling man his way does not belong. It does not belong to man who is walking even to direct his step.**

When humans do it their way, the way they want to selfishly do it, rather than the way God tells us to do it, there will be consequences.

For example, God tells us to worship Him alone, not money. But when a selfish and sinful person worships money they will do anything to have more. They make bad investments, lie to banks, or flat out steal. This collective sinfulness caused the 2008 U.S. recession and millions of people lost half of their life's savings when banks collapsed and stocks crashed.

Another example is the modern family. God tell us to love and honor our spouses. But human selfishness and sin causes someone to have an affair, destroying a family and forcing the ex-spouse and kids alike to endure years of suffering and adverse consequences.

Biblical truth shows us that Yahweh is love and that He cares for us. He doesn't cause trails, temptations, or suffering. And again, let's not forget that suffering is a result of (1) human sin, (2) Satan, or (3) chance and unforeseen circumstances.

March 27th Satan Causes Suffereing

"The whole world is lying in the power of the wicked one" (1 John 5:19)

The bible reveals to us a simple truth: that Satan is the ruler of this world. Satan and his demons mislead people into sin and evilness. Satan and his demons have caused so much suffering.

For an example of suffering caused by pure evil, think of all the thousands of people killed each week by narcotic traffickers and drug dealers as cocaine grown in

Colombia is flown from Venezuela into Central America, then transported through Mexico to the hands of a despicable drug dealer who sells it to a teenager at the local high school.

War, murder and rape are other ways Satan and his Demons have managed to wreak havoc on the earth and fill it with pain and suffering.

Biblical truth shows us that Yahweh is love and that He cares for us. He doesn't cause trails, temptations, or suffering. And let us not forget that suffering is a result of (1) human sin, (2) Satan, or (3) chance and unforeseen circumstances.

March 28nd Chance and Unforeseen Circumstances Cause Suffering

"I returned to see under the sun that the swift do not have the race, nor the mighty ones the battle, nor do the wise also have the food, nor do the understanding ones also have the riches, nor do even those having knowledge have the favor; <u>because time and unforeseen occurrence befall them all.</u> For man also does not know his time. Just like fishes that are being taken in an evil net, and like birds that are being taken in a trap, so the sons of men themselves are being ensnared at a calamitous time, when it falls upon them suddenly" (Ecclesiastes 9:11-12)

Accidents happen. People find out they are allergic to bee stings when the antidote is not available. Motorcycle riders know that they take their lives into their own hands every time they turn on their bikes. A car pops a tire and runs off the road…etc. Today's scripture tells us that we are all vulnerable to chance occurrences and unforeseen anomalies.

My teenage daughter just talked to my wife and I recently about this very subject of suffering. She was concerned about how a loving God could allow this world to be so bad and why would He cause so much suffering. It was a very real and heart felt conversation. We explained to her that God does not cause suffering and showed her the causes of suffering. However, <u>just knowing the causes of suffering doesn't make suffering go away. But for sure, knowing the causes of suffering prevents you from blaming Yahweh and drifting away from Him.</u>

Your suffering is either part of the devil's schemes, the consequences of your sin or the sins of others, or a result of chance occurrences and unforeseen circumstances. Please never blame Yahweh for suffering.

<u>March 29th Understanding Death from a Biblical Perspective</u>

"That is why, just as through one man sin entered into the world and death through sin, and thus death spread to all men because they had all sinned" (Romans 5:12).

Death entered the world as a consequence of sin and is a sad reality of life. But most people don't understand what happens when you die.

The modern church hypocritically lies and tells people that when you die you go instantly to heaven to live forever. They imply that everyone goes to heaven, except maybe Hitler or Osama Bin Laden etc. (I am being ironic) Also, some Catholics go to purgatory where they suffer and work out penance (punishment) until they are righteous enough to get into heaven. But this is all incorrect.

The bible tells us that when you die you go to "Hades" or "Sheol" where you are powerless and conscious of nothing, awaiting the coming of God's Kingdom, resurrection and judgement. Death is described many places in the bible as going to sleep. Some will sleep for thousands of years before being resurrected for judgement. Others, who die just before the arrival of God's Kingdom, will only sleep a short time.

Everyone Dies. Well, at least that used to be the case. But since we are living in the last days, there will be many of us who endure through the great tribulation and fear inspiring Day of Judgment, and who will be able to live forever. Whether you will live forever or die tomorrow, it is important to know what Yahweh's plan for death entails because it can give you hope during this time of trouble and will help you recognize false religion and their false doctrines.

March 30th Biblical Words for Grave / Death

"She'ol and the place of destruction themselves do not get satisfied; neither do the eyes of a man get satisfied" (Proverbs 27:20).

In order to study death you need to become familiar with two Greek words and one Hebrew word which are frequently mistranslated by faker Christian organizations as "hell."

Origin	Word	Meaning
Greek	Hades	Common Grave
Hebrew	Sheol	Common Grave
Greek	Gehenna	Total Destruction, Lake of Fire

In summary, Sheol and Hades describe the same thing. The bible tells us that people who have died are waiting or resting in "Hades" or "Sheol." They are dead and conscious of nothing. They are then awakened (resurrected) into life or judgment. Of those resurrected to everlasting life, most will be resurrected to live in paradise. Sadly, those resurrected for judgment are sent to "Gehenna" for complete destruction.

March 31th There is no such thing as Purgatory

"All that your hand finds to do, do with your very power, for there is <u>no work</u> nor devising nor knowledge nor wisdom in She′ol, the place to which you are going" (Ecclesiastes 5:10).

There is no work or knowledge or wisdom in Sheol. This is an important scripture for Catholics to know. The Catholic Church falsely teaches that when people die, many go to purgatory, an interim location between heaven and earth where humans work out their righteousness.

Today's scripture tells us that there is no work in the grave. So it impossible for man to work out his salvation through punishments in a non-existent place called purgatory.

The concept of purgatory is an assimilation of Greek mythology and their belief in the underworld.

Purgatory is not a word found in the bible nor is it a biblical truth. When you die and are in Sheol (pit, hole, grave), you are conscious of nothing and therefore do not work.

April 1st Both the Good and Bad Go to Sheol / Hades as our Bodies return to Dust

"In the sweat of your face you will eat bread until you return to the ground, for out of it you were taken. For dust you are and to dust you will return" (Genesis 3:19).

Everyone goes to the common grave, but our physical bodies return to dust.

Only through the amazing power of our wonderful God, Yahweh, are we able to be resurrected again.

Because the common grave is where everyone awaits a resurrection and judgment, both the righteous and the unrighteous go to Sheol / Hades.

A great scripture for understand this truth is when Job is afraid of God's anger and says that he would rather be dead and in Sheol. **O that in Sheol you would conceal me, That you would keep me secret until your**

anger turns back, That you would set a time limit for me and remember me!" (Job 14:13). Job was a righteous man who Yahweh favored. Certainly, if Job knew he would be going to Sheol then it must be a place for good people as well as bad people.

April 2nd The Dead are Unconscious and Silent

"For the living are conscious that they will die; but as for the dead, they are conscious of nothing at all, neither do they anymore have wages, because the remembrance of them has been forgotten" (Ecclesiastes 9:5)

Today's scripture reveals to us that that those who are dead are conscious of nothing at all.

The dead are not able to think. (Psalm 146:4) **His spirit goes out, he goes back to his ground; In that day his thoughts do perish.** This is a good scripture for those who claim to be dead and wake up to tell grandiose stories about their experience. These people were never fully dead. They may have had no heart beat or electrical activity for a short time, both of which can be elongated with the cold, but there was enough life giving blood and oxygen for them to survive once their system restarted.

Although I don't want to ever put Yahweh in a box, these people's memories of heaven and the light at the end of the tunnel are either demonically inspired, self-accrediting dreams about their preexisting false expectations, or memories made by psychologists and religious leaders who ask leading questions. The bible tells us that when you die your body stops and you are no longer conscious of anything. It is blackness.

Hades or Sheol are silent. (Psalm 115:17) **The dead themselves do not praise Jah, Nor do any going down into silence.**

April 3rd The Dead are Emotionless and Powerless

"Also, their love and their hate and their jealousy have already perished, and they have no portion anymore to time indefinite in anything that has to be done under the sun" (Ecclesiastes 9:6).

The dead are dead and do not have emotions. This means that dead people do not become evil spirits who have evil opinions and harbor resentment against the living. They have no emotions. They are dead.

The dead are not able to scare you, hurt you, kill you, and haunt you. (Isaiah. 26:14) **They are dead; they will not live. Impotent in death, they will not rise up.** The dead have no power. Voodoo witch doctors who live in grass huts and modern day catholic priests with gold rings and comical hats all ignore this truth that the dead are impotent. Many cultures in Africa even spend fortunes during burial ceremonies so that their dead loved one is happy with his burial so that he is appeased and will not be angry with them and haunt them as a ghost. This is not factual. The dead are impotent. There is no reason to pray to them, be in fear of them, worry about them, say rosaries to them, and donate money on their behalf. The dead are dead.

April 4th The Bible Forbids Spiritism

"Do not turn yourselves to the spirit mediums, and do not consult professional foretellers of events, so as to become unclean by them. I am Yahweh YOUR God" (Leviticus 19:31).

Yahweh forbids spiritism.

Spiritists do not communicate with the dead but communicate with demons who are pretending to be the dead. As we read previously, Satan and his demons can transform themselves into angels of light or other things to mislead the earth[11]. Their only goal is to take people away from true worship of Yahweh the almighty. Yes, it is a scary theme. Yes, demons can talk like your dead loved one or feared one. Yes, demons have power and strength. This is why Yahweh warns us not to give the devil a foot hold. This is why Yahweh warns us against getting involved in spiritism.

YHWH detests spiritists. (Deuteronomy 18:10-12) **There should not be found in you anyone who makes his son or his daughter pass through the fire, anyone who employs divination, a practitioner of magic or anyone who looks for omens or a sorcerer, or one who binds others with a spell or anyone who consults a spirit medium or a professional foreteller of**

---

[11] 2 Corinthians 11: 14-15

events or anyone who inquires of the dead. For everybody doing these things is something detestable to Yahweh, and on account of these detestable things Yahweh your God is driving them away from before you.

April 5th The Bible Forbids Talking to Dead People

"Now the works of the flesh are manifest, and they are fornication, uncleanness, loose conduct, idolatry, practice of spiritism, enmities, strife, jealousy, fits of anger, contentions, divisions, sects, envies, drunken bouts, revelries, and things like these. As to these things I am forewarning YOU, the same way as I did forewarn YOU, that those who practice such things will not inherit God's kingdom" (Galatians 5:19-21).

Spiritism is listed as one of the evil works of the flesh which prevents people from entering the kingdom of God.

If you are catholic or orthodox and pray to - or ask help from - or worship - or adore dead saints, then you are practicing Spiritism and are absolutely doing what Yahweh forbids and detests. You are comparable with a Satanist and a voodoo witch doctor because you at least have access to and claim to believe inspired scriptures. Repent, stop trying to communicate with the dead saints, stop giving praise and worship and false credit and power to dead humans and demons. Worship the only true, living god, Yahweh.

April 6th Death is described as Sleeping

""""Why are YOU causing noisy confusion and weeping? The young child has not died, but is sleeping" Mark 5:39.

The bible describes many people who are dead as sleeping. Today's scripture records the words of Jesus who is explaining that the dead girl is only sleeping.

Lazarus's death is another example where Jesus himself compares death and being in Sheol with sleeping. (John 11:11-14) **He said these things, and after this he said to them: "Lazarus our friend has gone to rest, but I am journeying there to awaken him from sleep." Therefore, the disciples said to him: Lord, if he has gone to rest, he will get well." Jesus had spoken, however, about his death. But they imagined he was speaking about taking rest in sleep. At that time, therefore, Jesus said to them outspokenly: "Lazarus has died."**

Stephen dies and Luke, under inspiration of Holy Spirit, describes it in Acts 7:60 as falling asleep: **then, bending his knees, he cried out with a strong voice: "YHWH, do not charge this sin against them." And after saying this he fell asleep [in death].**

April 7th Gehenna is Total Destruction

"And do not become fearful of those who kill the body but cannot kill the soul; rather, fear him who can destroy both soul and body in Gehenna" (Matthew 10:28).

"Gehenna" is synonymous with destruction and or the lake of fire. Figuratively, Gehenna means total destruction. Literally, Gehenna or the Valley of Hinnom was a deep ravine outside of Jerusalem where people tossed their trash and filth. In biblical times, the trash and filth were burning all the time. It was a great literal representation of destruction.

After the first death where people go to Sheol or Hades, everyone is resurrected for judgement. The righteous are given paradise and the unrighteous are given a judgement of destruction. These unrighteous ones are sent to the second death which is total destruction or the lake of fire. (Revelations 20:13-14) **And the sea gave up those dead in it, and death and Hades gave up those dead in them, and they were judged individually according to their deeds. And death and Hades were hurled into the lake of fire. This means the second death, the lake of fire. Furthermore, whoever was not found written in the book of life was hurled into the lake of fire.**

April 8th The Ungodly go to Gehenna for Complete Destruction

These very ones [the unrighteous] will undergo the judicial punishment of everlasting destruction from before the Lord and from the glory of his strength" (2 Thessalonians 1: 9).

The ungodly will be resurrected and punished with total destruction. How sad it is that they will not be given everlasting life. How sad it is that they did not honor Yahweh during their lives.

Many immature Christians like to think that everyone will go to heaven. But this is false doctrine. The bible tells us over and over again that **"unrighteous persons will not inherit God's Kingdom"** (1 Corinthians 6:9). So please live your life in a righteous way so that during the resurrection you will be judged and found worthy of paradise, not destruction.

April 9th Timeline of Dying

And he said to him: "Truly I tell you today, You will be with me in Paradise" (Luke 23:43).

Most Christian churches do not understand the timeline of dying. When you die you are dead, conscious of nothing, dust. You go to paradise after the resurrection, not immediately after you die.

Let's take a close look at what Jesus said in today's scripture. Please note that there is a punctuation mark after the word "today." If there was no punctuation mark, then Jesus would be saying that that day (immediately after dying) they would be in paradise. But because there is a comma (or a pause) after today, Jesus is saying something similar to "right now in this moment I am saying that when you are resurrected you will receive paradise." Many churches say things like "she is now looking down on us from heaven." This is not so. Your loved one is dead and in Hades / Sheol, black, conscious of nothing, dust, waiting to be resurrected.

April 10th There is no Such Thing as Everlasting Torture in a Fiery Hell

"So he called and said, "Father Abraham, have mercy on me and send Lazarus to dip the tip of his finger in water and cool my tongue, because I am in anguish in this blazing fire" (Luke 16: 24).

Most faker Christian churches do not understand death and say that it involves cruel, everlasting fiery torment. The faker Christian church uses Luke 16:22-26 and the parable of "the rich man" and "Lazarus" to scare people into going to church.

First of all, a loving God judges justly, and would never give everlasting torment as a punishment to someone who did not love Him. The inability to inherit paradise and being given total destruction is sufficiently severe, but just.

Secondly, this scriptural parable was recorded to emphasizes the importance of honoring Yahweh and that having the text of the bible is enough for anyone to find Yahweh.

Thirdly, this parable is very figurative and not to be taken literally. Spiritism is forbidden throughout the bible so why would the rich man plead to "father Abraham?" We just spent a week studying how Sheol/Hades are silent, dark, powerless, unconscious. There is no way for the rich man to be aware. Jesus is clearly giving a non-literal illustration.

Let us summarize all we have studied this week: Someone dies. This is the first death. They are in Sheol or

Hades, asleep in death, conscious of nothing, powerless. They will wait until the resurrection where they will be judged. If they are judged worthy, they get everlasting life. If they are judged unworthy of everlasting life they will go to Gehenna, the lake of fire, for total destruction. This is the second death. The dead are not tormented by fire. They are not in purgatory working out their salvation and praying to dead saints. They are not in heaven floating on clouds with fat baby angels with wings and bows and arrows.

April 11th Resurrection and Judgement

"And I have hope toward God, which hope these [men] themselves also entertain, that there is going to be a resurrection of both the righteous and the unrighteous." (Acts 24:15)

There are many incorrect misunderstandings within the churches and denominations of the Christiandom concerning what happens after someone dies and is judged. Many churches falsely say that when you die you go instantly to heaven to live forever. Everyone goes to heaven, except maybe Hitler or Osama Bin Laden [of course I am being ironic]. Some Catholics go to purgatory first where they suffer and work out penance (punishment) until they are righteous enough to get into heaven. This is all wrong.

Biblical truth reveals that <u>everyone</u> is resurrected, individually judged face to face based upon their works, and receives a just verdict of everlasting life or destruction.

Many false religions say that when you die you immediately will live forever in heaven or in paradise. This is wrong. The bible clearly states that we will all be raised up for a resurrection, a resurrection into everlasting life or into judgment and destruction. That is why it is important to honor Yahweh with all your heart, mind, soul, strength and to be obedient.

The bible clearly teaches that everyone dead (both the righteous and unrighteous) will be resurrected so that Jesus can render a face to face judgment to them based upon the deeds of their life. Jesus will separate the sheep from the goats. The sheep will go to everlasting life and the goats will go to everlasting destruction.

Thankfully, it is not our responsibility to judge others. Jesus sees their hearts, knows extenuating circumstances, and will render a fair, just verdict. Even though it is not our job to judge, we do not want to be ignorant to the process of resurrection and judgment.

Everyone dead will be resurrected. There will be a resurrection of the righteous and unrighteous.

Both the righteous and wicked will be judged. (Ecclesiastes 3:17) **So I said in my heart: "The true God will judge both the righteous and the wicked, for there is a time for every activity and every action."**

April 12th The Dead will be Resurrected for Individual Judgement

"And the sea gave up those dead in it, and death and Ha′des gave up those dead in them, and they were

judged individually according to their deeds" (Revelation 20:13).

Today's scripture reminds us that the dead will be resurrected for judgement. We see that Hades (translated as "Grave") gives up its dead so that they can be judged according to their deeds. When God's Kingdom comes, the dead will be resurrected from the grave to be judged for their deeds. It doesn't matter if the dead person has been dead for three thousand years or three days. Only Yahweh has the power to raise the dead.

Today's scripture also reminds us that we will all be judged based upon our deeds and conduct.

Are your deeds and daily conduct a reflection of your love for Yahweh?

April 13th Judgement is made to Your Face

"You well know that Yahweh your God is the true God, the faithful God, keeping his covenant and loyal love to a thousand generations of those who love him and keep his commandments. But those who hate him he will repay <u>to their face</u> with destruction. He will not be slow to deal with those who hate him; he will repay them <u>to their face</u>" (Deuteronomy 7: 9-11).

Judgment will be in your face and individual.

Yahweh is the only true God. And as the only true God, Yahweh alone is worthy of our love and worship and praise.

The reason that everyone is judged "to their face" is that everyone must know and see that Yahweh alone is the only true God, even if they only see or accept this fact during the last few seconds before being destroyed.

Do you acknowledge that Yahweh alone is God and is worthy of love and worship?

April 14th You will be Judged According to Your Deeds

"And I saw the dead, the great and the small, standing before the throne, and scrolls were opened. But another scroll was opened; it is the scroll of life. The dead were judged out of those things written in the scrolls according to their deeds" (Revelation 20:12).

You will be judged according to your deeds, not from your perspective but from God's perspective. If you were to judge your own deeds from your own perspective you would probably assess that you are perfect in every way and that all your decisions were wise. But this is not the case. We will all be perfectly judged from our all-knowing God's perspective, based upon His rules for conduct, His Biblical principles. How sad it would be if He found that our deeds and conduct were not in accordance with the loving principles explained to us through the Bible.

Our goal is to have our names written in the "scroll of life." This means that when we are judged, we will receive a merciful verdict of everlasting life.

How do your deeds and conduct compare with biblical standards?

April 15th Yahweh has Delegated Judging to Jesus

"For just as the Father raises the dead up and makes them alive, so the Son also makes alive whomever he wants to. For the Father judges no one at all, but he has entrusted all the judging to the Son" (John 5: 21-22).

Yahweh has the power and authority to resurrect and judge. But we learn from today's scriptures that the responsibility of judging has been entrusted to Jesus. Because Jesus is zealous for his father, we can expect Jesus to render favorable judgement to those who also loved Yahweh and lived their lives in accordance with Biblical principles.

Jesus will judge the living and the dead. (2 Timothy 4:1-2) **I solemnly charge you before God and Christ Jesus, who is destined to judge the living and the dead, and by his manifestation and his kingdom, preach the word, be at it urgently in favorable season, in troublesome season, reprove, reprimand, exhort, with all long-suffering and [art of] teaching.**

April 16th You Reap what you Sow

"For we must all appear before the judgment seat of the Christ, so that each one may be repaid according to the things he has practiced while in the body, whether good or bad" (2 Corinthians 5:10).

We will be repaid according to our conduct. If we were bad and disrespected our God Yahweh and our neighbors then we will receive destruction. If we were good and loved our God Yahweh and our neighbors then we will receive life.

Because all authority has been given to Jesus we know that Jesus will be a righteous and all-knowing judge. He knows our hearts and our conduct. We cannot fool Jesus or Yahweh. So we will be repaid in accordance with how we pay. We will reap what we sow.

What would Jesus say about your heart and deeds these days?

Exercise faith in Jesus. (John 11:25) **Jesus said to her: "I am the resurrection and the life. He that exercises faith in me, even though he dies, will come to life."** It is essential to point out that Jesus's expression is not "having faith in me" but is "exercising faith in me." Exercising implies work and a deliberate effort.

April 17th Two verdicts: Everlasting Life or Destruction

"Do not marvel at this, because the hour is coming in which all those in the memorial tombs will hear his voice and come out, those who did good things to a resurrection of life, those who practiced vile things to a resurrection of judgment" (John 5:28-29).

At the judgement, there will be only two verdicts: Everlasting life or Destruction.

There is no "do over."

There is no "better next time."

There is only life or destruction.

How sad it will be for those who did not live their lives in accordance with Yahweh's principles.

How wonderful it will be for those who loved Yahweh and their Neighbors in accordance with Biblical principles.

Which verdict do you want to receive?

April 18th Are you a Sheep or a Goat

"When the Son of man arrives in his glory, and all the angels with him, then he will sit down on his glorious throne. And all the nations will be gathered before him, and he will separate people one from another, just as a shepherd separates the sheep from the goats. And he will put the sheep on his right hand, but the goats on his left. (46) **And these will depart into everlasting cutting-off, but the righteous ones into everlasting life.** (Matthew 25:31-33,46)

When the Kingdom of God comes Jesus and the angels will separate people as sheep or goats. The sheep follow their shepherd, Jesus, and live their loving lives in accordance with biblical truth. The goats are the ones who live their lives their way, or worshiped false gods.

This is an easy to understand illustration. Those who are sheep will receive everlasting life. Those who are goats receive destruction.

Are you a sheep or a goat?

April 19th The Road to Destruction is Large

"Go in through the narrow gate; because broad and spacious is the road leading off into destruction, and many are the ones going in through it; whereas narrow is the gate and cramped the road leading off into life, and few are the ones finding it" (Matthew 7:13)

Large is the road to destruction and narrow is the road leading to everlasting life.

If you are a luke-warm Christian or a non-Christian you should not take this scripture lightly. It is unwise to think that all roads lead to God or that all paths and all journeys lead to the same place.

Only those who take the narrow way, who love Yahweh and live in accordance with Biblical principles, will inherit life.

Which road are you on?

April 20th I Never Knew You

"Not everyone saying to me, 'Lord, Lord,' will enter into the kingdom of the heavens, but the one doing the will of my Father who is in the heavens will. Many will say to me in that day, 'Lord, Lord, did we not prophesy in your name, and expel demons in your name, and perform many powerful works in your name?' And yet then I will confess to them: I

never knew YOU! Get away from me, YOU workers of lawlessness" (Matthew 7:21-23).

Faker Christians will not enter the Kingdom.

Many people say they do not believe in God. They will. This is because everyone will be resurrected for judgment. Some ask why would a loving God resurrect someone only to send them off to destruction?

The answer is simple. Yahweh deserved honor and glory and respect and worship and praise. And He will get it from everyone. He gets it now from those who love him and will continue to love Him forever. And those who could care less about Him now will certainly give Him respect when they see His remarkable grandeur and glory as they realize that they choose poorly. Sadly, many will regret that they followed false traditions of the church instead of doing what Yahweh says through the bible.

April 21th A Living Soul

"On this account I say to you: Stop being anxious about your <u>soul</u> as to what you will eat or what you will drink, or about your bodies as to what you will wear. Does not <u>soul</u> mean more than food and the body than clothing" (Matthew 6:25).

There are many incorrect ideas about the "soul" circulating within the faker Christian church. The laws of logic tell us that they all could be wrong, but they certainly cannot all be right. So, let's look at what we know and can prove from the bible.

The bible clearly teaches that:

1. A soul is a living creature or a living being
2. Animals and humans are souls (living creatures)
3. Our souls (lives) belong to Yahweh
4. Only Yahweh can kill our soul

That is it. This is what we can know for sure. The bible doesn't teach about dying and going to purgatory where we suffer for as long as we need to in order to be purified of our sins. This is a false and tormenting teaching of the Catholic church.

Let's look at the above four concepts in greater detail…

April 22th Soul: A Living Being

"YHWH God proceeded to form the man out of dust from the ground and to blow into his nostrils the breath of life, and the man came to be a living soul" (Genesis 2:7).

"Soul" is translated from the Hebrew word "Nephes" and the Greek word "psyche." "Nephes" is found in the bible 754 times and Psykhe occurs 102 times. Nephes means breath as in "has breath" or "is a breathing creature." Psykhe is familiar to most of us because of words like psychology and is related to mind. Soul is having a mind and the breath of life, a living creature.

Genesis 2:7 is a good scripture to study because it clearly uses the word Nephes as a living creature, person, being or soul. Let's look at it from several translations. Please note that Nephes has been translated into "living person," or "living creature," or "living being," or living soul".

New Living Translation: Then the LORD God formed the man from the dust of the ground. He breathed the breath of life into the man's nostrils, and the man became a living person.

Young's Literal Translation: And YHWH God formeth the man -- dust from the ground, and breatheth into his nostrils breath of life, and the man becometh a living creature.

Holman Christian Standard Bible: Then the LORD God formed the man out of the dust from the ground and breathed the breath of life into his nostrils, and the man became a living being.

There are hundreds of examples of "soul" in the bible so if you need to do additional research then please do so.

April 23rd Soul: Animals and Humans are Souls (Living Creatures)

"It is even so written: 'The first man Adam became a living soul.' The last Adam became a life-giving spirit" (1 Cor. 15:45).

Animals and humans are souls (living creatures). Today's scripture tells us that Adam became a living creature. Please note that Adam, the first man, "became" a soul. It doesn't say that he had a soul. He became a soul. Becoming a soul means becoming a living creature.

People are (souls) living creatures. (1 Pet. 3:20) **In Noah's days, a few people, that is, eight souls, were carried safely through the water.**

Animals also are (souls) living creatures. We see this in many scriptures. Below you can read a few examples:

Animals are (souls) living creatures. (Genesis 1:20) **God went on to say: 'Let the waters swarm forth a swarm of living souls.'** Obviously if YHWH calls fish souls then the meaning of the word soul must be living creature.

The same word for soul is used for man and animals. (Leviticus 24:17-18) **In case a man strikes any soul of mankind fatally, he should be put to death without fail. And the fatal striker of the soul of a domestic animal should make compensation for it, soul for soul.**

April 24th   Soul: Our Souls (Lives) Belong to Yahweh

"Look! All the souls—to me they belong. As the soul of the father so likewise the soul of the son—to me they belong. The soul that is sinning—it itself will die" (Ezekiel 18:4).

Today's scripture reminds us that all souls belong to Yahweh. And if they sin, they die.

A (soul) living creature can be killed. (Matthew 10:39) **Whoever finds his soul will lose it, and whoever loses his soul for my sake will find it.** We are encourages to die to ourselves and to live for Yahweh.

If we live for Yahweh in this world then we will inherit the kingdom. If we only live for ourselves in this world then we certainly will not have the opportunity to inherit the kingdom of God. In other words, if we are bad in this world we will be destroyed during the judgement.

April 25th Soul: Only Yahweh can Destroy our Souls

"And do not become fearful of those who kill the body but cannot kill the soul; but rather be in fear of him that can destroy both soul and body in Gehenna" (Matthew 10:28).

Only Yahweh can kill our soul

Only Yahweh can kill our soul. This is a very important scripture because it tells us that man can kill our body but man can't kill our souls. So when our bodies die, our souls do not die. Our soul can only be destroyed by Yahweh in Gehenna.

What happens to our soul during the time between when we die and when we are resurrected to everlasting life? Great question? The bible doesn't tell us exactly how that works, but we know for sure that when we die, we rest and wait in unconsciousness in Hades or Sheol until the judgement. After judgement, we receive either destruction in Gehenna or everlasting life. If our souls is destroyed in Gehenna then it is obviously mortal and destroyable. This proves that the Catholic church's tradition of the "immortal soul" is not biblical. But if our souls are not destroyed in Gehenna, then we can assume that our souls (our lives as living creatures) will keep on living during everlasting life. In this sense, our souls live forever.

How the resurrection process specifically works is unknown. Are we resurrected young or old or in new bodies or born again as babies? I don't even want to speculate about how we are resurrected. I don't want to put Yahweh in a box or to limit His abilities. Yahweh is in charge of that amazing process. But we can trust in Yahweh who made this system and have confidences that the joys of the resurrection are worth any sacrifice me make in this current world to remain obedient and loyal to Yahweh.

Let's summarize what we learned about the soul: A soul is a living creature or a living being. Animals and humans are souls (living creatures). Our souls (lives) belong to Yahweh. Only Yahweh can kill our soul.

April 26th Don't Put God in a Box… or a Statue

"Therefore, since we are the children of God, we should not think that the Divine Being is like gold or silver or stone, like something sculptured by the art and design of humans" (Acts 17:29).

Don't put Yahweh into a box. Don't limit Yahweh to a statue or idol. Although Yahweh manifests Himself sometimes through various means, He is an invisible spirit.

Most churches hypocritically teach you that it is OK to pray to saints or to their statues or necklaces. They falsely say that it is OK to have idols in your church or house and that it is OK to have a cross in your house or church or around your neck.

Biblical truth tells us that saints are dead and powerless. Statues and jewelry and images are powerless. We are commanded to pray to and worship Yahweh and Yahweh alone.

Yahweh made the world in six days and rested on the seventh (not because he needed to rest but to set a perfect example for us). He is all powerful, all knowing, and timeless. If we make a statue of an old guy with a great beard and worship it then we are limiting Yahweh. Yahweh can't be limited. **<u>Yahweh can't be put in a box</u>**. That is why Yahweh tells us over and over again never to make anything so as to worship it.

April 27th Yahweh Doesn't Live in Man Made Structures

"But will God truly dwell upon the earth? Look! The heavens, yes, the heaven of the heavens, themselves cannot contain you; how much less, then, this house that I have built" (1 Kings 8:27).

Yahweh is not contained in a building.

Yahweh doesn't live in a manmade place like a house, temple, or church. (2 Samuel 7:6-7) **For I have not** dwelt in a house from the day of my bringing the sons of Israel up out of Egypt to this day, but I was continually walking about in a tent and in a tabernacle. During all the time that I have walked about among all the sons of Israel, was there a word that I spoke with one of the tribes of Israel that I commanded to shepherd my people Israel, saying, 'Why did YOU people not build me a house of cedars?'**

Yahweh must me worshiped in truth. (John 4:24) **God is a Spirit, and those worshiping him must worship with spirit and truth.**

If Yahweh can't be contained in a huge building, then he certainly can't be contained in a picture, or image, or an idol or a statue. Yahweh is everywhere, all-knowing and all powerful. We do not have special access to Yahweh when we are in front of a cross at the local cathedral. The cross is inaccurate and has no power. We do not have special access to Yahweh when we are looking at a statue of Jesus being tortured. The statue has no power. We do not have special access to Yahweh when we are holding a pendant or rosary or necklace. The pendant or rosary or necklace has no power. We do not have special access to Yahweh when we pray to a statue of a dead saint or to a statue of Jesus' mother, Mary. The saints and Mary are all dead. They have no power.

April 28th Don't Make Images and Statues and Worship Them

"I am Yahweh your God, who have brought you out of the land of Egypt, out of the house of slaves. You

must not have any other gods against my face. You must not make for yourself a carved image or a form like anything that is in the heavens above or that is on the earth underneath or that is in the waters under the earth. You must not bow down to them nor be induced to serve them, because I Yahweh your God am a God exacting exclusive devotion, bringing punishment for the error of fathers upon sons, upon the third generation and upon the fourth generation, in the case of those who hate me; but exercising loving-kindness toward the thousandth generation in the case of those who love me and keep my commandments" (Exodus 20:2-6).

Yahweh commands us not to make images of things and worship them. This is a direct quote from the Ten Commandments. So there is nothing to say, nothing to argue. We must not make statues and forms and worship them. Period.

Worshiping a statue (form or idol) of a false god, a cross, a saint, Mary, or Jesus are all forbidden. We must worship Yahweh and Yahweh alone.

April 29th Worship the Creator, not the Creation

"... even those who exchanged the truth of God for the lie and venerated and rendered sacred service to the creation rather than the One who created, who is blessed forever. Amen" (Romans 1:25).

We all worship something. Some worship money, their stomach, their careers, their possessions. When we worship things made by man or rather than the only true

God, we are not giving Yahweh His proper respect and love.

The same goes for nature. We are supposed to worship the creator, not things created. Yes, the creation is wonderful, but the Creator is still greater.

April 30th Yahweh Doesn't Share His Glory

"I am Yahweh. That is my name; and to no one else shall I give my own glory, neither my praise to graven images" (Isaiah 42:8).

Yahweh doesn't share his glory with powerless images.

So, when someone worships an image or an idol they are taking away that which is due only to Yahweh. This is not good. Yahweh is a loving God, but He is also jealous. He shouldn't have to share his glory with anything. He alone is worthy our prayers and praise and worship.

Do you have a favorite statue, painting, image, idol? Do you pray to this statue, painting, image or idol? If so, you should stop immediately. Yahweh doesn't share his glory or praise.

In a huge catholic cathedral in Paris I once encountered a very creepy statue of Pope Paul VI. (A creepy statue of a creepy man. Google him.) I was surprised to see a woman kneel down in front of it and begin to pray and cry. What was she thinking? We are supposed to pray to YHWH, the living God. We are not supposed to pray to a statue of an evil and dead faker Christian Pope.

You can't go anywhere in the world without finding a catholic cathedral or faker Christian church or a prayer room which doesn't have a statue of a saint or Jesus being tortured or Mary holding Jesus. We are supposed to pray to YHWH, the living God. We are not supposed to pray to a statue of a dead person.

Sadly, millions of people visit their local cathedral every day to pray to powerless statues of their patron saints or some silly variation of the famous "Virgin of Guadalupe." We are supposed to pray to YHWH, the living God. We are not supposed to pray to a statue of dead and powerless people.

May 1st Guard Yourselves from Idols

"Little children, guard yourselves from idols" (1 John 5:21).

John's words are so simple and yet so profound. Protect yourself from idols.

Of course, John is warning us to protect ourselves from statues made in the likeness of false and powerless gods. But idols can also take other forms. They can be religious statues which put Yahweh in a box. They can be materialistic possessions which take away our attention from God.

Yes, it is possible for a material possession (a house, car, bike, phone, watch) to become an idol. You always think about it. You work for it. You can't wait to own it. Perhaps it has become an idol to you. Remember, we are told to love people and use things, not love things and use people.

It is so easy for people to be seduced by images, ideas, possessions. The mass media marketing systems take advantage of this truth by seducing you to want and worship their product.

Be careful what you worship. Guard yourselves from idols.

May 2nd Idols are Powerless

"Look! All of them are something nonexistent. Their works are nothing. Their molten images are wind and unreality" (Isaiah 41:29).

Images and Idols have no power and are nothing.

Idols and carved images have no power and are valueless. (Habakkuk 2:18) **Of what benefit has a carved image been, when the former of it has carved it, a molten statue, and an instructor in falsehood? When the former of its form has trusted in it, to the extent of making valueless gods that are speechless?**

Idols have no power and those who make them will also become powerless in death. (Psalm 115:3-8) **but our God is in the heavens; Everything that he delighted [to do] he has done. Their idols are silver and gold, the work of the hands of earthling man. A mouth they have, but they cannot speak; Eyes they have, but they cannot see; Ears they have, but they cannot hear. A nose they have, but they cannot smell. Hands are theirs, but they cannot feel. Feet are**

theirs, but they cannot walk; They utter no sound with their throat. Those making them will become just like them, All those who are trusting in them.

How sad it is that people misfocus their worship towards powerless, inanimate objects rather than to the all-knowing, all-powerful, living God, Yahweh.

May 3rd Christians should be Known for their love, not Gold Necklaces

"There are, in fact, many other things also which Jesus did, which, if ever they were written in full detail, I suppose, the world itself could not contain the scrolls written" (John 21:25).

Let's get practical for a moment. Jesus is awesome. We love Jesus. Jesus was a perfect example for us. Jesus is at the right hand of Yahweh. The very last verse of the book of John tells us in today's scripture that if all the stories about Jesus were written down, the scrolls would fill the world.

But if Jesus was so wonderful, why do faker Christians make images and statues and necklaces of the means by which he was tortured. Satan sadistically enjoyed torturing Jesus. And you aren't much better when you wear a necklace with the image of our suffering savior.

Faker Christians are recognized by cross necklaces. True Christians are recognized by love. (John 13:35) **By this all will know that YOU are my disciples, if YOU have love among yourselves.**

Imagine you had a brother who you love very much who was killed in a motorcycle accident. Would you wear a necklace of a crashed motorcycle? That is perverted. That is not how you honor your brother. Then why would you do that with Yahweh's son.

Faker Christians love images of Jesus being tortured. If you love Jesus then you want to think of his wonderful works of love. You don't want to think of the day he was tortured to death. 90% of paintings in faker churches and cathedrals and art museums are of Jesus being tortured. If you love Jesus then these images make you sad.

May 4th Yahweh will Destroy Idol Makers

"Every man has behaved so unreasoningly as not to know. Every metalworker will feel ashamed because of the carved image; for his molten image is a falsehood, and there is no spirit in them. They are vanity, a work of mockery. In the time of their being given attention they will perish" (Jeremiah 51:17-18).

Yahweh will pay back image makers by destroying them. This is scary but just. Yahweh shares His glory with no one. And so those who carve and paint idols will be held responsible for all the stumbling blocks they placed before people, pulling them away from true worship.

Idols are powerless and anyone who trusts in them will also become powerless in death. (Psalm 135:15-18) **The idols of the nations are silver and gold, the work of the hands of earthling man. A mouth they have,** but they can speak nothing; Eyes they have, but they can see nothing; Ears they have, but they can give ear to nothing. Also, there exists no spirit in their mouth. Those making them will become just like them, everyone who is trusting in them.

May 5th Yahweh Will Destroy Graven Images

"And I will cut off your graven images and your pillars from the midst of you, and you will no more bow down to the work of your hands" (Micah 5:13).

On the Day of Judgment, Yahweh will destroy graven images and idols. This means anything dedicated to false gods, in representation of false gods, or made to be prayed to or worshiped will be destroyed. This list includes statues and paintings and crosses and mosques and pyramids….

Yahweh wants you to use your mind to realize that the wooden thing you pray to is powerless and detestable. (Isaiah 44:14-15) **There is one whose work is to cut down cedars. He selects a certain type of tree, an oak, and he lets it grow strong among the trees of the forest. He plants a laurel tree, and the rain makes it grow. Then it becomes fuel for a man to make fires. He takes part of it to warm himself; He builds a fire and bakes bread. But he also makes a god and worships it. He makes it into a carved image, and he bows down before it.**

If you own a cross or rosary or idols you are a faker Christian. Throw them away, clean up your life, and realize that our loving father, Yahweh, is not empowered or accessed through your images and idols.

If you think it is more effective to pray with a cross or rosary in your hand you are wrong. You don't need a cross or rosary to access your loving Father in heaven.

If you think it is OK to pray to a statue or to a saint or to a dead person then you are a fake Christian. You don't need a statue or a saint to access your loving Father in heaven.

Throw away your idols, statues, crosses, rosaries, clean up your life, and realize that our loving father, Yahweh, requires exclusive devotion.

May 6th Don't Show off your Generosity

"So when you give to the needy, do not announce it with trumpets, as the hypocrites do in the synagogues and on the streets, to be honored by others……(Matthew 6:2).

The other day I was reading the "Harvard Magazine" and was sad to see that the magazine had 8 pages full of the names of the people who made donations to Harvard. Out of the approximate 4000 donations made, only 611 (or 15%) were mentioned as anonymous!

Giving generously is fine, ethical, and loving. But Jesus commanded us to do it anonymously. So if you want to help others by giving away material things, doing charity, or by donating money, just do it and keep it to yourself! Don't be a faker Christian by making a show of your generosity.

You can also encourage others to be charitable, to donate, or to help others in need without bragging about the specifics of your previous donations.

Do not forget that our heavenly Father, Yahweh, sees your fine deeds and will repay you for the good you have done out of your heart, and not because of lower motives likes getting an emotional "applause" from men!

It is important to remember the parable of the poor widow mentioned in Mark 12:41-44. No contribution is too small if it is commensurate with your abilities and well-motivated.

May 7th Christians Should be Recognized by Holiness, Not their Necklace

"Consider what sort of people you ought to be in holy acts of conduct and deeds of godly devotion" (2 Peter 3:11).honors

Stop showing off how holy you are by having a shameful gold cross on your neck. Don't think that the bigger the necklace, the greater the holiness. It only makes a person look like a rapper. Better start showing Yahweh your true heart by your actions. The church falsely teaches that it is OK to have a cross in your house or church or around your neck and to pray to it and to worship it.

Biblical truth tells us that Yahweh is not pleased with your cross necklace or statue.

Jesus died for our sins by being nailed to what the original Greek text called a "stauros" (σταυρός) or a "zylon" (ξύλον). Although these words are translated into English as a single, vertical stake or beam or pole, both of these words have been falsely translated by the early church as cross.

But before we study the history and meaning of these words, let's make a quick summary of the Bible's disdain for religious statues:

Yahweh clearly tells us in Exodus 20 and Deuteronomy 5 not to make images and statues of things and worship them. Yet, the faker protestant and catholic churches love to make images of a suffering and or dead and powerless Jesus on a cross and worship it. They pray to the cross. They pray at the cross. They finish prayers by making the sign of a cross.

The instrument of Jesus death is not something to celebrate. If your son was innocent yet put to death in the electric chair or via lethal injection would you walk around with a gold electric chair or medical syringe hanging proudly around your next? Of course not!

May 8th Displaying a Cross or Jesus on a Cross Exposes Jesus to Public Shame

"...but have fallen away, it is impossible to revive them again to repentance, because they nail the Son

of God to the stake again for themselves and expose him to public shame" (Hebrews 6:6).

Already, through a clear biblical commandment (in the 10 Commandments) and practical reasoning (Hebrews 6:6), we see that a cross is not something in which Yahweh delights. Now let's dig deeper into our already skeptical understanding of the cross by looking at the meaning of "stauros" or "zylon" using some of the most trusted dictionaries available.

Stauros is found in the bible as Strong's Concordance word number 4716. The Vines Complete Expository Dictionary says it is:

> *an upright pale or stake." On such malefactors were nailed for execution. Both the noun and the verb stauroo, "to fasten to a stake or pale," are originally to be distinguished from the ecclesiastical form of a two beamed "cross." The shape of the latter had its origin in ancient Chaldea, and was used as the symbol of the god Tammuz (being in the shape of the mystic Tau, the initial of his name) in that country and in adjacent lands, including Egypt. By the middle of the 3rd cent. A.D. the churches had either departed from, or had travestied, certain doctrines of the Christian faith. In order to increase the prestige of the apostate ecclesiastical system pagans were received into the churches apart from regeneration by faith, and were permitted largely to retain their pagan signs and symbols. Hence the Tau or T, in its most frequent form, with the cross-piece*

lowered, was adopted to stand for the "cross" of Christ.

What this tells us is that the original "stauros" was a wooden stake, more like a short telephone pole. The apostate church in the third century changed the meaning of the "stauros" to cross in an attempt to increase membership. By the way, I find it ironic that "Thomas Nelson," one of the largest faker Christian "den of thieves" book publishing companies in the world prints the Vines Complete Expository Dictionary which acknowledges that the "stauros" meant upright stake, not a cross.

Below are a few more trusted definitions or stauros:

The Thayer Greek Lexicon's first definition is "an upright stake, especially a pointed one (Homer, Herodotus, Thucydides, Xenophon)."[12]

NAS exhaustive Concordance defines stauros as "an upright stake."[13]

The Strong's Exhaustive Concordance defines stauros as "from the base of histemi; a stake or post (as set upright), i.e. (specially), a pole or cross"[14]

Stauroó (Strongs word 4717) is the verb form of Stauros. Thayer Greek Lexicon defines it as (1) "to stake, drive down stakes" or (2) to fortify with driven stakes,

---

[12] http://biblehub.com/greek/4716.htm (Thayer's)

[13] http://biblehub.com/greek/4716.htm (NAS Exhaustive)

[14] http://biblehub.com/greek/4716.htm (Strong's Exhaustive)

to palisade."[15] It is interesting to see that the verb for Stauroó means to drive in stakes… like you were making a fence, not make crosses or cross beams.

Vines defines Xylon (Strong's word 3586) as "wood, a piece of wood, anything made of wood" (see STAFF, STOCKS), is used, with the rendering "tree," (a) in Luke 23:31, where "the green tree" refers either to Christ, figuratively of all His living power and excellency, or to the life of the Jewish people while still inhabiting their land, in contrast to "the dry," a figure fulfilled in the horrors of the Roman massacre and devastation in A.D. 70 (cp. the Lord's parable in Luke 13:6-9; see Ezek. 20:47, and cp. Ezek. 21:3); (b) of "the cross," the tree being the stauros, the upright pale or stake to which Romans nailed those who were thus to be executed, Acts 5:30; 10:39; 13:29; Gal. 3:13; 1 Pet. 2:24".[16]

Strong's Exhausted Concordance defines Xylon as "from another form of the base of xestes; timber (as fuel or material); by implication, a stick, club or tree or other wooden article or substance -- staff, stocks, tree, wood."

Now is it easier to see that when the bible writers use the word stauros or xylon they are referring to the completely upright wooden stake upon which Jesus died for our sins.

---

[15] http://biblehub.com/greek/4717.htm (Thayer's)
[16] Vines Complete Expository Dictionary, Thomas Nelson, Nashville, 1996, Page 642

Secular historians even agree that 1st century Romans killed people with a single vertical torture stake, not a cross.

May 9th Jesus' Torture Stake looked like a T or t

"Pilate wrote a title also and put it on the torture stake. It was written: "Jesus the Nazarene' the King of the Jews." Therefore many of the Jews read this title, because the place where Jesus was impaled was near the city; and it was written in Hebrew, in Latin, in Greek. However, the chief priests of the Jews began to say to Pilate: "Do not write 'The King of the Jews,' but that he said, 'I am King of the Jews.'" Pilate answered: "What I have written I have written" (John 19:19-22).

The sign which Pilate wrote above Jesus may have made his vertical torture stake look from a distance like a T or a t. However, this sign was not a cross beam upon which Jesus body and weight hung. It was merely a sign.

It is sad to see that the truth about our savior was hidden by the Catholic Church in the first centuries after his death. This wasn't too hard since the people were not allowed to have a copy of the bible to read the truth for themselves.

Sadly, the faker church has had almost 2000 years to cover up the truth that Jesus was killed on a vertical, singular piece of wood. For all of you who see the hypocrisy and lies of the church this cover up is easy to understand. For those of you who grew up with crosses and painting of the cross all over your houses, churches, and museums, it is harder to believe this truth. Please do your own research to see for yourself that the cross was a pagan symbol adopted by a false church.

Please stop worshiping a cross, stop praying to a cross and stop wearing a cross. Please clean up your life, your wardrobe, your house and throw away every cross you have. Please know that history and the original texts of the bible show that Jesus died on a singular, vertical piece of wood. This was a sad and painful time for our savior and we should honor Yahweh by not having an inaccurate symbol of how His son died around our necks, in our homes, or at the place of our worship.

May 10th Yahweh says to Worship Him Alone

"You must not make for yourself a carved image or a form like anything that is in the heavens above or that is on the earth underneath or that is in the waters under the earth. You must not bow down to them nor be induced to serve them, because I YHWH your God am a God exacting exclusive devotion" (Exodus 20: 4-5).

The hypocritical church says that it is ok to pray to Mary and to worship and adore Mary. The hypocritical church says that Mary can help you because she is the most important person in Heaven.

Biblical truth reveals that Mary is dead (resting) and is powerless. We are commanded to pray to and worship Yahweh and Yahweh alone.

Mary was a wonderful woman who had such a pure heart that she was chosen by Yahweh for the amazing privilege and responsibility of being the mother of Jesus, Yahweh's son. Yet, Mary is the source of so many theological mistakes.

We should not worship dead people or dead saints. We are not supposed to worship Jesus. We are not supposed to worship Mary. We are supposed to worship God alone.

May 11th God doesn't Share His Glory with Mary

"I am Yahweh. That is my name; and to no one else shall I give my own glory, neither my praise to graven images" (Isaiah 42:8).

Yahweh shares his glory with no one... not even Mary.

Yahweh doesn't share his glory with dead saints, and he won't share his glory with Mary. If you worship or glorify Mary then you are violating Biblical commandments.

Take a few minutes to memorize this wonderful scripture.

May 12th Misconceptions about Mary

"But he had no intercourse with her until she gave birth to a son; and he called his name Jesus" (Matthew 1:25).

Mary had sexual intercourse and is no longer a virgin. The bible clearly states that Joseph had intercourse with his wife after Jesus was born.

The Greek goddess Artemis from Ephesus was known for being an eternal virgin. This pagan concept of eternal virginity was assimilated by Catholics towards Jesus' mother.

Mary had other children. The bible clearly states that Jesus had siblings. (Matthew 12:46) **While he was yet speaking to the crowds, look! His mother and brothers took up a position outside seeking to speak to him.**

Read Matthew 13:55 to see the names of some of Jesus's brothers. **"Is this not the carpenter's son? Is not his mother called Mary, and his brothers James and Joseph and Simon and Judas?"**

Do some research on your own to see that the writer of the books James and Jude were Jesus' brothers.

Mary died almost 2000 years ago. As we studied in a few weeks ago, the dead are powerless and conscious of nothing. Therefore, Mary has no power and we should not worship her, pray to her, or give glory to her.

May 13th The Bible Forbids Praying to or Worshipping Mary

"It is in vain that they keep worshipping me, for they teach commands of men as doctrines" (Matthew 15:9).

Praying to, venerating, and worshipping Mary are all unbiblical traditions of the Catholic Church.

Praying to Mary is outside the will of Yahweh.

Venerating Mary is outside the will of Yahweh.

Glorifying Mary is outside the will of Yahweh.

Making statues of Mary to worship is outside the will of Yahweh.

The catholic churches' immoral and unbiblical adoration of Mary alone is sufficient for me to say with a clean conscious that all Catholics are fakers. Shame on you if you pray to Mary rather than to Yahweh. Satan has won. He has fooled you into worshiping someone else, besides Yahweh. Shame on you if you go to a cathedral and pray and worship before a statue of a dead and powerless woman. Did you forget about the ten commandments where it says to only worship God and to not make idols? Where is your sense of reasoning?

Sadly, so many Catholics pray to Mary. Praying to Mary is wrong. The bible tells us to only pray to Yahweh.

May 14th Only Pray to Yahweh

"Do not be anxious over anything, but in everything by prayer and supplication along with thanksgiving let YOUR petitions be made known to God" (Philippians 4:6).

Prayer goes to Yahweh and to Yahweh alone.

The hypocritical church says that it is OK to pray to Jesus or to saints or to Mary or to dead popes.

Biblical truth tells us to pray only to Yahweh, but in the name of Jesus.

In the next few days we are going to learn about (1) acceptable locations of prayer and (2) to whom you must direct your prayer.

May 15th Pray Anywhere, but Discreetly

"Also, when YOU pray, YOU must not be as the hypocrites; because they like to pray standing in the synagogues and on the corners of the broad ways to be visible to men" (Matthew 6:5).

Jesus tells us to pray in a hidden place. But where?

Location of prayer is almost unimportant. Please don't think that to have your prayers heard you need to be in a church or in front of a statue or image. The power to hear and answer prayer comes from Yahweh, the hearer of prayers, and not from the cathedral or statue of a dead Saint or Jesus's mother.

A prayer made in a cathedral is actually less likely of being answered than a prayer made in your car. If you are in an old, huge, finely decorated Cathedral (think of Notre Dame Cathedral, Paris or St. Peter's Basilica in Rome) then you are surrounded by statues and images and inside a place where false doctrine and lies have been preached by Catholic Priests for hundreds of years, misleading thousands of thousands of people away from the truth and onto the path that leads to death and judgment. But if your heart is in the right place, then Yahweh will hear your prayer despite being in such a blatantly evil place. If you are praying in your car, then perhaps no one knows what you are doing and in fact you are in a hidden place or private room. This is more in line with what Jesus directed us to do. But don't forget, Yahweh sees the heart. So pray from the heart.

May 16th Yahweh is called the Hearer of Prayers

"O Hearer of prayer, even to you people of all flesh will come" (Psalm 65:2).

Yahweh is the hearer of prayers.

Prayer does not go to false gods or to anyone else. Yes there are bad examples in the bible of people doing silly things to win the approval of false gods. But we know that these false gods have no power. A great example of praying and yelling out to false gods who have no power is when Elisha challenges the prophets of the false god Baal to see if false god Baal will send down fire from the sky to consume a burnt offering. (1 Kings 18:26) **So they took the young bull that he gave them. Then they dressed it, and they kept calling upon the name of Baal from morning till noon, saying: "O Baal, answer us!" But there was no voice, and there was no one answering.**

All of the heroes of the faith prayed to Yahweh. Abraham prayed to Yahweh. Moses prayed to Yahweh. Joshua prayed to Yahweh. Daniel prayed to Yahweh. Paul prayed to Yahweh. I hope you get the pattern.

Not one person in the entire bible prayed to the messiah. And so we should not pray to Jesus, either.

If you pray to Jesus then you are wrong and outside the will of Yahweh. Faker Christians all over the world pray to Jesus. Yes, we are to give thanks and ask for things in Jesus' name. But Yahweh is the hearer of prayers. He is the giver of power and blessings.

If you pray to Mary, you are wrong and outside the will of Yahweh. Mary was a wonderfully blessed woman, but she has been dead now for almost 2000 years. She has no power. She is resting in Hades and will be resurrected when Yahweh calls all of those who also have died.

If you pray to inanimate things (images or statues or the cross) then you are wrong and outside the will of Yahweh. Prayer need to be directed to Yahweh who is not confined to a building or an image or a statue.

If you pray to Saints, you are wrong and outside the will of Yahweh.

I want to extent today's "Word of Wisdom" and tell a sad personal story. My Catholic father recently died and out of respect for the rest of my family we decided to attend the funeral, knowing it was going to be a hypocritical church tradition, not a reflection of biblical truth. During the service, the Catholic priest asked us to all extend our arms out towards the casket and said "please join me in begging the saints to fling open the gates of heaven and welcome in our dear brother." In one sentence, this priest made so many theological errors. I wonder if he had ever read the bible. Certainly, he was ignoring it. Why would the priest beg the saints to help my father get into heaven? The saints are dead and powerless and also awaiting the resurrection. We are supposed to pray to Yahweh and only to Yahweh.

In an attempt to add respect and power to the church, they established the tradition of praying only in the church and praying to inanimate things. This is silly and unbiblical. The church loves to pervert biblical truth to better serve itself.

May 17th Jesus Prayed Often, but Only to Yahweh

"Jesus spoke these things, and, raising his eyes to heaven, he said: "Father, the hour has come; glorify your son, that your son may glorify you" (John 17:1).

Jesus prayed to God, his Father, not to himself. Jesus's longest recorded prayer is found in John 17 and is directed to Yahweh.

Jesus prayed all the time. There are many examples in the bible when Jesus went off to pray. Matthew 14:23 is one example, of many, when Jesus went someplace by himself to pray. Jesus also had a heartfelt prayer in Gethsemane: **"Then Jesus came with them to the spot called Gethsemane, and he said to the disciples: "Sit down here while I go over there and pray." And taking along Peter and the two sons of Zebedee, he started to be grieved and to be sorely troubled. Then he said to them: "My soul is deeply grieved, even to death. Stay here and keep on the watch with me." And going a little way forward, he fell upon his face, praying and saying: "My Father, if it is possible, let**

this cup pass away from me. Yet, not as I will, but as you will" (Matthew 26:36-39).

We can learn a lot from Jesus' example of praying from the heart, and only to Yahweh.

May 18th Jesus taught us to Whom we must Pray

"YOU must pray, then, this way: 'Our Father in the heavens, let your name be sanctified. Let your kingdom come. Let your will take place, as in heaven, also upon earth" (Matthew 6:9-10).

Jesus showed us that we should pray to YHWH.

Jesus prayed to his Father, not to himself. Jesus' model prayer teaches us to pray to Yahweh.

It is in style these days at protestant churches to pray to Jesus. But this is unbiblical and a slap in Yahweh's face. Jesus is the created, the son. Yahweh is God, the Creator, the Father. We must not pray to or worship anyone else besides Yahweh.

May 19th Pray to Yahweh, but in Jesus' Name

"And in that day YOU will ask me no question at all. Most truly I say to YOU, If YOU ask the Father for anything he will give it to YOU in my name" (John 16:23).

When we are thankful we should pray to Yahweh and give thanks in the name of Jesus. (Ephesians 5:20) **always giving thanks to our God and Father for everything in the name of our Lord Jesus Christ.**

The name of Jesus is powerful. Jesus is powerful. But all of the power of Jesus' name and all the power that Jesus has is from Yahweh. By referencing Jesus' name at the end of our prayers we are implying "I am in a right standing before you Yahweh and am able to offer up this pray of supplication or thanksgiving only because of the access given to me by the ransom of Jesus." It is an admittance of humility, of the need for Jesus' sacrifice, and an acknowledgement that without Jesus' sacrifice we would never be able to have a right standing before Yahweh, our grand creator.

May 20th Be Fruitful and Multiply

"And God proceeded to create the man in his image, in God's image he created him; male and female he created them. Further, God blessed them and God said to them: "Be fruitful and become many and fill the earth and subdue it..." (Genesis 1:27-31).

Yahweh made man and woman and told them to be fruitful and multiply. The hypocritical church teaches that it is OK to not have children. They even teach that if you love God and want to serve Him full time it is best if you become a monk or nun or priest and dedicate your life to celibacy.

Biblical truth commands us to get married to someone who loves Yahweh and to raise a lot of Christian children together. Don't become a priest or nun. Be fruitful and multiply.

Please note that YHWH made the family before He made the church and its organization.

May 21th Don't Link Yourself to Non-Christians

"Do not become unevenly yoked with unbelievers. For what fellowship do righteousness and lawlessness have?" (2 Corinthians 6:14).

Yahweh loves marriage but He wants you to marry someone who loves Him as much as you do. The rule for Christian marriage is that you are only supposed to marry another Christian.

How sad and hard it is for Christians who marry atheists or people from other religions.

It is so much better to be alone then to be married to someone stupid.

May 22nd The Bible Prophesied about Nuns and Priests in the Evil Catholic Church

"However, the inspired utterance says definitely that in later periods of time some will fall away from the faith, paying attention to misleading inspired utterances and teachings of demons, by the hypocrisy

of men who speak lies, marked in their conscience as with a branding iron; <u>forbidding to marry</u>, commanding to abstain from foods which God created to be partaken of with thanksgiving by those who have faith and accurately know the truth" (1Timothy 4:1-3).

The bible does say that Satan and his demons will mislead the faker Christian church (in this case the catholic church) in the final times to make celibacy part of their doctrine. How amazing, yet sad, that it came true.

Priests of Yahweh had children. Prophets of Yahweh had children.

<u>**Nowhere**</u> in the bible does it say that if you love Yahweh you must become celibate.

Today's scripture is a prophecy of the "later periods of time," which is now. This prophecy says that the apostate church will have "misleading inspired utterances and teachings of demons." We see that these apostate Christian fakers are hypocrites and liars who have no consciences. They incorrectly forbid marrying.

The Catholic Church violates biblical commands and mandates that if you love Yahweh and want to serve Him, you must be celibate. Men become celibate priests. Women become celibate nuns. This is a ploy by Satan to ensure that people who love Yahweh do not marry and reproduce and make godly offspring who also love and serve Yahweh in the future. It is obvious that Satan is using the false teachings of the Catholic Church to kill off anyone that is predisposed to love and serve Yahweh. This fact is black and white in the bible.

The Catholic Church is outside the will of Yahweh. No wonder there are so many sex scandals associated with the Catholic Church. Sadly, about 90% of all priest and nuns are either sexually active, have violated their vow of celibacy, or enjoy porn. Wake up people and leave the Catholic Church. How many of your sons and daughters need to be raped by sexually perverted men who teach false doctrine (which was predicted 2000 years ago in Paul's warning to Timothy) before you get out?

Sadly enough, if you look at the last part of 1 Timothy 4:3 you will notice that this demonically inspired teachings will also forbid eating foods which God created to be partaken of with thanksgiving. This is exemplified through the Catholic church's policy of not eating meat on Fridays. All around the world Catholics eat only fish on Friday. Ok…back to our subject.

If you think you have a calling to become a celibate priest or nun then you are wrong. You do not have a calling from Yahweh but you ate too much pizza the night before and your mind is all over the place. Working for the Catholic Church is outside the will of Yahweh.

May 23rd   Singles have more time to focus on Yahweh

"For I am already being poured out like a drink offering, and the due time for my releasing is imminent. I have fought the fine fight, I have run the course to the finish, I have observed the faith" (2 Timothy 4:6-7).

Yes, the bible mentions singleness. But this is for someone who has a special calling which allowed that person to focus on serving Yahweh. Joshua son of Nun never married and was able to serve Yahweh with all this strength. Paul was able to constantly serve Yahweh as an apostle and overseer. These men had special missions which benefited from complete devotion to Yahweh.

If you think you have a calling to stay single to "make more money" or "work on yourself" or to "have more time for help at your faker Christian church" then you are wrong.

If you think you are called to be single, then it better be so that you can do something amazingly hard in service to Yahweh. Someone with a calling from Yahweh to be single is someone Yahweh will use and pour out like a drink offering in His service.

People with the gift of singleness learn a foreign language and become missionaries. They become elders in the church and work 24 hours a day for Yahweh.

Likely you don't have the gift of singleness, but you will need to be patient. Finding a Christian man is so hard these days. Sadly, too many men contribute to the $57 billion pornography industry[17] or play video games 20 hours a week[18] like children. These men don't know the first thing about the bible or being a Godly man. Finding a godly man is going to be hard. Don't settle

---

[17] https://wsr.byu.edu/pornographystats
[18] http://www.addictions.com/video-games/alarming-video-game-addiction-statistics/

and marry a loser. You will be so much happier as a lonely single than as someone who is yoked together with a faker Christian or non-Christian.

May 24th Follow Biblical Truth not Man-Made Traditions

"In reply he said to them: "Why is it YOU also overstep the commandment of God because of YOUR tradition?" (Mathew 15:3)

Please love the truth. Don't love the traditions of men over the commandments of God.

Leave false religion today!

Celibate priest and nuns and all sort of monks, no matter which denomination, are outside the will of Yahweh. Leave false religion, get married to someone who loves Yahweh, and raise godly children. Be fruitful and multiply.

May 25th The Greatest is the One who Serves

"So he sat down and called the twelve and said to them: "If anyone wants to be first, he must be last of all and minister of all" (Mark 9:35).

The modern day church falsely tells us that "true religion" includes a well-paid hierarchy of priests and ministers and bishops who all learned the truth during seminary. The higher your rank in the church, the more God loves you and the more likely it is that your prayers are heard. The true religion is led by the Pope, who is perfect and speaks for God. True religion is powerful in the world and is a strong economic and political power.

Biblical truth tells us that the Kingdom of God is not a part of THIS world. God gave us guidelines for organizing true religion until His kingdom comes. If your organization doesn't look like what the bible describes as true religion then you are not a part of true religion. Leave that denomination as soon as possible.

The 1st principle of true religion is that if you want to be great you need to serve.

Jesus tells us that the 1st will be last. (Matthew 19:30) **But many that are first will be last and the last first.**

May 26th True Servants of God Must Be Humble

"Humble yourselves, therefore, under the mighty hand of God, that he may exalt YOU in due time" (1 Peter 5:6).

Yahweh's servants must be humble.

If you are selfish you love yourself. If you are humble, you are free to love God and your neighbor.

Yahweh is love. Serving Yahweh is about love. Yahweh's organization must be about love. The "true religion," as defined by the bible, must be about love. It is not about power. It is not about being a celebrity. It is not about kissing the ring. It is not about you or making you feel good. It is about Yahweh and putting Him first.

Are your church leaders humble, or is it all about them? What about you? Are you humble?

May 27th The Kingdom of God is not about "Power"

"But he said to them: "The kings of the nations lord it over them, and those having authority over them are called Benefactors. YOU, though, are not to be that way. But let him that is the greatest among YOU become as the youngest, and the one acting as chief as the one ministering. For which one is greater, the one reclining at the table or the one ministering? Is it not the one reclining at the table? But I am in YOUR midst as the one ministering." (Luke 22:25-27).

Leaders in Satan's world love power. But Jesus came to serve.

If your organization is about power, then it can't be a representative of God's Kingdom. Those who love Yahweh and want to represent Yahweh are obedient to biblical principles, humble, and loving.

Is your church about obedience, service, humility, and love?

May 28th Yahweh is in Charge of the Kingdom of God

"That people may know that you, whose name is Yahweh, You alone are the Most High over all the earth" (Psalms 83:18).

Yahweh is sovereign over all the earth. He is the grand creator of all things and the only True God.

Yahweh's son, Jesus, is also amazing and wonderful. But it is not about Jesus, it is about Yahweh. Yahweh is superior to Jesus.

Yahweh is the head of Jesus. (1 Corinthians 11:3) **But I want YOU to know that the head of every man is the Christ; in turn the head of a woman is the man; in turn the head of the Christ is God.**

Do you place God first in your Life?

May 29th Jesus is King in the Kingdom of God

And Jesus approached and spoke to them, saying: "All authority has been given me in heaven and on the earth" (Matthew 19:18).

Yahweh has given all authority to Jesus. Jesus is now the Leader of God's Kingdom and the head of the congregation of true Christians.

Let us look at a few other scriptures about Jesus.

Jesus is Yahweh's son. (Matthew 3:17) **"Look! Also, there was a voice from the heavens that said: "This is my Son, the beloved, whom I have approved."**

Jesus is the head of the Congregation. (Colossians 1:18) **...and he is the head of the body, the congregation. He is the beginning, the firstborn from the dead, that he might become the one who is first in all things.**

Jesus has all things (except Yahweh) in subjection under him. (1 Corinthians 15:27-28) **For [God] "subjected all things under his feet." But when he says that 'all things have been subjected,' it is evident that it is with the exception of the one who subjected all things to him. But when all things will have been subjected to him, then the Son himself will also subject himself to the One who subjected all things to him, that God may be all things to everyone.**

May 30th Christians are Obedient

"For this is what the love of God means, that we observe his commandments; and yet his commandments are not burdensome" (1 John 5:3).

Real Christians live in accordance with biblical principles.

Obedience is Essential. Yahweh's rules are designed to give you peace and joy and abundant, everlasting life.

Hypocrites follow traditions of men not the bible. Matthew 15:3 **In reply he said to them: "Why is it YOU also overstep the commandment of God because of YOUR tradition?"**

I can't stress obedience enough. The bible is so clear on this point. You must be obedient to what Yahweh says through the scriptures. You can't be a Christian and in a right standing with Yahweh if you are disobedient.

May 31st Clean, Undefiled, Spotless

"The form of worship that is <u>clean</u> and <u>undefiled</u> from the standpoint of our God and Father is this: to look after orphans and widows in their tribulation, and to keep oneself <u>without spot</u> from the world (James 1:27).

Real Christians keep themselves spotless, literally and figuratively.

Does your worship look "clean and undefiled" or does it look like the world?

Is your life "spotless" or has the world made your dirty?

Today's scripture is very practical. It says that we must be spotless in this dirty world. It is impossible to be in the dirty world and remain clean. Remember, it is easier to stain a clean person than it is to make a stained person clean. So please keep yourself spotless in this dirty world.

June 1st Observe what Jesus Taught

"Go therefore and make disciples of people of all the nations, baptizing them in the name of the Father and of the Son and of the holy spirit, <u>teaching them to observe all the things I have commanded YOU. And, look! I am with YOU all the days until the conclusion of the system of things" (Matthew 28:19-20).

Real Christians teach what Jesus taught.

Jesus taught that the Kingdom of God, as organized and described from the bible, must have Yahweh as the head, Jesus as the delegated leader, and people who live their lives in accordance with biblical principles, not worldly norms.

For example, Popes are not mentioned in the bible and are outside the will of Yahweh. Bishops are not mentioned in the bible and are outside the will of Yahweh. Female Elders and Overseers are outside the will of Yahweh. If your organization has a pope or a cardinal or female elders and clergy then it is outside the will of Yahweh.

June 2nd Christians are not part of this World

"I request you, not to take them out of the world, but to watch over them because of the wicked one. They are no part of the world, just as I am no part of the world. Sanctify them by means of the truth; your word is truth…" (John 17: 15-18).

Yahweh's people should not be a part of the world. This means they should be politically neutral. They should not be power brokers.

Jesus was not part of this world and said in his famous John 17 prayer that his followers would also not be a part of this world.

Are you a part of this world or do you try to mind your own business and keep yourself physically and spiritually clean?

June 3rd Christians don't look like the World

"Consequently I entreat YOU by the compassions of God, brothers, to present YOUR bodies a sacrifice living, holy, acceptable to God, a sacred service with YOUR power of reason.-And quit being fashioned after this system of things, but be transformed by making YOUR mind over, that YOU may prove to yourselves the good and acceptable and perfect will of God. (Romans 12:1)

True Christians are not supposed to be fashioned by the system of things. They are not supposed to look like the world, dress like the world, talk like the world, be selfish like the world, serve themselves and worship money like the world.

The reason true Christians don't want to be fashioned by worldly systems is that the world is lying in the power of Satan. (1 John 5:19) **We know we originate with God, but the whole world is lying in the [power of the] wicked one.**

Are you fashioned after God or do you look like the people of this world?

June 4th Christians are not Friends with the World

"Friendship with the world is enmity with God" (James 4:4).

If your religion is a power broker in the world then it is not in accordance with biblical principles and is not the true religion. The Catholic Church fought hundreds of wars and killed thousands, if not millions of men. The Catholic Church and the Holy Roman Empire make Hitler and Mussolini look like kind hearted idealists.

Just think of Lutheran chaplains in Germany praying for god to bless their soldiers as they went off to kill Americans. Or just think of Lutheran chaplains in the USA praying for god to bless their soldiers as they went off to kill Germans. Should make you think. Every other denomination presumes to be fighting on God's side and takes up weapons against other Christian brothers who also wrongly assume they are on God's side. Who decides which side has God's blessing?

June 5th Built Upon a Solid Foundation of Truth

"In answer Simon Peter said: "You are the Christ, the Son of the living God." In response Jesus said to him: "Happy you are, Simon son of Jonah, because flesh and blood did not reveal [it] to you, but my Father who is in the heavens did. Also, I say to you, You are Peter, and on this rock-mass. I will build my congregation, and the gates of Hades will not overpower it" (Matthew 16: 16-18).

Yahweh's church would be built on the truth that Jesus is God's son.

Many faker Christian organizations claim that the interpretation of Matthew 16:16-18 is that the church would be built upon Peter, and they therefore make up a genealogy of all popes dating back to Peter the disciple. This is wrong. The rock mass that Yahweh's congregation will be built upon is Jesus and knowledge that Jesus is God's son.

It is essential to have a good foundation when building any project, house, shed, castle. The house of our faith can't be built upon false ideas like the trinity, papal infallibility, ignoring the sabbath… The house of God must be built upon a foundation of truth.

June 6th Build your House on a Solid Foundation

"Therefore everyone that hears these sayings of mine and does them will be likened to a discreet man, who built his house upon the rock-mass. And the rain poured down and the floods came and the winds blew and lashed against that house, but it did not cave in, for it had been founded upon the rock-mass" (Matthew 7: 24-25).

This beautiful verse from Jesus is a great help for life. How so? He is simply telling us that having a solid foundation of knowledge and belief is essential for personal success and happiness. Your heart and mind have to go hand in hand with what God tells you so that no stupid and untrue idea can tickle your ears and blow away your faith.

Is your faith "built on a solid rock-mass" or are you easily persuaded, influenced by the ideas and philosophies of the world?

June 7th Jesus is the Cornerstone

"But he looked upon them and said: "What, then, does this that is written mean, 'The stone which the builders rejected, this has become the chief cornerstone'? Everyone falling upon that stone will be shattered. As for anyone upon whom it falls, it will pulverize him" (Luke 20:17-18).

Jesus is the chief cornerstone that the builders of the apostate church rejected. But what exactly does this mean?

A corner stone is precise. This means that when building a structure, the cornerstone is the first stone placed on the foundation. All other stones are placed against it and measured against it. Jesus is our perfect example and everything we do must be measured off of his example.

Because Jesus was rejected, we see that the "church" doesn't use Jesus' example as a cornerstone. They use their own traditions and false teaching as their foundation.

Be careful, everyone falling upon Jesus the cornerstone will be "shattered" and Jesus will "pulverize" anyone He falls on. This is a reference to how Jesus would smash the hypocritical church leaders of his time by pointing out their false teachings. He called them hypocrites, vipers, foxes, unwashed vessels. This is also a reference to the great judgement when Jesus, the perfect judge, will separate the sheep from the goats. He will pulverize those who rejected his example as the cornerstone and followed their own traditions and false teachings.

June 8th Jesus is a Stumbling Stone

"It is to YOU, therefore, that he is precious, because YOU are believers; but to those not believing, "the identical stone that the builders rejected has become [the] head of [the] corner," and "a stone of stumbling and a rock-mass of offense." These are stumbling because they are disobedient to the word. To this very end they were also appointed" (1 Peter 1:7-8).

Jesus was the stone of stumbling and many will trip and fall because they misuse, abuse, or ignore him.

If you ignore a big stone in your path you are going to trip over it. If you are like the Jews who ignored Jesus then eventually you will trip over him.

A hypocritical church leader who teaches traditions and false doctrine can argue with and kick against the truth as much as they want, but they will never win. The solidness of the truth trips many and causes them to stumble.

Just think of how the Pharisees fought against and were threatened by Jesus. They kicked the corner stone and even had Jesus murdered. They will stumble during the great judgement when they will receive their just reward.

One can fight against and ignore the truth as much as they want. But eventually, they will have to deal with it. And when they do, they will stumble and trip.

June 9th A Little Stone will Destroy World's Empires

"You kept on looking until a stone was cut out not by hands, and it struck the image on its feet of iron and of molded clay and crushed them. At that time the iron, the molded clay, the copper, the silver and the gold were, all together, crushed and became like the chaff from the summer threshing floor, and the wind carried them away so that no trace at all was found of them. And as for the stone that struck the image, it became a large mountain and filled the whole earth" (Daniel 2: 34-35).

We have been discussing rocks and stone for the past few days... build your faith upon a solid rock foundation of truth. Jesus is the cornerstone and we must use his example as the standard. Jesus was the stone of stumbling and many who fight the Truth of God will trip over or be smashed by this stone of stumbling.

Today's scripture is the final scripture about Biblical stones. The scripture is from the book of Daniel when Daniel interprets Nebuchadnezzar's dream about the world empires.

We read that in the final days (which is now) a little stone will destroy the world's empires. Since this little stone is not made by hand, it will be made by God. This little stone will do Yahweh's work on earth, and then will become big and strong and have a large family. This little stone is the Chieftain prophesied in the end of Ezekiel and it will be wonderful to see, in our life time, a representative of Yahweh on earth again acting on His behalf.

June 10th Jesus' Financial Philosophy

"YOU received free, give free" (Matthew 10: 8).

Jesus reminds us that the standard for Christian ministry is "free."

So if your so called denomination charges for books, charges for magazines, charges for bibles, and charges for conferences, then they are not a representation of the organization Jesus wanted.

Furthermore, if your ministers or priests make as much money as lawyers, politicians, and chief financial officers then they are outside the will of Yahweh and do not reflect the way Jesus wanted his church to be organized.

How much money did Jesus make a year? What was his retirement plan? Did he live in the house next to the cathedral and drive a Cadillac? Jesus was a man of little means. In fact, almost all of Yahweh's servants were poor.

June 11th You Can't Serve God and Money

"No one can slave for two masters; for either he will hate the one and love the other, or he will stick to

the one and despise the other. YOU cannot slave for God and for Riches" (Matthew 6: 24-25).

You can't worship Yahweh and money.

Did you know that a retired priest can earn more money than a practicing doctor or lawyer? Who cares if you believe in the Yahweh or not, stay a priest long enough and you can retire to absolute luxury.

If your religion takes up offerings they are outside the will of Yahweh. Yahweh's organization should be run based off of voluntary, discreet, not mandatory, donations. Did you know that in some places there are church taxes which are automatically deducted from your salary? For example, in Germany, depending upon the state you live in, 8-9% of your income is automatically deducted from your salary as "Kirchensteuer," what means "church tax."

In 2012, the Catholic Church received 5.2 million euros and the Protestant Church received 4.6 million euros only from German Church Taxes. Isn't this Nauseating? These churches disregard the commandments of Yahweh so they can follow the traditions of men. Electronic fund transfers to the Vatican bank is not in the bible.

True religion should give away truth for free. If you believe that what you write has the power of life and death then you should give it away for free. Does your religion give away bibles and study materials or does it charge for them? If it charges money, then it is outside the will of Yahweh.

June 12th True Religion's Dressing and Grooming Standards

"and clothe yourselves with the new [personality], which through accurate knowledge is being made new according to the image of the One who created it" (Colossians 3:10).

True religion is clothed with the new personality, one which becomes more and more like Jesus' personality.

Although the inner person is so much more important than the outer person, the way you dress says something about you. Let's do some common sense analysis of what the bible says and point out a few easily identifiable bad examples out there: Catholic leadership, evangelical Protestants, and the Jews.

We don't know for sure if Jesus was rich or poor. But the bible tells us he owned a seamless tunic (John 19:23). A seamless tunic took about six months of hard work to make. So Jesus had the equivalent of a thousand dollar handmade suit. What this means to us is that Jesus did not wear funny clothes. So, if you wear a comical looking hat like the pope, you are not doing what Jesus did. Neither did Jesus go to the other extreme and dress too casually. So if you are the faker protestant church minister who wears jeans and a t-shirt then you are not doing what Jesus did.

Jesus was dressed in accordance with his culture and customs, but he was dressed nicely and cleanly and respectably. Jesus wanted to reflect the dignity and cleanliness of his father. So don't dresses like a penguin or a crow, as do all the fakers in the Catholic Church?

And don't dress like a punk teenager as do the fakers in the protestant church. Dress in something clean and nice and respectable in accordance with the best of your cultural customs.

How do leaders in your denomination dress?

June 13th No Funny Hats

"For a man ought not to have his head covered, as he is God's image and glory; but the woman is man's glory" (1 Corinthians 11: 7).

Funny hats are not biblical. Paul never wrote a message to the early church leaders saying "in order for everyone to know that you are a super Christian, you must wear a funny hat." But he did write the opposite in 1 Corinthians 11:4: **Every man that prays or prophesies having something on his head shames his head**.

Yahweh instructs us that men should not cover our heads at all.

If you wear a Yamaka or Kippah then you are outside the will of Yahweh. If you wear a comical hat as part of your ridiculous priest outfit then you are outside the will of Yahweh. Read the bible, get rid of your ridiculous clothes, quit your job, and repent. Honoring Yahweh should not be a part of a carnival show.

June 14th Be Clothed with Love

"Accordingly, as God's chosen ones, holy and loved, clothe yourselves with the tender affections of compassion, kindness, lowliness of mind, mildness, and long-suffering" (Colossians 3:12).

True religion is clothed with holiness.

True religion is clothed with love. (Colossians 3: 14) **But, besides all these things, [clothe yourselves with] love, for it is a perfect bond of union.**

Yahweh has a great imagination and His creation is wonderful and colorful. Faker Christians and Catholics and orthodox leaders as well as orthodox Jews evidently hate color, joy and brightness. The bible never says to wear funny clothes and dress like a penguin or crow. The bible never says to wear a funny hat.

Let us review the Words of Wisdom since the 25th of May. Yahweh wants his worshipers to be:

- humble (the first will be last)
- be neutral (not mixed up in politics because Yahweh's kingdom is not of this world)
- built upon the knowledge of Jesus being Yahweh's son (upon this rock I will build my church)
- be generous (you have received freely so give freely)
- dressed cleanly and with dignity (modest), not in funny outfits (cloth yourself with love)
- be loving (to Yahweh and neighbor)

Is this what you look like?

June 15th Baptism is Important

"Go, therefore, and make disciples of people of all the nations, baptizing them in the name of the Father and of the Son and of the Holy Spirit" (Matthew 28:19).

Baptism is important. Otherwise Jesus would not have told us to make disciples and to baptize.

The hypocritical church tells you that it is acceptable to get baptized as an infant or as a lukewarm Christian.

Biblical Truth tells us that we are to learn and become obedient to bible principles. Next, we must become a disciple of Jesus, following his footsteps closely. Then we can get baptized by someone who has the authority to baptize.

Being baptized symbolizes becoming a new person. As your old self enters the water you die to your old self and are symbolically washed cleaned. Your new personality emerges, completely focused on honoring Yahweh with your life.

Baptism requires three things:

1. A decision by someone mature who accepts the word of God, lives in accordance with biblical principles, and who wants to dedicate his life to honoring Yahweh
2. Water submersion

3. A male baptizer who accepts the word of God and lives in accordance with biblical principles

Of course, there are exceptions. And I would never want to put Yahweh in a box. But trust me, the exceptions are rare.

June 16th Baptism is for the Obedient or those filled with God's Power (Holy Spirit)

"Or do you not know that all of us who were baptized into Christ Jesus were baptized into his death? So we were buried with him through our baptism into his death, in order that just as Christ was raised up from the dead through the glory of the Father, so we also should walk in a newness of life. If we have become united with him in the likeness of his death, we will certainly also be united with him in the likeness of his resurrection" (Romans 6: 3-5).

Baptism symbolizes the death of our old selves and being made alive to our new selves. It represents a decision to serve Yahweh which can only be made by a mature and obedient person.

Baptism requires a decision by someone mature who accepts the word of God, lives in accordance with biblical principles, and who wants to dedicate his life to honoring Yahweh.

First, you accept the truth and then you are baptized.

Baby baptism means nothing. Your baby didn't even understand what was going on, let alone make a life-long decision to serve Yahweh. Teach your child to be a disciple of Jesus and when he / she is old enough to fully comprehend what this requires and means, they can get baptized to symbolize their commitment.

Baby baptism isn't biblical. There isn't one example of a baby being baptized in the bible. It is impossible for a baby to understand the word of Yahweh, accept the word of Yahweh, decide to live according to biblical principles, and then to dedicate himself and undergo baptism.

All baptisms in the bible involve mature people aware of the decision they are making. Baptisms are only for those wise enough to fully understand that they are making a lifelong commitment to live for Yahweh. This can only be done by truly zealous and wise adolescent children or adults.

Jesus was God's perfect son, and yet he was baptized when he was 30. You are not better than Jesus. Your children are not better than Jesus. Your infant's baptism means nothing in the eyes of Yahweh. Only when baptism comes from your child's heart, when he or she is truly committed to loving and serving Yahweh, does Yahweh accept the baptism.

June 17th Baptism Requires Submersion

"During those days, Jesus came from Nazareth of Galilee and was baptized in the Jordan by John. And immediately on coming up out of the water, he

saw the heavens being parted and, like a dove, the spirit coming down upon him. And a voice came out of the heavens: "You are my Son, the beloved; I have approved you" (Mark 1:9-10).

Baptism requires water submersion and coming out of the water.

Although the most important aspect of your baptism is your heart, the physical messiness of being submerged and wet and messy and "coming up out of the water" (Mark 1:10) makes being made new more symbolic, more real, and more like what Jesus did.

Again, I don't want to put Yahweh in a box. But having a porn-addicted faker protestant minister splash a few drops on your forehead doesn't cut it. You should do what Jesus did and Jesus was dunked and came out of the water.

June 18th Only a Man with Authority should Baptize

"… and make appointments of elders in city after city, as I instructed you: if there is any man free from accusation, a husband of one wife, having believing children who are not accused of debauchery or rebelliousness. For as God's steward, an overseer must be free from accusation, not self-willed, not quick-tempered, not a drunkard, not violent, not greedy of dishonest gain, but hospitable, a lover of goodness, sound in mind, righteous, loyal, self-controlled…" (Titus 1:5-8).

Baptism is done by a male baptizer who accepts the word of God and lives in accordance with biblical principles

Since the leaders of the true religion, as defined in the bible, are men, baptism must be conducted by a man. The baptizer must be a ministerial servant, elder (older man) or overseer. Baptisms by a woman do not count because no woman has authority over a man to preside or officiate at his baptism.

Baptism must be conducted by a righteous man with authority. This is common sense. Would you want a hypocritical man who molests children, doesn't pay his taxes, and has no respect for the word of God baptize you? Of course not. You want your baptism to be done by someone who lives his life consistent with biblical principles. Not everyone in the bible baptized. John baptized many, to include Jesus (Matthew 3: 1-5 and 16-17). There is no biblical record of Jesus baptizing anyone. But Jesus' disciples baptized many.

Your adult baptism by hypocritical or unqualified representatives of the Christendom means nothing. Being baptized into a denomination that prays to saints, worships statues and or Mary, celebrates pagan holidays, violates clear bible principles, and teaches false doctrine means nothing. Learn what the bible really teaches. And when you fully comprehend what this requires and means, get baptized (for the first time) to symbolize your new life serving Yahweh.

June 19th Born Again

"In response Jesus said to him: "Most truly I say to you, unless anyone is born again, he cannot see the Kingdom of God" (John 3:3).

Baptism signifies being born again. This isn't a literal birth but a symbolic birth. Being totally submerged and wet and messy is a more accurate way to symbolically become new or be born again.

Since we are talking about baptism, an outward sign of an inward disposition of purity and commitment to honoring Yahweh, let's talk about two modern day variations of superficial and non-sustentative transformations: (1) being "born again" and (2) "accepting Jesus as Lord and savior." Both can be done without having the slightest idea about what being a disciple actually means.

For years many modern-day protestant faker churches preach and teach that being "born again" is the end all be all - "non-plus-ultra." If you are born again then you are in. No exceptions. You are going to heaven for sure. But like everyone else in their denomination, they are not transformed into a more Christ-like person, they are not obedient to the word of God, they love the world, they don't love their neighbor, and they are certainly not disciples of Christ. Jesus did not say make people "born again." He said make "disciples."

A disciple follows Jesus's example. A disciple studies and knows the bible, and lives in obedience with the bible. So, unless you study the bible, know the bible, and are obedient to biblical principles, you have not been reborn.

Many faker Christians roam the world trying to get people to "accept Jesus as their savior." They corner you at a shopping center and ask you if you have "accepted Jesus as your Lord and savior." Of course, the guys that ask this have no idea what they are talking about. Jesus said make disciples, he did not say badger people until they feel so bad that they cry out and admit that they need help, only for you to abandon them, not explain to them what the bible really teaches, and then run off to your other faker Christian friends to brag about "leading someone to Jesus."

These people are immature and need to grow up. It is not about them or you, it is about Yahweh. It is about loving Him with your all, and loving your neighbor as yourself. You don't have the first idea what it takes to be a real Christian, a disciple of Jesus. Study the bible, know the bible, be obedient to biblical principles. Then, once you are sure you get it, teach this to others. Obedience to and love for Yahweh takes years to teach, not two minutes at a shopping mall.

Baptism symbolizes your commitment to Yahweh. That means you bear Yahweh's name and reputation. If you live a clean life, like a true disciple of Jesus, and have love for one another, then you glorify the name of Yahweh. But if you are disobedient and unclean and worldly, then you blaspheme the name of Yahweh. The 10 commandments listed in Exodus 20 and Deuteronomy 5 warn us to not blaspheme the name of Yahweh. This doesn't simply mean don't say His name like a curse word, which many of you do and tolerate. It means don't be called by His name or associated with His name and be a hypocrite, a faker, worldly, without love, or disobedient.

Shame on the millions of faker Christians out there who have been baptized because that think they are worthy of being associated with Yahweh and yet who live immoral, dirty, worldly, unloving and disobedient lives. You blaspheme the name of Yahweh every day and slap Him in the face with your hypocrisy and disobedience.

June 20th Blood is Sacred

"For the life of every sort of flesh is its blood, because the life is in it. Consequently, I said to the Israelites: "You must not eat the blood of any sort of flesh because the life of every sort of flesh is its blood. Anyone eating it will be cut off" (Leviticus 17:14)

Life is in the blood. Back in the times of the law, blood sacrificed to Yahweh is what made a sacrifice valuable.

The hypocritical modern day church tells us that it is acceptable to eat or drink or put someone / something else's blood into our bodies.

Biblical Truth tells us that it is unquestionably forbidden to eat or drink or put someone / something else's blood into our bodies.

Life is sacred. Life is in the blood. Therefore, blood is sacred.

June 21st Jesus was the Last Blood Sacrifice

"Also, he took a cup and, having given thanks, he gave it to them, saying: "Drink out of it, all of YOU; for this means my 'blood of the covenant,' which is to be poured out in behalf of many for forgiveness of sins" (Matthew 26:27-28).

Jesus' blood poured out as the great Passover lamb saves all who believe in him and exercise faith in him.

The blood of the Passover sheep saved the Israelites during the time of Passover. (Exodus 12:13) **And the blood must serve as YOUR sign upon the houses where YOU are; and I must see the blood and pass over YOU, and the plague will not come on YOU as a ruination when I strike at the land of Egypt.**

We no longer practice the sacrificial laws since Jesus was the last accepted sacrifice. But if the law tells us that blood is required to make a sacrifice, then the underlying Biblical principles remind us that blood is sacred.

June 22nd Abstain from Blood

"For the holy spirit and we ourselves have favored adding no further burden to YOU, except these necessary things, to keep abstaining from things sacrificed to idols and from blood and from things strangled_ and from fornication._ If YOU carefully keep yourselves from these things, YOU will prosper. Good health to YOU" (Acts 15:28-29).

The bible tells us to abstain from blood.

The above scripture is authoritative. With the help of Yahweh's power (spirit) the older men (elders) of the early church say that we must abstain from blood. So what does that mean for you?

True Christians don't drink blood.

True Christians don't eat blood.

True Christians don't accept blood transfusions.

True Christians don't accept vaccinations with blood in it.

There are four fractions in blood: Platelets, Plasma, Red Blood Cells and White Blood Cells. True Christians don't accept or use or eat or drink or inject any part of blood.

The medical community is reinforcing the bible's requirement to not mix blood. Science is proving that blood transfusions aren't that safe. This reinforces biblical truth and prevents patients from having complications from someone else's blood or from blood that doesn't match. Bloodless surgeries are becoming more and more common and successful. Bloodless surgeries collect all the blood which flows from the wound or surgery site, clean it, then and put it back into the patient's body during the surgery. Thus people are able to have a major surgery without accepting someone else's blood.

Many cultures and countries have traditional sausages and dishes including blood. These foods are unbiblical and outside the will of Yahweh. Don't eat them again.

Some cultures believe it is macho to drink blood. It is not macho. It is unbiblical and outside the will of Yahweh. Don't do it.

Blood is sacred and should not be played with, manipulated, consumed or transfused. Honor Yahweh with your blood.

June 23rd Communion is Symbolic

"Also, he took a loaf, gave thanks, broke it, and gave it to them, saying: "This means my body which is to be given in YOUR behalf. Keep doing this in remembrance of me." Also, the cup in the same way after they had the evening meal, he saying: "This cup means the new covenant by virtue of my blood, which is to be poured out in YOUR behalf" (Luke 22:19-20).

Hypocritical churches teach that during communion the bread mysteriously turns into the body of Jesus and the wine mysteriously turns into the blood of Jesus.

Biblical Truth tells us to honor Jesus' ransom sacrifice by living a pure and obedient life, not by falsely presuming your powerless and faker Christian priest has turned a wafer into Jesus' skin and wine into his blood.

During Jesus' final meal he started a tradition which many call Communion or the Eucharist.

Communion is symbolic. This is not open to interpretation.

Many Christian denominations falsely believe that when you participate in communion the bread mysteriously changes into the body of Christ and the wine mysteriously changes into the blood of Christ. These denominations say that only members of their group can partake of the bread and wine because only they understand the miracle that mysteriously occurs when they "partake of the emblems."

Here is a quote from catholic online which explains that they think the bread becomes Jesus's body and the wine his blood: "Recalling these words of Jesus, the Catholic Church professes that, in the celebration of the Eucharist, bread and wine become the Body and Blood of Jesus Christ through the power of the Holy Spirit and the instrumentality of the priest."[19]

June 24th A Litteral Interpretation of Communion is Unbiblical

"For the holy spirit and we ourselves have favored adding no further burden to YOU, except these necessary things, to keep abstaining from things sacrificed to idols and from blood and from things strangled_ and from fornication._ If YOU carefully keep yourselves from these things, YOU will prosper. Good health to YOU" (Acts 15:28-29).

---

[19] http://www.catholic.org/clife/jesus/eucharist.php

If you actually believe you are drinking Jesus' blood then you are a cannibal and are violating Yahweh's will.

If what Catholics believe is true then each time a priest does his magical prayer on the wafer and it becomes the living body of Jesus, the priest performs a miracle. According to catholic tradition and requirements, after leading communion three times, the priest would have done three miracles, making him eligible for sainthood. That means every priest should be a saint. Perhaps when they are dead, we can make a medal of them to wear around our necks and pray to them?

Sometimes the bible is not definitive about if a scripture is literal or symbolic. However, when a scripture is presumed to be literal, and by being literal, it violates biblical principles, then this cannot be so because the bible does not contradict itself. Therefore, the communion scriptures must be symbolic.

Since a literal interpretation of communion would mean that we are eating human flesh (cannibalism) and drinking blood (which is also forbidden) then we can know, definitively, that communion cannot be literal.

We are supposed to think of and remember Jesus' broken body (like bread broken in half) and his poured our blood. We are not supposed to do a miraculous prayer to turn a wafer into Jesus' skin so we can become cannibals.

Please know that eating the actual body and drinking the actual blood of Jesus is impossible, weird, super creepy, and a violation of biblical laws and principles.

Communion is symbolic. Think of Jesus' life and sacrifice when you have bread and drink wine. But better yet, the best way to honor Jesus' sacrifice is to live a life consistent with the living word of God.

June 25th The Bible is Inspired

"All Scripture is inspired of God and beneficial for teaching, for reproving, for setting things straight, for disciplining in righteousness, so that the man of God may be fully competent, completely equipped for every good work" (2 Timothy 3:16-17).

The Word of God is inspired. Sadly, faker churches and ministers falsely teach that the bible is full of wisdom, that it may or may not be relevant for today, and that it may or may not be inspired by God.

Biblical Truth implores us to treasure the scriptures, study the scriptures, meditate on the scriptures, and live our lives in accordance with the inspired and powerful words of the scriptures.

The bible is where a true Christian gets his or her authority. The bible is either inspired or not. If it is inspired, then you better obey it. If you don't think it is inspired, then you better change your mind soon, before you disqualify yourself from the love of God and everlasting life.

The Bible is not to be interpreted or played with. It is to be obeyed.

June 26th Yahweh will Accomplish His Purposes

"So my word that goes out of my mouth will be. It will not return to me without results, But it will certainly accomplish whatever is my delight, And it will have sure success in what I send it to do" (Isaiah 55:11).

You can't stop the word of Yahweh from being accomplished. You can't hide the word of God or destroy it. If Yahweh predicts something through one of His prophets then for sure it is going to happen.

This is what makes the bible so scary and also what makes it so wonderful.

Do you know prophecies in the bible are yet to be unfulfilled? You better find out. Because they are for sure going to be fulfilled and perhaps you need to prepare for them.

June 27th The Law will be Fulfilled

"Indeed, it is easier for heaven and earth to pass away than for one stroke of a letter of the Law to go unfulfilled" (Luke 16:17).

The word of Yahweh will be fulfilled.

We are so blessed in modern days to have the bible so easily available. But this has not always been the case.

For hundreds of years, the bible was hidden from the people and kept only for the priests to use and interpret. This is how the Catholic Church could cheat the people by selling "indulgences" to forgive sin. This was how the Catholic Church was able to claim a lie about the Pope being infallible. If there is any doubt about papal infallibility then check out the endless list of papal mistakes, scandals, and excommunications.

The Catholic Church has locked away other inspired writings. The Catholic Church has tried to hide the name of Yahweh. The Catholic Church has even added non-inspired books to what they call the canon of bible literature.

Despite Satan's efforts to hide the word of God, it is available now more than ever. Thanks to a German named Luther, the bible was translated into a common language which has now become standard. Thanks to another German named Gutenberg, the printing press could more quickly make bibles for more people to read. Thanks to archeologist who continue to find manuscripts, we know that the Old Testament translations we use now are 99% the same as the scrolls which Jesus himself would have read.

When the oldest copy of the Bible was discovered in Egypt (called the Sinai Codex) the Vatican then displayed their almost complete version (called the Vatican Codex), which is a few years older. Both copies are wonderful.

But how sad is it that the Vatican did not admit to even having their original manuscript until the Sinai Codex was found and announced publicly. If the Vatican cared about knowing, teaching, sharing, and doing the will of Yahweh, they would have long ago announced the presence of that codex. And let me remind Vatican leaders of one more thing: Yahweh knows all the other inspired and stolen documents you have locked within your walls. May Yahweh rebuke you.

June 28th God's Word will not pass Away

"A Heaven and earth will pass away, but my words will by no means pass away" (Mark 13:31).

Thankfully, the Word of Yahweh will not pass away.

The cannon of the bible is not a perfect story because it involves imperfect men and Satan, the deceiver, trying his best to sabotage YHWH's sovereignty. But what we now have is enough to know YHWH and to live in accordance with His principles.

There are good translations of the bible and there are terrible, watered-down translations of the bible. But even in the worse translation of the bible you can find every single biblical principle you need to make YHWH proud of you. Even in a terrible translation you can see that a true Christian should not eat blood, should not watch an R Rated movie, should not fight in a war in support of a secular political nation, should not pray to dead people or Mary, and should not worship images or statues or crosses.

I recommend you use a bible which has Yahweh or YHWH written in it about 7000 times.

Any translator who shows respect to the name of YHWH will also show respect to the words of YHWH.

My wife and I now use online bible reference web-sites which allow us to read the bible in its original language from the oldest scrolls known to exist. We do not fully speak Hebrew, Aramaic, or Greek, but because of these web sites and programs we can study the bible word for word. I can't recommend this enough. These sites are wonderful.[20] The bible was meant to be read, not translated. Sadly, the church doesn't teach Hebrew or Greek because it cares more about being relevant and contemporary. But so much is lost in translation and reading Yahweh's word straight from the source is wonderful.

June 29th God's Word is Alive

"For the word of God is alive and exerts power and is sharper than any two-edged sword and pierces even to the dividing of soul and spirit, and of joints from the marrow, and is able to discern thoughts and intentions of the heart" (Hebrews 4:12).

The word of God is alive. This is why two people can read the same scripture and both can learn and apply two different ideas. There is so much wisdom and life changing truth in the scriptures.

Sadly, many faker Christians think they are smarter than Yahweh and can interpret the bible. They claim that the bible is wrong and then they say things to tickle the ears of the people at the expense of slapping Yahweh in the face.

---

[20] www.scripture4all.org

June 30th Don't Play with God's Word

"In reply he said to them: "Why is it YOU also overstep the commandment of God because of YOUR tradition?" (Matthew 15:3)

The modern church says that it is acceptable to play with the bible since it is full of wisdom and may or may not be relevant for today and may or may not or be inspired by God.

Biblical Truth tells us not to be content with watered down spiritual milk from a faker Christian denomination. We must seek and study and meditate upon hearty spiritual food.

One of the reasons this devotional needed to be written is because 99% of the people in Christian churches don't know what the bible teaches. They are being led by ministers and priests who don't know what the bible actually teaches, and have become satisfied with drinking spiritual milk (for babies) each week rather than eating a spiritual steak (for the mature believer).

Most churches waters down the truth of the bible or exchanges it for the traditions of man.

July 1st The Blind Leading the Blind

"Let them be. A blind guide is what they are. If, then, a blind man guides a blind man, both will fall into a pit" (Matthew 15:14).

Sadly, most people in faker Christian churches are blind, being led by those who are also blind.

Sadly, reading and knowing the Bible is no longer a requirement when studying Theology. What should you learn from a faker church leader who does not even know the source of wisdom?

If you go to a highly liturgical church it is probable that you have no idea what the bible teaches. All high liturgy denominations are lukewarm Christian making machines which spend so much effort in peripheral matters that those in the pews never learn anything new or important from the word of God. How sad it is that a 10 year old catholic boy and his 40 year old catholic father both only know that Noah save two of every animal, Moses parted the red sea, Jesus is God, and Mary is the most powerful person in heaven. Do your own research to find that Noah saved not just two but seven of every clean animal, Moses did not part the Red Sea but parted the "Sea of Reeds" or the "Sea of Papyrus," Jesus is not god but is Yahweh's son, and Mary is dead and powerless.

Satan has won in those churches by creating people who have become satisfied with mediocrity and accept rituals rather than the life changing wisdom and understanding available if they would only open their pristine, expensive, leather-bound King James Bible.

July 2nd Beware of False Prophets

"Be on the watch for the false prophets that come to YOU in sheep's covering, but inside they are ravenous wolves. By their fruits YOU will recognize them. Never do people gather grapes from thorns or figs from thistles, do they? Likewise, every good

tree produces fine fruit, but every rotten tree produces worthless fruit; a good tree cannot bear worthless fruit, neither can a rotten tree produce fine fruit. Every tree not producing fine fruit gets cut down and thrown into the fire. Really, then, by their fruits YOU will recognize those [men]"** (Matthew 7: 15-20).

Beware of faker, evil Christians (wolves) dressed in sheep's clothing. They will teach you traditions of men rather than the word of God. Test what they say. Compare it to the bible. If what your minister says violates the word of God then leave that church immediately.

July 3rd Truth Twisters were Predicted 2000 Years Ago

"I know that after my going away oppressive wolves will enter in among YOU and will not treat the flock with tenderness, and from among YOU yourselves men will rise and speak twisted things to draw away the disciples after themselves. "Therefore keep awake" (Acts 20:29-31).

Beware of faker Christian churches which twist the truth. Indicators that your denomination twists Biblical truth are when it…

- Hides the name of God, YHWH (pronounced Yahweh)
- Teaches the unbiblical doctrine of the trinity even though the truth is that YHWH is the only, true God, Jesus is His son, and holy spirit is another way to describe YHWH's power

- Teaches a lie about Christmas being Jesus' birthday even though it is a pagan holiday to celebrate the winter solstice
- Teaches a lie about Easter being Jesus' resurrection even though Jesus was killed during Passover (Nissan or Abib the 14th) and not during a pagan holiday to celebrate a false fertility god
- Teaches lies about YHWH causing suffering when in fact suffering is not caused by our loving Father but is caused by Satan, sin, and time / unforeseen circumstance
- Teaches unbiblical lies about death and instantaneously going to heaven
- Teaches unbiblical lies about your soul being immortal and floating up to heaven
- Teaches unbiblical lies about hell-fire and judgment and purgatory
- Encourages unbiblical prayers to and worship of images and crosses
- Violates truth and biblical commandments by using the cross for worship
- Shamefully worships Mary, not Yahweh alone
- Shamefully prays to Jesus, Mary, and or saints rather than to Yahweh alone
- Violates biblical requirements to be fruitful by mandating celibacy for clergy, monks, and nuns
- Worthlessly baptizes babies, kids, and adults who don't understand or live lives in accordance with biblical principles
- Doesn't honor Yahweh by teaching that blood is sacred

- Reprehensibly teaches a lie about bread and wine miraculously turning into Jesus' body and blood when celebrating communion
- Ignores Yahweh's commandment for a Saturday Sabbath and created a sacrilegious tradition for a "Lord's day" on Sunday

Does your denomination Twist the Truth? And if so, why are you still a part of that denomination?

July 4th Ear Ticklers were Predicted 2000 Years Ago

"For there will be a period of time when they will not put up with the healthful teaching, but, in accord with their own desires, they will accumulate teachers for themselves to have their ears tickled; and they will turn their ears away from the truth, whereas they will be turned aside to false stories" (1 Timothy 4:3-4).

Human selfishness will cause men to accumulate teachers who don't tell the truth but tell them what they want to hear. Indicators that your denomination tickles ears are when it…

- Is not obedient to Biblical principles
- Worthlessly baptizes babies, kids, and adults who don't understand or live lives in accordance with biblical principles
- Doesn't believe that the bible is living and active, follows the traditions of men over the

principles of the bible, and changes key words and texts in bible translations
- Waters down the truth of the bible
- Supports unbiblical wars and political systems via military chaplains
- Doesn't understand or teach the Kingdom of God
- Tolerates lies from other false religions and doesn't have the courage to stand for the truth

Does your denomination teach Biblical truth or tickle your ears? And if tickles your ears, why are you still a part of that denomination?

July 5th Yahweh will Open Your Eyes & Ears

"I, Yahweh, have called you in righteousness; I have taken hold of your hand. I will safeguard you and give you as a covenant for the people. And as a light of the nations. For you to <u>open the blind eyes</u>, to bring the prisoner out of the dungeon. And those sitting in darkness out of the prison. I am Yahweh. That is my name; I give my glory to no one else, and the <u>ears of the deaf will be unstopped</u>" (Isaiah 42:6-8).

The good news is that Yahweh will open the eyes and ears of those whose hearts are worthy of finding and serving Him.

Jesus literally fulfilled this scripture by helping the blind see, the deaf hear, and setting free those captive to sin and ignorance.

So, if you want to know the truth, seek it. Yahweh will give you eyes to see it and ears to hear it.

July 6th Eat a Steak, Don't Drink Milk.

"We have much to say about him, and it is difficult to explain, because you have become dull in your hearing. For although by now you should be teachers, you again need someone to teach you from the beginning the elementary things of the sacred pronouncements of God, and you have gone back to needing milk, not solid food. For everyone who continues to feed on milk is unacquainted with the word of righteousness, for he is a young child. But solid food belongs to mature people, to those who through use have their powers of discernment trained to distinguish both right and wrong" (Hebrews 5:11-14).

To have eyes that see and ears that hear you need to feed on solid spiritual food.

Just as babies, drink milk and adults eat solid food, spiritual babies drink milk from weak sources and mature believers feed upon the solid biblical food of the scriptures.

Do you seek watered down messages from your minister every week at a church service or do you have a hearty bible study program where you are daily seeking out solid biblical truth?

July 7th Seek Yahweh 1st

"Keep on, then, seeking first the Kingdom and his righteousness, and all these other things will be added to you" (Matthew 6:33).

Seeking the Kingdom of Yahweh must be your priority, not your 2nd or 3rd or your 10th.

Yahweh deserves our best time, our best energy. He doesn't deserve our left-overs.

Yahweh is always there. He is as close to us as we want Him to be. We must choose to be close to Him and to make Him our priority.

Please take a few seconds to memorize today's scripture.

July 8th The Prayers of Bad Husbands are Hindered

"YOU husbands, continue dwelling in like manner with them according to knowledge, assigning them honor as to a weaker vessel, the feminine one, since YOU are also heirs with them of the undeserved favor of life, in order for YOUR prayers not to be hindered" (1 Peter 3:7).

This scripture is great because it reminds all of us that Yahweh's love is undeserved (grace). And it further reminds men that if they want their prayers not to be hindered, they need to treat their wives well.en

Men:

- The heart of a woman is so fragile that you must deliberately work with all your strength and discipline to never misuse or hurt this fragile and loving heart.
- Never, never, never hurt a woman's heart.
- YHWH doesn't like it when you mistreat his daughters.
- Do not date for fun. Dating is a word or concept not found in the bible and results in hurting a woman's precious heart.
- Do not flirt or tease or lead on a woman. This builds false expectations and results in hurting a woman's precious heart.
- Stop having sexual or immoral preferences about women. It is wrong to focus on a certain type of woman rather than on her heart. For example… to only say "I like blonds" or "I like big breasts" or "I like short hair." Don't focus on things that fade away with age. Your preference should be for someone who loves YHWH. Imagine the self-esteem complexes you will cause if the woman who gives her heart to you is a brunette, with little breasts and long hair. She will not feel loved or cherished because you were evil and had a preference for body types and colors.
- Your true preference should only be to marry a zealous, like-minded Christian who lives in accordance with biblical principles. Women who love Yahweh are beautiful. So, finding that type of a woman is a true blessing.
- Your wife should be your standard for beauty. She is the only one you should ever love and

desire and treasure and look at-period. Honor her before you even find her.

July 9th Jesus Sets the Standards for Sexuality

"You heard that it was said: 'You must not commit adultery.' But I say to you that everyone who keeps on looking at a woman so as to have a passion for her has already committed adultery with her in his heart" (Matthew 5:27-28).

Women everywhere must be extra thankful to Jesus whose example and teachings valued women so much. The law never said flat out that a man should only have one wife. Yet the biblical principles at work remind us that marriage is sacred and that love should be pure.

Jesus' words during what many call the "sermon on the mount" definitively tell us that a man should only have one wife and that he must remain absolutely loyal to her. The expressions "so as to have passion for her" obviously means not to lust or covet, but it also touches upon the truth that the eyes see, then the heart wants.

Jesus is telling men to stop looking at any woman (on the street, in the car beside you, on TV, on the advertisement, or in a magazine) because it will entice your heart to sin.

Polygamy is officially declared immoral and outside the will of Yahweh. Jesus tells you to not even look at woman who is not your wife. This is because you are supposed to honor your wife and keep love pure. If you have a second wife it would be impossible to not look at her. Therefore, Jesus is mandating that men are to only have one wife.

Sexual sin and lust will prevent you from entering the Kingdom of God. When Jesus says in Matthew 5:29 that it would be better to have one eye then have both and be thrown into Gehenna (meaning total destruction) it is obvious that Yahweh doesn't tolerate sexual sin and lust.

Masturbation is immoral. Don't do it. In my opinion, Jesus' reference to the right hand in Matthew 5:30 is a discreet way of saying don't masturbate. Control your sexual urges, wait until you are married, and make a lot of wonderful love with your equally yoked, obedient, loving, real Christian wife.

Women, aren't you glad that Jesus' seven sentences about lust demand men to be loyal to their wives, outlaw polygamy, forbid masturbation, and demand purity within marriage?

July 10th Jesus Loves and Values Women

"There were also women watching from a distance, among them Mary Magdalene as well as Mary the mother of James the Less and of Joses, and Salome, who used to accompany him and minister to him when he was in Galilee, and many other women who had come up together with him to Jerusalem" (Mark 15:40-41).

Jesus valued women by allowing them to be a part of His entourage. For example, consider the women traveling with Him when Jesus went to Jerusalem.

Yahweh loves women and has designed a special role for them. They are not to lead the church or family. This is a man's job. Yahweh wants women to be empowered, loved, and led by Godly men.

The heart of a woman is a special gift from Yahweh and its unique and wonderful design is a remarkable image of perfection and love.

A woman becomes attracted to the one she loves. She is not influenced at first by handsomeness or beauty but as a result of her love, she develops an unchangeable attraction for the one she has chosen to love. This purity of love is a gift from Yahweh.

All women that truly love God and honor him with their life style are beautiful. They are made in Yahweh's image and designed to be a helpmate to men.

As a father, I am trying hard to teach my daughter how to grow up in this terrible world. I want her to see what right looks like in the family by being a good leader and provider. I want her to see the love I have for her mother, and for Yahweh. I want her to know she is loved and that Yahweh loves her. I want her to know that to Yahweh, she could never be more beautiful. But too often she is insecure about her looks or figure or hair or glasses and doesn't think she is, in fact, beautiful. We struggle to find a balance between taking care of her appearance and not trying to look like the "stars" of this world. It is a struggle to keep her from thinking like the world.

July 11th Yahweh Dignifies Women

"Yahweh then said this to Moses: "The daughters of Ze·lo′phe·had are correct. You should by all means give them the possession as an inheritance among their father's brothers and transfer their father's inheritance to them. And tell the Israelites, 'If a man dies without having a son, you must then cause his inheritance to pass to his daughter" (Numbers 27: 6-8).

How wonderful it is that Yahweh dignified women by mandating that women share in the inheritance.

Even in the 21st century, many countries and cultures still treat women like property, no better than a car or a farm animal. In British history, we sadly find countless cases of women getting thrown out of their houses by the new male heir just after the patriarch died. Primogeniture is not biblical.

Women were so loved that they were the first to see and experience the resurrection: Mark 16:1-6.

Yahweh loves and dignifies women.

July 12th Yahweh Designed Women to be Wives and Mothers

"Likewise let the aged women be reverent in behavior, not slanderous, neither enslaved to a lot of wine,

teachers of what is good; that they may recall the young women to their senses to love their husbands, to love their children, to be sound in mind, chaste, workers at home, good, subjecting themselves to their own husbands, so that the word of God may not be spoken of abusively" (Titus 2:3-5).

Women were designed to be helpmates, run the household, and raise wonderful Godly children. Yahweh's design for a woman is to be a worker at home.

Many women are "liberated" these days and want the responsibilities of men, the work of men, and the role of men. But this is not the way a family was designed. Men provide and women run the household. Disasters occur when a mother spends all her time with her career and can't train and develop her kids into Christian adults.

July 13th Men Should Provide and be the Leaders of the Family

"Certainly, if anyone does not provide for those who are his own, and especially for those who are members of his household, he has disowned the faith and is worse than a person without faith" (1 Timothy 5:8).

Yahweh doesn't want women to be the providers. Yahweh requires men to provide.

What this means is that all the "dead beat husbands" out there who do not work to provide for their families or who make their wives work to provide for the families are worse than unbelievers. Yahweh places great importance upon accepting your role in life and the woman's role is not to be the provider.

Of course, there are extenuating circumstance like death and divorce. But these should be the exception, not the standard.

July 14th We must all Accept our God Given Roles

"But I want YOU to know that the head of every man is the Christ; in turn the head of a woman is the man; in turn the head of the Christ is God" (1 Corinthians 11:3).

While every part of the body works together, there can only be one head. The leader of the woman is the man.

Women need to accept their role in Yahweh's family. (Ephesians 5: 21-23) **Be in subjection to one another in fear of Christ. Let wives be in subjection to their husbands as to the Lord, because a husband is head of his wife as the Christ also is head of the congregation, he being a savior of [this] body.**

Being in subjection to a Godly man is wonderful. He loves you, cares for you, and provides for you. Who wouldn't want to work for or be partnered with a real Christian man? What a source of strength and love a real Christian man must be. So, don't be afraid of the word subjection. (1 John 4:18) **There is no fear in**

love, but perfect love casts fear out, because fear restrains us. Indeed, the one who is fearful has not been made perfect in love.

Women should be under the leadership and responsibility and care of their husbands. (Colossians 3:18) **"YOU wives, be in subjection to [your] husbands, as it is becoming in [the] Lord".**

Women, let's be very honest. Being in subjection to a stupid man is very, very hard. And sadly, most men these days are stupid. No wonder modern and liberated women want to lead and assume the man's role. Don't make a mistake and marry a stupid man or a boy. I know that is very hard to find a godly man out there, but it is 100 times better to be lonely than to be linked together with someone stupid.

July 15th Christian Women must Marry Christian Men

"Do not become unevenly yoked with unbelievers. For what fellowship do righteousness and lawlessness have? Or what sharing does light have with darkness" (2 Corinthians 6:14).

The difficulty of living a life with someone stupid is why our loving Father reminds us to only marry someone who believes the bible and who lives in accordance with biblical truth. The bible warns us not to be unequally yoked with nonbelievers.

In the sad case that you are married to someone stupid or you violated biblical guidance and did not marry someone who lives their life in accordance with biblical principles, you must love them so well that they come into the truth. (Peter 3:1-2) **In like manner, YOU wives, be in subjection to YOUR own husbands, in order that, if any are not obedient to the word, they may be won without a word through the conduct of [their] wives, because of having been eyewitnesses of YOUR chaste conduct together with deep respect.**

July 16th Women Should not Teach from the Pulpit

"For God is [a God], not of disorder, but of peace. As in all the congregations of the holy ones, let the women keep silent in the congregations, for it is not permitted for them to speak, but let them be in subjection, even as the Law says. If, then, they want to learn something, let them question their own husbands at home, for it is disgraceful for a woman to speak in a congregation. What? Was it from YOU that the word of God came forth, or was it only as far as YOU that it reached? If anyone thinks he is a prophet or gifted with the spirit, let him acknowledge the things I am writing to YOU, because they are the Lord's commandment" (1 Corinthians 14:33-37).

Women are not supposed to teach or talk from the pulpit in a Christian congregation.

This last sentence of today's scripture is essential. A woman not speaking in the congregation is the Lord's commandment, not man's. Yahweh is simply saying that men must accept their role as leaders, they must accept their responsibility over women, and they must take the lead.

Yahweh values the education of women. The design of the temple allowed for women to have a place so that they could listen to the Law. They were required to know the law and have it in their heart so that they could teach it to their children. (Deuteronomy 6:4-7) **Listen, O Israel: YHWH our God is one YHWH. You must love YHWH your God with all your heart and all your soul and all your strength. These words that I am commanding you today must be on your heart, and you must inculcate them in your sons and speak of them when you sit in your house and when you walk on the road and when you lie down and when you get.**

The bible further explains that women are not to teach in a congregation or exercise authority over men. This means they are not supposed to run a church. (1 Timothy 2:12) **I do not permit a woman to teach, or to exercise authority over a man, but to be in silence.**

Women should not go to seminary and become ordained minister for faker Christian denominations. If your church is led by a woman, then your church is outside the will of Yahweh.

July 17th Women Can and Should Make Disciples

"Go, therefore, and make disciples of people of all the nations, baptizing them in the name of the Father and of the Son and of the Holy Spirit" (Matthew 28:19).

If a woman is living a life in accordance with biblical principles, then she is required to study and know the bible and to "make disciples of all men" in accordance with the great commission.

Doing this means that a woman who honors Yahweh can teach and instruct and lead bible studies for other women and couples.

Women should only teach men who don't know the bible with the help of their husbands, or in safe numbers.

Women must wear head coverings if they teach in the presence of men. (1 Corinthians 11: 3-6/10) **But I want YOU to know that the head of every man is the Christ; in turn the head of a woman is the man; in turn the head of the Christ is God. Every man that prays or prophesies having something on his head shames his head; but every woman that prays or prophesies with her head uncovered shames her head, for it is one and the same as if she were a [woman] with a shaved head. For if a woman does not cover herself, let her also be shorn; but if it is disgraceful for a woman to be shorn or shaved, let her be covered / That is why the woman ought to have a sign of authority upon her head because of the angels.**

July 18th A Gentle Spirit

"Do not let your adornment be external the braiding of hair and the wearing of gold ornaments or fine clothing but let it be the secret person of the heart in the incorruptible adornment of the quiet and mild

spirit, which is of great value in the eyes of God" (1 Peter 3:3-4).

Yahweh wants women to have a gentle and mild spirit.

All true Christian women are beautiful. This truth is regardless of age, size, color, nationality and is because a woman who loves Yahweh is radiant. No amount of BOTOX or starvation or elective surgeries or physical exercising can ever compare.

Most men are evil these days. Advertisements and the media exploit this evilness to make women insecure about themselves and to entice them to do dumb things or to wear immodest things in order to find a man, get attention, or gain social acceptance.

Yahweh did not make women to be two meters tall with 10% body fat. He made a woman's body strong and feminine. Stop being fashioned after evil magazines, Hollywood / worldly stars, and the expectations of immoral men who want you to be insecure about yourself, dress like prostitutes, buy their products, and vainly fight to look like someone else.

Quit being like the trashy women of the world! Dress modestly, be feminine and beautifully modest.

Quit being like the sad women of this world who think of nothing else besides their appearances.

July 19th Fatness is Good, not Bad

"Why do YOU people keep paying out money for what is not bread, and why is YOUR toil for what

results in no satisfaction? Listen intently to me, and eat what is good, and let YOUR soul find its exquisite delight in fatness itself" (Isaiah 55:2).

Christians should be healthy, exercise and treat the temple of our bodies with respect. But we don't need to follow the examples of the world and be excessive about physical fitness.

Nowhere in the bible does it say that putting yourself under stress to be skinny is good. Making crazy diets or trying to copy anorexic (unhealthy) fashion models from evil magazines is not encouraged in the bible.

In fact, the bible says many times that fatness is good. Today's scripture is just one example.

Please note that being overweight is also not healthy or beautiful.

Please have a balance that honors our creator by taking care of your temple, being healthy and feeling well.

July 20th Military Chaplains Serve Governments, not God

"Adulteresses, do YOU not know that the friendship with the world is enmity with God? Whoever, therefore, wants to be a friend of the world is constituting himself an enemy of God" (James 4:4).

Hypocritical churches teach us that it is OK to serve as a chaplain in the military of your country.

Biblical Truth tells us that Chaplains serve Satan and his delegated representatives in the nations in contrast to the will of Yahweh and in violation of biblical principles.

Shame on the thousands of faker Christian military chaplains out there who think they represent the living God YHWH. The very fact that you are a part of such a worldly organization exemplifies that you are not a representative of the living God, YHWH. You are immoral, dirty, worldly, unloving and disobedient. You blaspheme the name of YHWH every day and slap Him in the face with your hypocrisy and disobedience.

Let me reuse an idea from a previous Word of Wisdom so you can see how it is impossible to be a real Christian and work for the military.

A faker Christian wants to make a difference in the world so he joins the military of one of the corrupt governments of this world and serves as a chaplain. He prays for soldiers who go off to war in support of that nation's objectives. But to maintain his job he never has the courage to say that his government, the war, or his commanders are immoral.

He would likely do his best to be politically correct. This faker chaplain is likely as ambitious and as concerned about advancing in rank as the average atheist infantry officer to whom he volunteered to minister.

This faker chaplain knows stories of the bible like a well-educated child but doesn't live in accordance with biblical principles. This faker Christian supports his nation at the cost of watering down the truth of the scriptures. This faker Christian feels like he is bold when he says "and I pray this in Jesus' name" and yet is such a faker that he doesn't even know or use or try to glorify the name of Yahweh.

And if he does know the name of Yahweh, he is way too afraid to ever say it in public. That would be a career ender for sure. Do you see how working for a government is impossible if you truly love Yahweh and want to live in accordance with His principles?

Now let's imagine a civil war, one like the US Civil War. Just think about hypocritical Baptist chaplains in New York who prayed for God to bless their soldiers as they went off to kill their literal brothers from Virginia. Just think about hypocritical Baptist chaplains in Virginia who prayed for God to bless their soldiers as they went off to kill their literal brothers from New York.

How about an international example? Just think of Lutheran chaplains in Germany praying for God to bless their soldiers as they went off to kill Americans. Or just think of Lutheran chaplains in the USA praying for God to bless their soldiers as they went off to kill Germans. Who decides which side has God's blessing? Maybe the Pope does?

July 21st   Military Chaplains Serve Pagan Governments

"We know we originate with God, but the whole world is lying in the [power of the] wicked one" (1 John 5:19).

Military chaplains are all wrong, it doesn't matter what country you are from. And this includes the self-righteous USA. The United States is not a nation blessed by Yahweh. The USA is not Yahweh's nation. The USA is as immoral and as unclean in the eyes of Yahweh as China or Syria.

Shame on the USA's corruption, sex scandals in the white house, blood thirsty military, homosexual marriages, millions of abortions, and money worship. Although the currency of the USA has "in God We Trust" written on it, the God of the USA is money and materialism, not Yahweh. That is why the USA is a sinking ship. The USA has inflated their powerless God (money) above Yahweh, charged double interest for it to blood thirsty prostitutes throughout the world, and backed it up not with gold or silver but with worthless promises from corrupt politicians and immoral bank leaders.

If you think you can serve as a chaplain in any military force and represent Yahweh then you are simply wrong. The reason we don't want to be fashioned by worldly systems is that the world is lying in the power of satan.

July 22nd Satan's World is Heading towards Self Destruction

"every kingdom divided against itself comes to ruin, and every city or house divided against itself will not stand" (Matthew 12:25)

The "war hungry USA" doesn't have Yahweh's blessing just like ISIS, Al-Qaeda and the Taliban don't have Yahweh's blessing. A Muslim is simply following a false god and Mohammed his prophet as he wages war against faker Christians throughout the world. The American government is simply following the impulses of their false God mammon as they intervene all over the world. This is Satan's world and for a real Christian it is easy to see Satan (Muslims) fighting Satan (Americans) in a divided house. Because we know from today's scripture that a divided house cannot stand, we know that this system of things will eventually end. This is why true Christians are anxiously awaiting the Kingdom of God.

July 23rd Don't Draw the Sword

"Put your sword back in its place," Jesus said to him, "for all who draw the sword will die by the sword" (Matthew 26:52).

Jesus said not to live by the sword.

Yes, in years past, Yahweh blessed and mandated war. But the last time He approved of and mandated war was about 3000 years ago. And when Yahweh approved of these wars, He said so through a prophet who actually heard the words of Yahweh, to an anointed King, in a specific geographic location, to fulfill a covenant Yahweh made with His people. It has been a very long time since Yahweh anointed a king, sent messages through prophets to direct that king into war, and provided supernatural power for victory. Yahweh does not favor the USA as they kill Iraqis in search of weapons of mass destruction, which evidently did not exist. Honestly, the love of money is perhaps the ultimate weapon of mass destruction and it keeps blowing up daily in the houses of faker Christians around the world.

July 24th God's Kingdom is Not of this World

"Jesus said, "My kingdom is not of this world. If it were, my servants would fight to prevent my arrest by the Jewish leaders. But now my kingdom is from another place" (John 18:36).

Jesus kingdom is not of this world. If it were of this world, Jesus and his disciples would have fought for it.

We know that the Kingdom of Yahweh is not represented by any modern secular (and pagan) government. Of course, some governments give more freedom than others, provide more services than others. But as a real Christian, we are told to wait for God's Kingdom and to pray that "God's kingdom come, God's will be done, on earth as it is in heaven."

We cannot enthusiastically and wholeheartedly serve Satan's world and its governments while waiting for God's Kingdom. We must be neutral. Our spiritual citizenship is in the Kingdom of God.

July 25th God's Kingdom is the Only Solution

"YOU must pray, then, this way: "'Our Father in the heavens, let your name be sanctified. Let your kingdom come. Let your will take place, as in heaven, also upon earth" (Matthew 6: 9-10).

The only solution to the earth's problems is the Kingdom of Yahweh. This is why Jesus prayed for Yahweh's kingdom to come.

We are falsely told from faker churches that God runs the world, that many of the world's problems are caused by God, and that God's Kingdom will be when everyone goes to heaven.

Biblical truth reveals that God's kingdom is not of this world, that this world currently lies in the power of the evil one, and that because God's Kingdom is in heaven and on earth, and is coming soon, we should stay awake.

How sad it is that the apostate, faker churches out there do not know or use or sanctify the name of YHWH, yet they pray "let your name be sanctified" every day in church and during mass.

How sad it is that the apostate, faker churches out there do not know what the Kingdom of God really is. If you ask the average faker Christian, they will tell you that the kingdom is when we are all dead and living in heaven with Jesus. But that is not so. Jesus spoke so often about the Kingdom of God. Obviously, this was an essential item of the faith to understand. Let's look at the Kingdom of God this week.

July 26th   The Kingdom of God will Crush the Modern Day Systems

"And in the days of those kings the God of heaven will set up a kingdom that will never be brought to

ruin. And the kingdom itself will not be passed on to any other people. It will crush and put an end to all these kingdoms, and it itself will stand to times indefinite"** (Daniel 2:44).

The Kingdom of God will be a righteous government which will end all corruption and bring peace forever.

And from today's scripture, we see that the Kingdom of God will stand to times indefinite.

July 27th Jesus is King in the Kingdom of God

"And the seventh angel blew his trumpet. And loud voices occurred in heaven, saying: "The kingdom of the world did become the kingdom of our Lord and of his Christ, and he will rule as king forever and ever" (Revelation 11:15).

The Kingdom of God is when Yahweh will forever establish an incorruptible and loving monarchy with Jesus as the King of Kings.

The Kingdom of God will bring all peoples under Jesus' authority. (Psalm 110:1) **The utterance of Yahweh to my Lord is: "Sit at my right hand until I place your enemies as a stool for your feet.**

July 28th God's Kingdom will Last Forever

"And the kingdom and the ruler ship and the grandeur of the kingdoms under all the heavens were given to the people who are the holy ones of the Supreme One. Their kingdom is an indefinitely lasting

kingdom, and all the ruler ships will serve and obey even them" (Daniel 7:27).

The Kingdom of God will be an indefinitely lasting kingdom. This is hard for us to imagine as world powers seem to change every few hundred years.

Consider previous world powers like the Romans, the Greeks, the Babylonians and the Ethiopians. Italy is perhaps one of the most corrupt and mafia ridden nations in the world. Their economy is terrible and the people are impoverished. The government of Greece is bankrupt. Babylon is wiped of the face of the earth and is now dust in Iraq. Ethiopia is one of the poorest nations on earth. Jesus was correct when he said, **"in this way the last ones will be first, and the first ones last"** (Matthew 20:16.

Thankfully, God's Kingdom will not come to an end… but will last forever. What a blessing and what a source of hope.

July 29th Paradise

" And he said to him: "Truly I tell you today, You will be with me in Paradise" (Luke 23:43).

Jesus called the Kingdom of God paradise.

Please note that there is a punctuation mark after the word "today." If there was no punctuation mark then Jesus would be saying that that day (immediately after dying) they would be in paradise. But because there is a pause after today, Jesus is saying something similar to "truly right now, today, I am telling you, that when you are resurrected you will receive paradise."

Because the Kingdom of God is also called paradise, we begin to understand how wonderful it will be to live under the authority of a perfect, just and loving monarch.

July 30th Peace

"The wolf and the lamb themselves will feed as one, and the lion will eat straw just like the bull; and as for the serpent, his food will be dust. They will do no harm nor cause any ruin in all my holy mountain," YHWH has said" (Isaiah 65:25).

The Kingdom of God will bring everlasting peace. This, too, is so hard for us to fathom. We are all surrounded by war and violence and destruction and fear. The Kingdom of God will end all of this and will bring in everlasting peace. What a source of hope.

The Kingdom of God will cause war to cease. (Isaiah 2:4) **And they will have to beat their swords into plowshares and their spears into pruning shears. Nation will not lift up sword against nation; neither will they learn war anymore.**

July 31st Health & Prosperity

"With that I heard a loud voice from the throne say: "Look! The tent of God is with mankind, and he will reside with them, and they will be his peoples. And God himself will be with them. And he will wipe out

every tear from their eyes, and death will be no more, neither will mourning nor outcry nor pain be anymore. The former things have passed away" (Revelation 21:3-4).

The Kingdom of God will bring perfect health. This will be so wonderful. We have all been touched by cancer and disease. What a blessing it will be to live free of health problems. What a source of joy and hope.

The Kingdom of God will also bring prosperity. (Isaiah 65:21-24) **And they will certainly build houses and have occupancy; and they will certainly plant vineyards and eat [their] fruitage. They will not build and someone else have occupancy; they will not plant and someone else do the eating. For like the days of a tree will the days of my people be; and the work of their own hands my chosen ones will use to the full. They will not toil for nothing, nor will they bring to birth for disturbance; because they are the offspring made up of the blessed ones of YHWH, and their descendants with them. And it will actually occur that before they call out I myself shall answer; while they are yet speaking, I myself shall hear.**

August 1st God Gave the Earth to Men

"As regards the heavens, to Yahweh the heavens belong, But the earth he has given to the sons of men" (Psalm 115:16).

The Kingdom of God is on earth and in heaven. Sadly, most faker Christians think that the Kingdom of God will be when we are all resurrected and live like fat baby angels in heaven. But the truth is that the Kingdom of God will keep 99% percent of people on earth.

The Kingdom of God is on earth and in heaven. (Matthew 6:9-10) **"YOU must pray, then, this way: "Our Father in the heavens let your name be sanctified. Let your kingdom come. Let your will take place, as in heaven, also upon earth.**

August 2nd The Righteous will Live on the Earth Forever

"The righteous themselves will possess the earth, And they will reside forever upon it. (Psalm 37:29)

The righteous will live on earth forever. This may be new information for you. But it is true and found in the bible many places.

Today's Word of Wisdom will be short so you can spend more time thinking about and memorizing this scripture.

August 3rd The Meek will Inherit The Earth

"But the meek ones themselves will possess the earth, And they will indeed find their exquisite delight in the abundance of peace" (Psalm 37:11).

The meek will not go to heaven as fat babies but will inherit the earth. (Matthew 5:5) **"Happy are the mild-tempered ones, since they will inherit the earth.**

Most luke-warm Christians know this bible verse but don't understand the implications. Let me put it all together for you. During the resurrection, Jesus will separate the sheep from the goats, the righteous from the unrighteous. The unrighteous will go to total destruction and the righteous will live on a paradise earth in the Kingdom of God, where Jesus is the King of Kings.

August 4th   The Kingdom of God has Not Yet Arrived

"Jesus answered: "My kingdom is no part of this world. If my kingdom were part of this world, my attendants would have fought that I should not be delivered up to the Jews. But, as it is, my kingdom is not from this source" (John 18:36).

The Kingdom of God (KOG) has not yet begun since it is not a part of the current world system.

Jesus tells his disciples in Matthew 24 many "signs" or indicators of the imminence of His presence and the beginning of the KOG. We should pay attention to these indicators. (Matthew 24:32-33) **Now learn from the fig tree as an illustration this point: Just as soon as its young branch grows tender and it puts forth leaves, YOU know that summer is near. Likewise, also YOU, when YOU see all these things, know that he is near at the doors.**

Yet no one knows the day or hour of when the Kingdom of God will come. (Matthew 24: 36-39) **Concerning that day and hour nobody knows, neither the angels** of the heavens nor the Son, but only the Father. For just as the days of Noah were, so the presence of the Son of man will be. For as they were in those days before the flood, eating and drinking, men marrying and women being given in marriage, until the day that Noah entered the ark; and they took no note until the flood came and swept them all away, so the presence of the Son of man will be.

August 5<u>th</u> Yahweh will Vindicate His Name

"And I shall certainly sanctify my great name, which was being profaned among the nations, which YOU profaned in the midst of them; and the nations will have to know that I am YHWH," is the utterance of the Sovereign Lord YHWH, "when I am sanctified among YOU before their eyes" (Ezekiel 36:23).

When the Kingdom of God arrives, Yahweh will vindicate His sacred name. All of those who hated or rejected or acted against God will regret their poor decisions.

The Kingdom of God will bring rejoicing and glory and praise to YHWH. (Revelation 5:13) **And every creature that is in heaven and on earth and underneath the earth and on the sea, and all the things in them, I heard saying: "To the One sitting on the throne and to the Lamb be the blessing and the honor and the glory and the might forever and ever."**

August 6th   Remove the Reproach of His People

"He will actually swallow up death forever, and the Sovereign Lord YHWH will certainly wipe the tears from all faces. And the reproach of his people he will take away from all the earth, for Yahweh himself has spoken [it]" (Isaiah 25:8).

There are a few significant implications of this scripture.

(1) Yahweh will take away the reproach of His people. This is good news because those of us who are treated in this world like idiots or losers because we believe in and want to love and honor Yahweh will no longer have to deal with this evil reproach.

(2) Lovers of Yahweh are reproached. So if the world doesn't hate you and think you are crazy then you likely don't love and honor God.

Knowing that Yahweh will take pleasure in His people gives us hope. (Ezekiel 20:41) **Because of the restful odor I shall take pleasure in YOU, when I bring YOU forth from the peoples and I collect YOU together from the lands to which YOU have been scattered, and I will be sanctified in YOU before the eyes of the nations.**

August 7th Who will live in the Kingdom of God?

"Moreover, Isaiah cries out concerning Israel: "Although the number of the sons of Israel may be as the sand of the sea, it is the remnant that will be saved" (Romans 9:27).

Only a remnant will be saved.

Those who Yahweh remembers and calls will enter the Kingdom of God. (Job 13:15) **You will call, and I myself shall answer you. For the work of your hands you will have a yearning.**

Only those exercising faith in Jesus will be saved. (John 3:16) **For God loved the world so much that he gave his only-begotten Son, in order that everyone exercising faith in him might not be destroyed but have everlasting life**

Those who exercise faith in Jesus will enter the Kingdom of God. (John 11:25) **Jesus said to her: I am the resurrection and the life. He that exercises faith in me, even though he dies, will come to life.**

August 8th   The Unrighteous will not enter the Kingdom of God

"What! Do YOU not know that unrighteous persons will not inherit God's kingdom? Do not be misled. Neither fornicators, nor idolaters, nor adulterers, nor men kept for unnatural purposes, nor men who lie with men, nor thieves, nor greedy persons, nor drunkards, nor revilers, nor extortionist will inherit God's kingdom" (1 Corinthians 6:9-10).

Be warned, faker Christians and the unrighteous will not enter the Kingdom of God.

Sadly, everyone believes that they are getting into heaven. But this wrong for two reasons: Location and Exclusivity.

Location: The bible tells us that while the Kingdom of God is on heaven and on earth, practically everyone who inherits the kingdom of God will live on a paradise earth.

Exclusivity: The righteous will live in the Kingdom of God, not the unrighteous. Today's scripture reminds us that not everyone gets in. The unrighteous, fornicators, followers of false gods, adulterers, practicing homosexuals, thieves, the greedy, drunks, gossips, and extortionists will not get into the Kingdom of God but will be destroyed.

August 9th Call Upon the Name of God

"And everyone who calls on the name of Yahweh will be saved" (Acts 2:21).

Those who know and use and call upon the powerful name of Yahweh will enter the Kingdom of God.

Do you know, use, and call upon the powerful name of Yahweh?

August 10th Jesus Knows Who His True Followers Are

"Not everyone saying to me, 'Lord, Lord,' will enter the kingdom of the heavens, but the one doing the will of my Father who is in the heavens will. Many

will say to me in that day, 'Lord, Lord, did we not prophesy in your name, and expel demons in your name, and perform many powerful works in your name?' And yet then I will confess to them: I never knew YOU! Get away from me, YOU workers of lawlessness"** (Matthew 7:21- 23).

Jesus is the perfect and just judge. He sees and knows those who truly are his followers.

Faker Christians will not enter the Kingdom of God. Only those who are obedient and do the will of Yahweh will enter the Kingdom of God.

August 11th   Yahweh and Jesus will Rule in the Kingdom of God

"And the seventh angel blew his trumpet. And loud voices occurred in heaven, saying: "The kingdom of the world did become the kingdom of our Lord and of his Christ, and he will rule as king forever and ever" (Revelation 11:15).

Yahweh and Jesus will rule in the Kingdom of God.

Of course, Yahweh is in charge, but He has delegated all authority to Jesus. (Matthew 28:18) **And Jesus approached and spoke to them, saying: "All authority has been given me in heaven and on the earth.**

Jesus and his family are the seed of Abraham and the seed of David who will rule forever. (Psalm 89:3-4) **"I have concluded a covenant toward my chosen one; I have sworn to David my servant, 'Even to time indefinite I shall firmly establish your seed, And I will**

August 12th The 144,000

"And I saw, and, look! the Lamb standing upon the Mount Zion, and with him a hundred and forty-four thousand having his name and the name of his Father written on their foreheads"(Revelation 14:1).

Jesus will rule with the assistance of 144,000 specially selected people who will serve as kings and as priests. Only these 144,000 people will go to heaven. The rest of all people will inherit the earth.

The 144,000 will be kings over the earth. (Revelation 5:10) **and you made them to be a kingdom and priests to our God, and they are to rule as kings over the earth."**

When you are one of the 144,000 who will help rule with and serve Jesus from heaven then you will know it. Trust me, it is not you. So please get the idea of going to heaven out of your mind.

When you die and are resurrected, if you are found righteous, you will live forever on a paradise earth. If you are righteous and live through the imminent great tribulation, then you will live forever on paradise earth. Either way, the essential thing for gaining access to the wonderful Kingdom of God is to be righteous.

August 13th It is Forbidden to Say the Name of False Gods

"And YOU are to be on your guard respecting all that I have said to YOU; and YOU must not mention the name of other gods. It should not be heard upon your mouth. (Exodus 23:13)

Yahweh commands us not to even mention the name of a false god. If we can't even say their names, then for sure we are not supposed to honor them by naming things after them.

Sadly, the Romans turned the planets that Yahweh created into "gods" and worshipped them. Then the Catholic church named days of the week and months after those false, powerless gods in form of planets. Shame on the Catholic church for doing so.

Let's take a step back and say that Yahweh's timing is not our own timing.

Time is the word that men use to describe the power that makes thing change.

A short discussion about time may make us think and perhaps give us a better understanding of reality.

Time was split in half by Jesus, Yahweh's Son. Every date in the world is either Before the Common Era (BCE) or Common Era (CE), Before Christ (BC) or After Christ (AC). Christ split time in half.

Sadly, Satan owns the days of the weeks and months of the year because all the days of the week and months of the year are named after false, powerless gods or planets. Think about the names of the days or months and you will find they are named after planets and constellations and false gods.

If the early Catholic Church truly had honoring Yahweh in mind when they made the Gregorian calendar they would not have allowed the names of false gods to be used for days and months.

August 14th Biblical Time

"For a thousand years are in your eyes but as yesterday when it is past, And as a watch during the night" (Psalm 90:4).

How wonderful it will be when Yahweh's kingdom comes and we are no longer a part of Satan's evil system of things which includes mentioning the names of false gods whenever we discuss days and months.

There are so many calendar errors which dishonor Yahweh. We have already highlighted that Jesus was NOT born on the 25th of December. We know Jesus did NOT die for our sins during Easter. Jesus paid a ransom for us all on Passover, which according to the bible and the Jewish calendar is the 14th day of Nissan, not some random Sunday in the spring.

Yahweh's biblical calendar is a super accurate Lunar-Solar system. The days of the week have no names, with the exception of the 7th day which is called the Sabbath. The day begins at sundown, and ends about

24 hours later when the sun sets. In the winter, days had very little light. In the summer, there was a lot of light.

There was no time as in "5:00 in the morning." Time started at first light, which is why all the bible times are expressions like "in the 3rd hour" or "during the 6th hour." If sunrise is 0600 then the 3rd hour would be about 0900 and the 6th hour would be around 1200, noon. Because in modern times we so completely worship money and productivity and scheduling too many events into our completely overstressed out lives, Yahweh's system seems imprecise. But Yahweh's original system works perfectly for those who live simply and prioritize the family and loving and serving Yahweh. I don't understand how the catholic church in 1538 could justify throwing away Yahweh's calendar in order to adopt their Gregorian calendar with false pagan god names for days and months.

August 15th Yahweh's Timing is not Our Timing

"However, let this one fact not be escaping YOUR notice, beloved ones, that one day is with Yahweh as a thousand years and a thousand years as one day" (2 Peter 3:8).

With Yahweh, a day is like a thousand years.

For us, a thousand human years is almost unfathomable. We want faster internet, faster food, faster cars. We are in such a rush for the here and now that we can hardly think of what will happen in 1000 years.

Our loving Father is so magnificent and wise and powerful. Even time is controlled by Yahweh the true God.

August 16th Eternity in our Hearts

"Everything he has made pretty in its time. Even time indefinite he has put in their heart, that mankind may never find out the work that the [true] God has made from the start to the finish" (Ecclesiastes 3:11).

Yahweh has also placed the desire to live forever in man's heart.

Our brain's potential validates that Yahweh designed us to live forever. Humans use something like 10 percent of our brain. Imagine how smart we would be if we actually used 100% of our Yahweh given abilities. For example, a girl growing up in a multi-cultural family, learns three languages before she turns four years old and grows up to become a doctor. This smart girl uses 10% of her brain's potential. Down the street is an average American teenager boy who can only speak English, and not without using profanity every fifth sentence. He plays videogames and watches a lot of TV. This dumb boy uses only 5% of his brain. Of course, modern society has accepted mediocrity, but even the smart kid only uses a fraction of her brain. This must hint at a design whereby humans can learn and grow and think for centuries. Imagine if that smart kid has everlasting life and how smart she will be in 500 years.

How wonderful it will be to see Yahweh's Kingdom come. Yet, according to the bible, it has taken almost six thousand years since the fall of Adam and Eve to prove Satan wrong. But what are six thousand years to Yahweh, our eternal and timeless Father? They are like 6 days.

August 17th Giving Time to Repent

"Yahweh is not slow respecting his promise, as some people consider slowness, but he is patient with YOU because he does not desire any to be destroyed but desires all to attain to repentance." (2 Peter 3:9).

If Yahweh's Kingdom would have come yesterday or last year then there would have been no hope for you. But He continues to be patient. Perhaps one of the many reasons He is so patient is so you can read "Words of Wisdom," have your eyes opened to see church hypocrisies, learn biblical truth, and then return to Yahweh with all your heart.

Let us consider the loving patience of Yahweh. Our Father wants no one to perish.

Yahweh is patient and wants everyone to come into an accurate knowledge of Him. (1 Timothy 2:3-6) **This is fine and acceptable in the sight of our Savior, God, whose will is that all sorts of men should be saved and come to an accurate knowledge of truth. For there is one God, and one mediator between God and men, a man, Christ Jesus, who gave himself a corresponding ransom for all.**

Remember the illustration of the Math Teacher? Yahweh is the math teacher and the bible tells us the rules for doing the long division of life. Satan is the troublemaking student who proudly thinks he has a better way to do long division. Yahweh could have smashed Satan but instead He lets Satan prove that his way for doing long division is wrong. Only Yahweh's rules for life lead to joy and fulfillment and peace and love.

Yahweh could have smashed Satan for his disobedience but He decided to allow Satan to prove himself wrong. And that he has done. Satan has proven in the last six thousand years that man cannot rule himself and that only by living a life obedient to Yahweh's commandments will man have peace and health and be free from hunger and death and suffering.

Be warned, however. Yahweh's patience is running out. Time is running out. Please turn your hearts back to the Father (Malachi 4: 6) and do it soon.

August 18th Remember the Sabbath

"Remember the Sabbath day to keep it sacred. You are to labor and do all your work for six days, but the seventh day is a Sabbath to Yahweh your God" (Exodus 20:8-9).

Yahweh gave us the Sabbath as part of the ten commandments.

The hypocritical church says that the "Lord's day" is on Sunday.

Biblical truth reveals that Yahweh gave us the Sabbath so we would rest. He commanded that we honor the Sabbath on Saturday, and that we honor the Sabbath forever.

The best example of your time not being Yahweh's time is the Sabbath. Yahweh gave the Sabbath to humans and He gave it to us on day 7. The Jewish calendar uses numbers for its days. But the 7th day is special. It has a name. It is called the Sabbath. The Spanish language still calls it "Sabado" or Sabbath day. But in English, we call it Saturday, sadly named after the pagan false god saturn. The catholic church chose to ignore the Saturday Sabbath and now billions of faker Christians celebrate the "day of rest" on Sunday, a day named after the false sun god. If your time was like Yahweh's time then you would celebrate the Sabbath on Saturday, like Yahweh designed and like the Jews still celebrate.

August 19th The Sabbath is Made for Man

"Then he said to them: "The Sabbath came into existence for the sake of man, and not man for the sake of the Sabbath. So the Son of man is Lord even of the Sabbath" (Mark 2:27-28).

Yahweh made the sabbath for man to rest. I don't need to tell you how busy life can be. Statistically, it is a miracle that you are reading a daily devotional. Most people are too busy to take a few seconds to learn something each day, even if what they learn may have eternal benefits.

Our loving Father knows that we are prone to over action and to filling our days with too much. This is why He commanded us to rest one day a week. This much-needed-rest is a game changer / life changer. Please be obedient to God Almighty and rest on the Sabbath. You won't regret it.

August 20th Jesus came to Fulfil the Law

"Do not think I came to destroy the Law or the Prophets. I came, not to destroy, but to fulfill" (Matthew 5:17).

Jesus honored the Sabbath. The gospels are full of examples of Jesus honoring the Sabbath, but not being ridiculous and legalistic about following the Sabbath. Jesus still honored His father, rested, and loved others by doing good for them.

Jesus believed in the Sabbath and presumed the Sabbath would be honored up until the great tribulation and the coming of the kingdom of God. (Matthew 24:19-21) **Woe to the pregnant women and those nursing a baby in those days! Keep praying that your flight may not occur in wintertime nor on the Sabbath day; for then there will be great tribulation such as has not occurred since the world's beginning until now, no, nor will occur again.**

August 21st God's People will always Honor the Sabbath

"So there remains a Sabbath-rest for the people of God" (Hebrews 4:9).

Yahweh never delegated to faker early church "fathers" the ability to change the Sabbath from Saturday to Sunday. Constantine never had permission to change the Sabbath from Saturday to Sunday. But since Constantine was known to worship the sun god then it makes perfect sense that he changed the Sabbath to Sunday and renamed it "the lord's day."

The bigger question is why do billions falsely ignore the Sabbath and rest on the wrong day. Don't they care about what Yahweh wants and has ordered through the bible.

August 22nd Don't Follow Unbiblical Traditions

"In reply he said to them: "Why is it YOU also overstep the commandment of God because of YOUR tradition" (Matthew 15:3)?

Why do so many "Christians" care more about the traditions of men than they do about the commandments of Yahweh?

Please enjoy a gift from Yahweh and observe a Sabbath's rest from Friday sunset until Saturday at sundown. This is what Jesus did, and what Yahweh mandated for time everlasting.

August 23rd Satan is Misleading the Earth

"So down the great dragon was hurled, the original serpent, the one called Devil and Satan, who is misleading the entire inhabited earth..." (Revelations 12:9)

Your minister or priest does not have miraculous powers and is not full of holy spirit.

Biblical truth tells us that Satan is trying to mislead the entire world and his sophisticated ways have deceived many.

We know that "holy spirit" is Yawheh's power and that Yahweh's power is able to do anything. However, many are deceived by the works of the devil and think they are witnessing miracles from Yahweh.

Let's look at these examples in the next few days.

1. People who pray to the "lord" and the "lord" answers back
2. People who speak in tongues at faker evangelical churches
3. Faith healings at faker evangelical churches
4. Faith healings at "holy" catholic sites
5. Crying or bleeding statues
6. Exorcisms

August 24th Satan Pretends to Be God or Jesus

"If any prophet presumptuously speaks a word in my name that I did not command him to speak or speaks in the name of other gods, that prophet must die" (Deuteronomy 18:20).

Today, let us discuss people who pray to "the lord" and "the lord" answers back.

I have heard many faker Christians say things like "God told me to do this and that" or "I think God is telling me to do this or that."

In all of biblical history, Yahweh almost always only spoke through one prophet at a time. Statistical probability indicates that you are not the prophet for this generation.

The prophets Yahweh did choose were refined through suffering into being men of absolute purity and devotion to Yahweh. They were not sinful "soccer moms" who have fake breasts, a child's understanding of biblical principles, a criminal's obedience to biblical principles, and who pray that "the Lord Jesus" will make them richer so they can drive a nicer car to and from their gossip woman's group bible study. The prophets Yahweh chose were not faker Christian men who are lethargic husbands, pray to Jesus rather than Yahweh, who love to use fancy doctrinal terms in the pulpit right before having an affair with the youth director's wife.

Yahweh's prophets were amazing men of character who had to endure amazing things in order to publish the word of Yahweh. I doubt Yahweh is now speaking to faker Christians who love looking at porn, play violent video games, and couldn't quote 10 bible verses if their life depended upon it. Trust me, Yahweh did not tell you to buy the Cadillac or do an interpretive dance for your congregation during the Easter Sunday service.

If Yahweh speaks to you then there is no doubt about it. It makes me sick to hear people say "I think the lord is telling me to do this or that." Daniel saw an angel and fell to his face in fear. John saw an angel and fell on his face in fear. Moses spoke with Yahweh and his (Moses') face would glow. If you actually do hear voices then it is the voice of Satan pretending to be Jesus or Yahweh. Please repent, clean up your life and house and car and music and friends, study the bible, and the voices in your head will be replaced with your own sound thoughts which reflect and make decisions based upon biblical principles.

August 25th Satan Pretends to be an Angel of Light

"And no wonder, for Satan himself keeps transforming himself into an angel of light. It is therefore nothing great if his ministers also keep transforming themselves into ministers of righteousness. But their end shall be according to their works" (2 Corinthians 11:14,15).

Today, we will discuss people who speak in tongues at evangelical churches.

Satan and his demons are very successful when they transform themselves into false angels and ministers. This is an essential scripture for understanding the lies that many churches and leaders have been telling for years.

This devotional is an attempt to open the eyes of the ones whose hearts are rightly disposed to see the truth. The reason so many don't see the truth is that they follow the lies and false teachings of their ministers who are following demons pretending to be angels of light or ministers of righteousness.

If demons can overtake men and their entire personalities, as witnessed dozens of times in the four gospels, then it is easy for them to take over a faker Christian and make them talk nonsense for a few minutes in church to make a huge spectacle of themselves and become undignified.

August 26th Satan Tells You What You Want to Hear

"For there will be a period of time when they will not put up with the healthful teaching, but, in accord with their own desires, they will accumulate teachers for themselves to have their ears tickled; and they will turn their ears away from the truth, whereas they will be turned aside to false stories" (2 Timothy 4:3-4).

Satan has bombarded the world with many false religions which tell people what they want to hear.

The gifts of Holy Spirit were almost always given to help spread the Good News of the Kingdom of God (Mathew 24:14) in the first century. In modern days, Yahweh doesn't need to send his power to entire churches to get them to preach the good news in foreign languages. Bibles are available in hundreds of languages and 99% of the people groups of this world have access to the written word.

Furthermore, if your faker church really was a "spirit filled" church then don't you think that Yahweh would first use His power to cure your pastor of his porn addiction before he gave every strong-willed woman and disobedient man the ability to speak "gibberish" or nonsense to one another, without any benefit to the advancement of the Kingdom of God. I don't want to limit the amazing power and capabilities of Yahweh and say that the gifts of holy spirit are no longer available, but I will say that they are more like one in a billion and no one in your church is that one in a billion, let alone everyone in your church.

August 27th Faith Healings Don't Last

"Many will say to me in that day, 'Lord, Lord, did we not prophesy in your name, and expel demons in your name, and perform many powerful works in your name?' And yet then I will confess to them: I never knew YOU! Get away from me, YOU workers of lawlessness" (Matthew 7: 22-23).

Let us discuss faith healings in the evangelical church

All too often the faker evangelical church likes to heal people or have a guest minister swing through town to heal people.

I remember as a child a guest minister visiting town who asked us to raise our hands if we wanted to dedicate our lives more fully to "the lord." Of course, I raised my hand. This man then called me up front and laid his hand on my forehead and started praying aggressively and pushing me slowly and slowly backwards. I noticed two other men come from back stage and stand behind me. As this visiting pastor pushed my forehead back and back I felt the other two men move in behind me and trap my ankles so that I would fall. Their intent was for me to trip backwards and then they would drag me off stage to make a big show of "holy spirit" in front of the audience. I simply stepped over their feet, took a few steps backwards, exposed their fraud and walked away. The next time someone asks me if I want to serve Yahweh with more dedication, I will just keep that between Yahweh and myself.

I know firsthand a man who was healed at a "healing service" from his chronic knee problems. He felt so great and was so excited. Sadly enough, a month later his knees were bad again. Worse yet, he is still disobedient to biblical principles, is a negligent husband, doesn't provide for his wife, worships money and physical fitness, and has a huge lust problem. I guess that the healing never enticed him to go and sin no more. (John 5:14) **After this Jesus found him in the temple and said to him: "See, you have become well. Do not sin anymore, so that something worse does not happen to you."**

The human body is so much stronger than anyone thinks. Ask any policeman, soldier or a medical professional and they will tell you about people who have had the strength to run with broken legs or on broken feet. Adrenaline allows people to maximize their strength and minimize their pain. Hallucinogenic drugs such as LSD have given skinny drug addicts the strength to break handcuffs. The power of Satan and demon possession is no less powerful than the human will, human strength, adrenaline, or LSD.

A demon possessed man in the time of Jesus used to break chains. (Mark 5: 2-4) **And immediately after Jesus got out of the boat, a man under the power of an unclean spirit met him from among the tombs. His haunt was among the tombs, and up to that time, absolutely no one was able to bind him securely, even with a chain. He had often been bound with fetters and chains, but he snapped the chains apart and smashed the fetters; and nobody had the strength to subdue him.** If Satan can make a man break chains he can make your knees or shoulder feel better, giving you the impression that you were healed.

August 28th Beware of Wolves in Sheep's Clothing

"Be on the watch for the false prophets that come to YOU in sheep's covering, but inside they are ravenous wolves. By their fruits YOU will recognize them. Never do people gather grapes from thorns or figs from thistles do they? Likewise every good tree produces fine fruit, but every rotten tree produces worthless fruit" (Matthew 7: 15-17).

Beware of wolves who dress like your neighborhood priest or minister. By their fruits you will recognize them. You will know a faker church that does satanically enabled faith healings by its fruit.

If the church and its members have no true understanding of Yahweh and the Kingdom of God, are not obedient, and have no fruit in the lives of their members, then they clearly do not have Yahweh's blessing, to include the amazing power to theatrically heal people.

True Religion is recognized by its love, not by theatrics. (John 13:35) **By this all will know that YOU are my disciples, if YOU have love among yourselves.**

August 29th   Money Making Catholic Healing Locations

"He was teaching and saying to them: "Is it not written, 'My house will be called a house of prayer for all the nations'? But you have made it a cave of robbers" (Mark 11:17).

Today let us discuss faith healings at famous Catholic sites around the world.

Lourdes, France is home of one of the Catholic Church's most ridiculous money making ventures which exploits kindhearted, but ignorant and naive people. Check out the web site if you have a few minutes.

Satan evidently healed someone in the water years back and in modern times, all day long you can go to mass or take baths in the waters to heal yourself from whatever ailments you have. Beware of taxes and fees associated with visiting this site. But feel free to buy all kinds of rosaries and powerless catholic paraphernalia at the many gift shops. Shame on those who work at this unholy and evil place and especially those who volunteer in the gift shops.

At this den of thieves, they have set up a huge statue to the "Lady of Lourdes." As we studied in previous "Words of Wisdom," we are commanded to worship Yahweh, not a dead and powerless woman. Don't forget to stay at a catholic hotel or visit a local restaurant and eat a "John the Baptist burger" with some "Holy Spirit" sauce.

This place exploits naive, but perhaps pure-hearted tourists and is almost as sad as modern-day Jerusalem.

The worse thing is that despite the Catholic Church leaders knowing this place is a fraud and that any display of power actually comes from Satan, they keep selling tickets and rosaries so you can have a "nice experience" and pray to a dead and powerless Mary rather than to the living God, Yahweh.

Shame on the Catholic Church for making money off the power of Satan and for not exposing this fraud to the honest hearted ones you so frequently exploit.

August 30th Crying Statues

"For false Christs and false prophets will arise and will give great signs and wonders so as to mislead, if possible, even the chosen ones" (Matthew 24:24)

Crying statues are not from Yahweh. They are usually a statue of Mary or the false god Buddah. Would Yahweh empower a statue of a false god? Never.

Isn't it suspicious that crying statues have never been documented by professionals on video?

We have already discussed the fact that we are commanded to worship Yahweh, not statues. We know that Mary is dead, powerless, conscious of nothing, and awaiting the resurrection. Add all this together and it is obvious that crying statues get their "miracle" from Satan.

August 31st Satan can make you See Things

"Again the Devil took him along to an unusually high mountain and showed him all the kingdoms of the world and their glory. And he said to him: "All these things I will give you if you fall down and do an act of worship to me" (Matthew 4: 8-9).

When Satan tempted Jesus, Satan was powerful enough to make Jesus see the entire world.

If Satan can make Jesus, Yahweh's perfect and obedient son, see the entire world at once, Satan can easily make faker Christians see things that don't exist. This may explain some car accidents. But for sure it explains why people think they see catholic statues of Mary bleeding from its eyes.

September 1st Exorcisms

"Knowing their thoughts, he said to them: "Every kingdom divided against itself comes to ruin, and every city or house divided against itself will not stand. In the same way, if Satan expels Satan, he has become divided against himself; how, then, will his kingdom stand" (Matthew 12:25-26)?

Casting out demons exemplifies how much effort Satan and his demons go through to deceive humans and keep them away from the truth. Jesus and his disciples cast out many demons. When they cast out demons, they did so by using the power of Yahweh.

However, in modern times, a faker Christian drives out a demon with the sign of a cross and in the name of the trinity. We know from studying the Bible that a cross has no power, dishonors Jesus, and disappoints Yahweh. We know from the Bible that the trinity is unbiblical. So, if a man drives out a demon using a cross and the trinity then we know that he is not driving out the demon using the power of Yahweh. If the power does not come from Yahweh then it must be a show from Satan. This means that Satan is driving out demons. Satan's house is divided and will not stand.

<u>September 2nd Satan's is Getting Desperate</u>

"On this account be glad, you heavens and you who reside in them! Woe for the earth and for the sea, because the Devil has come down to you, having great anger, knowing that he has a short period of time" (Revelation 12:12).

Satan is desperate because he knows his time is short.

Take a look around at the state of this world and it is easy to see that Satan is giving his 100% best to steal, kill and destroy. He is desperate because he knows that his prominence is soon to end as the Kingdom of God is soon to arrive. Whether it is 30 days from now, or

30 years from now, we are in the final days and soon God will bring His Kingdom.

September 3rd Satan Pretends to be a Minister of Light

"And no wonder, for Satan himself keeps transforming himself into an angel of light. It is therefore nothing great if his ministers also keep transforming themselves into ministers of righteousness. But their end shall be according to their works" (2 Corinthians 11:14-15).

We know that Satan sometimes pretends to be a minister of righteousness.

Whether you want to believe it or not, Satan orchestrates a hugely sophisticated game of deception whereby one demon possesses a person, another demon makes a person feel miraculously faith healed, another demon speaks to a person and pretends to be God or Jesus, another demon misleads a man and speaks to him a plan to make a new religion which will pull billions of humans away from true worship, another demon tells a person to start a sect and then to have everyone commit suicide, another demon misleads church members into thinking that a cross and the trinity have power, and another demon leaves (or is exercised) out of a person when confronted by the powerless cross and trinity just to make a good show.

Countless other demons work to make men follow the traditions of men rather than the commandments of

YHWH. This game is so sophisticated that you better open your eyes to see it before it is too late.

September 4th Jesus is the Firstborn of Creation

"He is the image of the invisible God, the firstborn of all creation" (Colossians 1:15).

Jesus is called the first born of creation.

He was Yahweh's first creation, who existed from times indefinite before now, and thru him all things were made.

Jesus was a master builder in heaven and on earth.

Jesus helped Yahweh make all things. (Colossians 1:16) **because by means of him all other things were created in the heavens and on the earth, the things visible and the things invisible, whether they are thrones or lordships or governments or authorities. All other things have been created through him and for him.**

September 5th Jesus Helped Make Humans

"Then God said: "Let <u>us</u> make man in our image, according to <u>our</u> likeness, and let them have in subjection the fish of the sea and the flying creatures of the heavens and the domestic animals and all the earth and every creeping animal that is moving on the earth" (Genesis 1:26).

Jesus helped create humans and is referred to when Yahweh says of man let us make him in our image.

Many people know this scripture but they don't fully understand the implications of Jesus existing before his time on earth and the assistance he provided Yahweh during the creation.

September 6th Jesus Existed Long Before Becoming Human

"Jehovah himself produced me as the beginning of his way, the earliest of his achievements of long ago. From time indefinite I was installed, from the start, from times earlier than the earth. When there were no watery deeps I was brought forth as with labor pains, when there were no springs heavily charged with water. Before the mountains themselves had been settled down, ahead of the hills, I was brought forth as with labor pains, when as yet he had not made the earth and the open spaces and the first part of the dust masses of the productive land. When he prepared the heavens I was there; when he decreed a circle upon the face of the watery deep, when he made firm the cloud masses above, when he caused the fountains of the watery deep to be strong, when he set for the sea his decree that the waters themselves should not pass beyond his order, when he decreed the foundations of the earth, then I came to be beside him as a master worker, and I came to be the one he was specially fond of day by day, I being glad before him all the time, being glad at the productive land of his earth, and the things I

was fond of were with the sons of men" (Proverbs 8:22-31).

Today's scripture is long but amazing. Most people don't know this scripture. It is Jesus talking about his life before the Earth was created. It is a fantastic scripture.

It is fun to ponder the wonderful imagination of our loving Father Yahweh and His firstborn Jesus who helped Him create all the wonderful things we enjoy here on Earth. Just think of a juicy piece of corn. The seeds are so delicious and sweet. Now flip the seeds to the inside, make them red, round, and even sweeter and you now have a pomegranate. What unique seeds and what variations. Just think of an eagle soaring, or how a humming bird flaps its wings thousands of times a minute. Both are birds and yet so different. Cocoa and coffee beans are my two favorite vegetables. It is amazing how wonderful and complex the world's design is. Doctors still can't fully understand the human body. NASA can only take pictures of space, let alone build it, define it, regulate it, and name it. Our loving Father and His son truly are master builders.

September 7th Jesus was a Master Builder (not Just a Carpenter)

"Is this not the carpenter's son? Is not his mother called Mary, and his brothers James and Joseph and Simon and Judas? (Matthew 13:55).

Even during His time on earth, Jesus was a master builder.

Many know Jesus and his father Joseph to be carpenters.

Carpenter in this verse is from the original Greek word "Tektonos." This word is better translated as stone worker, master builder, craftsman, builder, and carpenter. Look it up if you are hesitant.

Tekton is the root word for rock as in the large rock masses under the earth's surface called "tectonic plates." So it would not be inaccurate to say Jesus worked to help his dad as a carpenter. But it would be more accurate to say he was a stone mason.

Jesus had to spend a lot of time with his education. He also knew a bit about his impending ministry. So it is logical that Jesus did not plan to inherit the family business and become a master-builder like Joseph. But nonetheless, Jesus was perfect and a wonderful son so there is no doubt that when possible, Jesus would help his father, Joseph, and his brothers with master building.

History reveals to us that during the time of Jesus there was plenty of need for master-builders and stone masons to construct buildings for the both the Romans and Jews.

In order to diminish the popularity and influence of the free masons, the Catholics began to translate "tektonos" into carpenter. Hundreds of years later people can see for themselves that the original scrolls say 'tektonos" or master builder / stone mason but they still can't get past their incorrect Sunday school idea that Jesus was a carpenter.

Jesus' significance and teachings and ransom are not changed if he was a carpenter or a painter or a master builder. But this one small example serves to illustrate the influence that Satan has had in the Catholic Church over the years to hide truth. This devotional is a small attempt to bring to light other, more essential lies and cover ups from false religions.

September 8th Satan is Misleading Churches away from Yahweh

"We know we originate with God, but the whole world is lying in the [power of the] wicked one" (1John5:19).

Hypocritical churches teach people that all churches and denominations basically lead to God.

Biblical truth tells us that we will know false religion by their bad fruit and should, as soon as possible, flee from false religion.

We should by all m-eans seek the truth before it is too late.

Today's scripture reminds us that this world is lying in the power of the evil one.

This truth is one which many do not want to accept. Of course, Yahweh is in charge and sovereign and all capable. But Satan runs the world right now. It only takes a minute to see that human governments have failed man, and that starvation, death, sin, and selfishness abound. Is this a reflection of our holy God of love? No way.

The only answer to the problems of this world is God's Kingdom, which will set it all straight again. That is why Jesus said in Matthew 9: 9-10 **YOU must pray, then, this way: "Our Father in the heavens, let your name be sanctified. Let your kingdom come. Let your will take place, as in heaven, also upon earth."**

Nothing short of YHWH's kingdom coming will end the evil effects of Satan upon the current system of things.

September 9th Beware of Wolves in Sheep's Clothing

"Be on the watch for the false prophets that come to YOU in sheep's covering, but inside they are ravenous wolves: (Matthew 7:15).

Beware of false religions, false teachers, and false doctrines. The world is full of many ideas about God. It is impossible that they are all right. The only way to test a prophet is to see if what he says corresponds with the Bible and with truth. 2000 years ago, Jesus warned his followers to be on the watch for those who claim to be prophets but who don't speak for Yahweh. They appear to be loving ministers, but on the inside, they are wolves.

Likely, your minister / priest is, in fact, a wolf in sheep's clothing. We recommend that you leave your church / cathedral / denomination immediately and live a life in accordance with biblical principles. A true Christian doesn't need a denomination but needs to be close to Yahweh.

September 10th A Tree is Known by its Fruit

"By their fruits YOU will recognize them. Never do people gather grapes from thorns or figs from thistles do they? Likewise every good tree produces fine fruit, but every rotten tree produces worthless fruit; a good tree cannot bear worthless fruit, neither can a rotten tree produce fine fruit. Every tree not producing fine fruit gets cut down and thrown into the fire. Really, then, by their fruits YOU will recognize those [men]" (Matthew 7:16-20).

A tree is known by its fruit. Just as a fig tree can't make mangos and a mango tree can't make figs, so a faker minister can't teach the truth and a truthful minister can't teach lies.

Because a tree is known by its fruit, it is easy to see if a minister is a false prophet (faker / hypocrite or a liar). Simply look at his fruits. Who cares if he has a PHD in Theology or graduated from a fancy seminary or university. If his fruits are hypocritical or unbiblical then beware, he is a wolf in sheep's clothing.

September 11th Christian Sects were Predicted 2000 Years Ago

"For there must also be sects among YOU, that the persons approved may also become manifest among YOU" (1 Corinthians 11:19).

The bible predicted over 2000 years ago that sects and false religion would become widespread. This certainly has come true in our lifetime. There are so called Christians who pray to Mary, not to Yahweh. There are so called Christians who don't honor the sabbath as Jesus did and as Yahweh commanded. There are so called Christians who have several wives even though Jesus said not to even look at another woman lustfully. There are so called Christians who are flamboyantly immoral and continually violate biblical principles. And of course, there are even Christian terrorist who hurt people and blow buildings up in the name of God. All of this is sad.

However, as today's scripture reminds us, there is also one redeeming quality that all of the sects and faker Christians have... they make it easy to see who are the real Christians. Their dirtiness makes it easier to see the peace, neutrality, cleanliness, integrity, love, and obedience of true followers of Yahweh.

September 12th Protestant Churches Peddle the Word of God

"for we are not peddlers of the word of God as many men are, but as out of sincerity, yes, as sent from God, under God's view, in company with Christ, we are speaking" (2 Corinthians 2:17).

Protestant churches which water down the word of God are peddlers of the Word of God. They tickle your ears by telling you what you want to hear. They make money from you by telling you what you want to hear. This is not the way it should be done.

Today's scripture tells us to speak with sincerity. I hope you feel the sincerity of this devotional. I know that more often than not my tone gets aggressive. But this is only a reflection of my zeal for Yahweh and my abhorrence of those who teach lies or false doctrine. I sincerely hope you learn bible truth and become closer to our loving Father, Yahweh. My sincerity is so deep that I have spent over 2 years making this "Words of Wisdom" devotional for you and have posted it on the internet for free.

September 13th Satan Blinds People's Minds

"If, now, the good news we declare is in fact veiled, it is veiled among those who are perishing, among whom the god of this system of things has blinded the minds of the unbelievers, that the illumination of the glorious good news about the Christ, who is the image of God, might not shine through" (2 Corinthians 4:3-4).

False religions are apostates who have drifted away from the truth into traditions of man. An apostate is "someone whose beliefs have changed and who no longer belongs to a religious or political group.[21]"

Apostates are veiled by Satan. Because they are wearing a figurative veil over their heads, they can't see or know the truth. They are blind to reality and refuse to see the truth.

---

[21] http://www.merriam-webster.com/dictionary/apostate

Sadly, we see from today's scripture that those who are blinded by Satan are perishing.

I hope and pray that many people will remove the veil of false beliefs so they can clearly see the reality of Yahweh's love and ways.

September 14th Mental Darkness

"They are in darkness mentally and alienated from the life that belongs to God, because of the ignorance that is in them, because of the insensitivity of their hearts" (Ephesians 4:18).

Apostates are mentally in the dark and alienate themselves from Yahweh. This is so very sad because now, more than ever, people have the opportunity, freedom, and ability to seek and find the "life that belongs to God."

Today we have more opportunity and freedom to seek God than ever before. Many nations have a freedom of religion. The bible is printed in almost every language.... but for sure in the top 200 most frequently used languages. The bible is cheap to purchase and free on the internet. We have so much potential to get to know the only true God. And yet, the easier it becomes to know God, the easier it is to be distracted by the things of the world or the tempo of life.

September 15th Jesus was harsh to so called Religious Teachers

"Woe to you who are versed in the Law, because you took away the key of knowledge. You yourselves did not go in, and you hinder those going in!" (Luke 11:52).

Jesus was loving and caring. Yet, to the hypocritical church leaders and scholars of his time, he was ruthless. This is because they taught one thing but did another. They were hypocrites and were misleading those who did not know better.

In modern times, using Jesus' tone and example, I say woe to those who are teachers and leaders in faker Christian churches and to those who are ordained seminary graduates. You have had within your grasp the truths of the bible but have never been able to fully see them or teach them. You will not inherit the kingdom and are sadly preventing others from going in.

September 16th From Bad to Worse

"But wicked men and impostors will advance from bad to worse, misleading and being misled" (2 Timothy 3:13).

Wicked men exist in abundance these days, both inside and outside of the church. Let us focus today on those imposters within the church.

Imposters within the Church advance from bad to worse, misleading the people in the pews (seats) and being misled by Satan, himself.

Yahweh forbids fornication. Yet it is now possible for homosexuals to be married in some churches.

The Catholic church encourages its billion followers to pray to and worship Mary, not Yahweh.

Yahweh tells us to love our neighbor. Yet it normal for denominations to send clergy to join the military to bless soldiers as they go off to fight for the financial interests of their secular nation.

As predicted over 2000 years ago, please beware of wicked men and imposters who are misleading and steering the church away from Yahweh.

September 17th Yahweh will Vindicate His Name

"A noise will certainly come clear to the farthest part of the earth, for there is a controversy that Yahweh has with the nations. He must personally put himself in judgment with all flesh. As regards the wicked ones, he must give them to the sword," is the utterance of Yahweh" (Jeremiah 25:31).

Yahweh will have a reckoning with false religion and with wicked men. As we read in today's scripture, Yahweh will judge the nations and the wicked, ultimately giving them the sword.

Yahweh is the only true God and is worthy of honor and praise and worship. He will not allow wicked people and nations to ignore Him forever. Although no one knows the day or the hour, He will one day soon vindicate His name.

Until then, it is never too late to repent of your sins and to seek Him and His ways.

September 18th Yahweh will Vindicate His People

"And YOU people will again certainly see [the distinction] between a righteous one and a wicked one, between one serving God and one who has not served him." (Malachi 3:18)

Yahweh will one day make a distinction between the goats and the sheep, the unrighteous and the righteous, false religions and the true religion.

A true Christian knows that this world and the people of this world hate them. They feel it and live it every day. How wonderful it will be when our righteous and loving Father vindicates His people and gives them life everlasting. What a reward.

September 19th Yahweh will Burn the Presumptuous Ones

"For, look! The day is coming that is burning like the furnace and all the presumptuous ones and all those doing wickedness must become as stubble. And the day that is coming will certainly devour them," Yahweh of armies has said, "so that it will

not leave to them either root or bough" (Malachi 4:1).

The bible discusses the "Day of Yahweh" quite often. This is when Yahweh will restore His kingdom and is what we all pray for when we say, **"may Your kingdom come, Your will be done, on earth, as it is done in Heaven"** (Matthew 6:10).

When Yahweh vindicates His name and His people, the wicked and presumptuous ones will become like stubble. They will be pulled up and destroyed as in a fire.

This scripture is important because it reminds all of us that someday, soon we hope, Yahweh's Kingdom will come, that it will end wickedness, and will restore a life of love and joy for those who were and are righteous.

September 20th There is Only One God

"I am YHWH, and there is no one else. With the exception of me there is no God" (Isaiah 45:5).

Yahweh is the only God. There is no other.

Hypocritical churches and false religions teach that God has many forms. For example, the god of Islam (allah) is the same as Yahweh. Or that there are many paths to God. Or that there is a little god in all of us.

Biblical truth tells us that Yahweh is the only God. There is no other God. All other so-called gods are false gods. You are either for Yahweh or against Yahweh. Period.

September 21ᵗʰ Jesus Causes Division

"Do YOU imagine I came to give peace on the earth? No, indeed, I tell YOU, but rather division" (Luke 12:51).

Jesus admits that he came to bring division between those who serve Yahweh and those who don't. This seems a bit contradictory at first. But it isn't.

If you love Yahweh with your all and your neighbor as yourself, then you are going to be different. You will stick out. And the world is going to see a reflection of God in you. And because of this, they are going to hate you.

Don't worry. Keep being loving and keep honoring Yahweh. Be obedient to biblical principles. And if people hate you and are mean to you then that simply means you are doing it right. Good job.

September 22ⁿᵈ Are You With or Against God?

"He that is not on my side is against me, and he that does not gather with me scatters" (Luke 11:23).

You are either for Jesus or against Jesus.

You are either for Yahweh or against Yahweh. Yahweh's family consists of the truth, His angels, His Kingdom, His son, and true worshipers. Satan's family consists of everything else.

When you see that everything is either for Yahweh or against Yahweh, it is much easier to live a life which honors Yahweh.

Islam: The false prophet Mohamed was deceived by Satan or one of his demons who pretended to be a god. I am sure that the false prophet Mohammed believed the voices in his head and that the false prophet Mohamed accurately wrote down what the voices said. Nonetheless, the voices in his head were not from YHWH but were from Satan or one of his demons pretending to be god. What the false prophet wrote down pulls people away from the truth of YHWH, and has caused war and strife and suppression and sadness ever since. Billions of Muslims have been misled from the truth of YHWH because of the lies that this false prophet wrote down. Satan has successfully misled a huge portion of the earth because of lies that he spoke through his false prophet. Please leave this false religion and seek YHWH, the loving God of Truth.

Hinduism: Hindus believe in a god for everything. This strictly violates the truth that YHWH is the only God. Satan again has successfully misled a huge portion of the earth because of this false religion and their belief in thousands of false gods. Please leave this false religion and seek YHWH, the loving God of Truth.

Buddhism: Worshiping a dead peaceful man and praying to a powerless statue of a fat guy is absolutely against the will of YHWH. Satan again has successfully misled a huge portion of the earth because of this false religion and their belief in that powerless, dead man.

Mormonism: Like Muslims, Mormons have a false prophet, Joseph Smith, who was deceived by Satan or one of his demons. I am sure that the false prophet Joseph Smith believed the voices in his head and I am sure that the false prophet Joseph Smith accurately wrote down what the voices said. Nonetheless, what this false prophet wrote down pulls people away from the truth of YHWH and violates biblical principles. Worse of all is that Mormons believe that there are other god's above YHWH, who created YHWH. Polygamy is outside the will of YHWH. Tolerating a year of sex and drinking and sin which allows men to appreciate the evils of the world is ridiculous and outside the will of YHWH. What they do and think and believe violates biblical truth. Satan again has successfully misled a huge portion of the earth because of lies that he spoke through one of his false prophets, Joseph Smith. Please leave this false religion and seek YHWH, the loving God of Truth.

September 23rd The Jews Abandoned Yahweh

"Look! YOUR house is abandoned to YOU" (Matthew 23:38).

Yahweh has stopped blessing the Hebrews.

"Political correctness" in the modern church teaches people that the Jews are God's people so who cares that they missed Jesus' coming. We must politically support the nation of Israel.

Biblical Truth tells us that Yahweh has abandoned the Israelites and has offered his hand to the obedient ones of the nations who want to worship Him in spirit and in truth.

It is said that the Hebrews are Yahweh's people. Jesus, himself, was a Hebrew. True, Yahweh made many covenants with the Jews. But sadly, the Hebrews were disobedient and left Yahweh. As a consequence of their disobedience, Yahweh disciplined them, as a loving Father, in an effort to bring them back into obedience and a right relationship. Yet, the Hebrews left Yahweh. Finally, Jesus was sent to model obedience and walking with Yahweh, and to be the final blood sacrifice, ending sacrifices for all time. After Jesus's sacrifice, Yahweh opened up the promises of the Kingdom of God to those right hearted ones from any nation.

The Jews do not have YHWH's favor any more. If you are a Jew and want to have the favor and love of your Creator, then you must become a true Christian and live a life obedient to biblical principles.

Yahweh cut off Judah. (2 Kings 23:27) **But YHWH said: "Judah, too, I shall remove from my sight, just as I have removed Israel; and I shall certainly reject this city that I have chosen, even Jerusalem, and the house of which I have said, 'My name will continue there.'"**

September 24th The Hebrews Left Yahweh

"And this house itself will become heaps of ruins. Everyone passing by it will stare in amazement and will certainly whistle and say, 'For what reason did YHWH do like that to this land and this house?'

And they will have to say, 'For the reason that they left Yahweh their God who had brought their forefathers out from the land of Egypt, and they proceeded to take hold of other gods and bow down to them and serve them. That is why YHWH brought upon them this entire calamity' (1 Kings 9:8-9).

The Hebrews left Yahweh. If they would have remained loyal and obedient, then they would have stayed with Yahweh. But they left Yahweh their God and now they follow the traditions of their elders.

Jesus correctly said that the Jews followed the traditions of men at the expense of neglecting the commandments of Yahweh. This can also be said of all major denominations because hypocrites follow traditions of men, not the bible. (Matthew 15:3) **In reply he said to them: "Why is it YOU also overstep the commandment of God because of YOUR tradition?**

September 25th   Yahweh Stopped Caring for the Hebrews

"For if that first covenant had been faultless, no place would have been sought for a second; for he does find fault with the people when he says: "'Look! There are days coming,' says Yahweh, 'and I will conclude with the house of Israel and with the house of Judah a new covenant; not according to the covenant that I made with their forefathers in [the] day of my taking hold of their hand to bring them forth out of the land of Egypt, because they did not continue in my covenant, so

that I stopped caring for them,' says Yahweh" (Hebrews 8:7-9).

Yahweh has stopped caring for the Hebrews. Wow. What a strong and sad scripture. Image how much your children would have to hurt you before you stopped caring for them. And yet, Yahweh is even more loving that we ever could be. For Yahweh to stop caring for his people, the Hebrews, then the Hebrews must have really hurt Him through their disobedience and disloyalty.

I hope and pray that we never sadden our loving heavenly Father by also being disobedient and disloyal.

September 26th The Hebrews Forsook Yahweh

"But you are among those forsaking Yahweh, Those forgetting my holy mountain, Those setting a table for the god of Good Luck, And Those filling up cups of mixed wine for the god of Destiny" (Isaiah 65:11).

The Israelites left Yahweh and sought after other, false gods. They were seduced by the world and the gods of the nations around them.

They even became superstitious and began to honor the false gods of good luck and destiny.

Sons of Israel (Jews in this scripture) are veiled. (2 Corinthians 3:14-15) **But their mental powers were dulled. For to this present day the same veil remains unlifted at the reading of the old covenant, because it is done away with by means of Christ. In fact,** down till today whenever Moses is read, a veil lies upon their hearts.

September 27th You Brought This On Yourself

"Have you not brought this on yourself, by abandoning Yahweh your God, while he was leading you in the way?" (Jeremiah 2:17).

There are significant consequences for leaving Yahweh.

The Jews abandoned Yahweh and they were taken into exile in Babylon. After repenting and being restored to the promised land, they again were disobedient and disloyal, following the traditions of men not the word of God. And now they have lost Yahweh's favor.

Jesus tells us definitively that the Hebrew leaders lost Yahweh's favor and that Yahweh was going to turn his favor to the nations. (Mathew 21:43) **This is why I say to YOU, the kingdom of God will be taken from YOU and be given to a nation producing its fruits.**

How sad it will be on judgement day for those who chose not to be obedient and loyal to Yahweh. There are significant consequences for leaving Yahweh.

September 28th You Should Have Listened

"**If only you would pay attention to my commandments! Then your peace would become just like a river And your righteousness like the waves of the sea**" (Isaiah 48:18).

The Jews have sadly lost the favor of Yahweh. Their sins brought this upon themselves. Yahweh has turned His attention to the gentiles. If only the Hebrews would have paid attention, their peace could have become just like a river, and their righteousness could have been like the waves of the sea.

Can you hear the sadness of God's words? Isn't it sad to see those you love make bad decisions? really leads the Catholic Church?

September 29th   The Catholic Church Follows the Traditions of the Popes, not the Word of God

"In reply he said to them: "Why is it YOU also overstep the commandment of God because of YOUR tradition?" (Matthew 15:3).

Based upon the "Words of Wisdom" of the past 300 days, we can see that the Catholic Church...

- Hides the name of God, Yahweh (pronounced Yahweh)
- Is not obedient to Biblical principles
- Is misled from the truth by Satan and his demons
- Doesn't discourage unwholesome entertainment
- Doesn't discourage evil friendships
- Promotes wars and is an influential part of the political systems of this world
- Is a den of thieves which seeks to make money off the word of Yahweh

- Doesn't understand the role and delegated authorities of Jesus
- Teaches the unbiblical doctrine of the trinity even though the truth is that Yahweh is the only, true God, Jesus is His son, and holy spirit is another way to describe Yahweh's power
- Teaches a lie about Christmas being Jesus' birthday even though it is a pagan holiday to celebrate the winter solstice
- Teaches a lie about Easter being Jesus' resurrection even though Jesus was killed during Passover (Nissan or Abib the 14th) and not during a pagan holiday to celebrate a false fertility god
- Teaches lies about Yahweh causing suffering when in fact suffering is not caused by our loving Father but is caused by Satan, sin, and time / unforeseen circumstance
- Teaches unbiblical lies about death and instantaneously going to heaven
- Teaches unbiblical lies about your soul being immortal and floating up to heaven
- Teaches unbiblical lies about hell-fire and judgment and purgatory
- Encourages unbiblical prayers to and worship of images and crosses
- Violates truth and biblical commandments by using the cross for worship
- Shamefully worships Mary, not Yahweh alone
- Shamefully prays to Jesus, Mary, and or saints rather than to Yahweh alone

- Violates biblical requirements to be fruitful by mandating celibacy for clergy, monks, and nuns
- Is not organized in accordance with biblical principles and guidelines established by early church leaders
- Worthlessly baptizes babies, kids, and adults who don't understand or live lives in accordance with biblical principles
- Doesn't honor Yahweh by teaching that blood is sacred
- Reprehensibly teaches a lie about bread and wine miraculously turning into Jesus' body and blood when celebrating communion
- Doesn't believe that the bible is living and active, follows the traditions of men over the principles of the bible, and changes key words and texts in bible translations
- Waters down the truth of the bible
- Doesn't teach the essential and honored role that Yahweh gives to women
- Supports unbiblical wars and political systems via military chaplains
- Doesn't understand or teach the Kingdom of God
- Doesn't use Yahweh's calendar but created an evil calendar which uses sacrilegious names for days of the week and months of the year
- Ignores Yahweh's commandment for a Saturday Sabbath and created a sacrilegious tradition for a "Lord's day" on Sunday

- Shamelessly uses fraudulent "miracles "and "gifts of the holy spirit" just to keep making money from faithful but naive people
- Doesn't understand Jesus' roll as the master-builder
- Tolerates lies from other false religions and doesn't have the courage to stand for the truth
- Never had Yahweh's favor and is obviously recognizable as not the true religion

Leaders of the Catholic Church need to beware, Yahweh sees the lies that you are teaching and the other lies you are covering up. (Isaiah 29:15) **Woe to those who go to great lengths to conceal their plans from YHWH. Their deeds are done in a dark place, while they say: "Who sees us? Who knows about us?"**

Biblical Truth: YHWH's followers are always obedient to the bible and are recognized by their love.

What YHWH says is inspired and true. Begin studying the bible so that you can honor Him with your life, decisions, thoughts, efforts, and heart, before it is too late.

Sep. 30th True Christians Are Recognized by Love

"By this all will know that YOU are my disciples, if YOU have love among yourselves" (John 13:35).

True Christians are recognized by their love. This is a wonderful scripture because it reminds us that the most important quality of a Christian must be love. We must have love, give love, and be recognized by love.

I must admit that the overall tone of this Devotional is aggressive, perhaps even negative. But this is because I love Yahweh and am so sad to see how traditions of men have slipped into the church and have pulled so many away from the truth.

Ezekiel 9 prophecies about how in the final times men will be sad, negative, and even sigh at the status of the world. My tone is just one example of this prophecy coming true in our lifetime.

Please don't forget that while we can be angry at hypocrisy and towards false traditions and doctrines which disrespect our loving Father, Yahweh, we must still love our neighbor. True Christians are known by their love.

October 1st   True Christians Recognize God's Sovereignty

"That people may know that you, whose name is Yahweh, You alone are the Most High over all the earth" (Psalm 83:18).

True Christians recognize Yahweh's sovereignty.

Psalm 83:18 is a beautiful scripture because it reminds us that (1) God's name is Yahweh, and (2) that Yahweh alone is God.

There are no other Gods. There is only the true God, Yahweh. All other gods are false gods.

Please take a moment and commit this scripture to memory.

October 2nd True Christians are Associated with God's Name

"Sym′e·on has related thoroughly how God for the first time turned his attention to the nations to take out of them a people for his name" (Acts 15:14).

True Christians are associated with Yahweh's name. This is because Yahweh has taken them for Himself, from the people of the nations. No longer is Yahweh prioritizing the Hebrews. As read in last week's Word of Wisdom, the Jews walked away from Yahweh by being disobedient and by following other false gods and the traditions of men.

In present times, Yahweh has called a people to himself from all over the world. They are the ones who know and use His name. They are the ones who are obedient to Biblical principles. They are the ones who are known for their love.

October 3rd True Christians Pray for God's Kingdom to Come

"YOU must pray, then, this way: "Our Father in the heavens, let your name be sanctified. Let your kingdom come. Let your will take place, as in heaven, also upon earth." (Matthew 6:9-10).

True Christians pray for the Kingdom to come, and they know what it means.

Most so-called Christians know this model prayer. Yet, most so-called Christians don't know what God's

Kingdom is. If you need a refresher then please go to May 25th through 29th.

How frightful, yet wonderful it will be when God's Kingdom comes. May we all have an extra dose of patients, strength, and love while we wait for it.

October 4th True Christians Prioritize the Word of God

"All Scripture is inspired of God and beneficial for teaching, for reproving, for setting things straight, for disciplining in righteousness, that the man of God may be fully competent, completely equipped for every good work" (2 Timothy 3:16-17).

True Christians accept and prioritize the Word of God.

The bible is not to be interpreted and played with. The bible is to understood and obeyed.

As we are reminded through today's Word of Wisdom, knowing the inspired scriptures will make the man of God fully competent and completely equipped for every good work.

Rather than going to Harvard or getting a Masters of Business Administration (MBA), a man should simply buy a Bible and study it every day for the rest of his life.

October 5th True Christians Love One Another

"I am giving YOU a new commandment, that YOU love one another; just as I have loved YOU, that YOU also love one another" (John 13:34).

True Christians love. This is the first and greatest commandment. We are to love Yahweh with all our heart, soul, mind, and strength. And we are supposed to love our neighbors as ourselves.

Today's scripture is a quote Jesus gives to his disciples. He tells them that they must love the way Jesus loved. The way Jesus loved and taught and gave of his time and life to the disciples was amazing. It is rare these days for people to invest so much love and time into the lives of someone else. Making disciples takes time and does not happens in minutes.

How are you following Jesus' example of pouring you time and love and life and wisdom into others?

October 6th True Christians are Out of This World

"Pilate answered: "I am not a Jew, am I? Your own nation and the chief priests delivered you up to me. What did you do?" Jesus answered: "My kingdom is no part of this world. If my kingdom were part of this world, my attendants would have fought that I should not be delivered up to the Jews. But, as it is, my kingdom is not from this source" (John 18:35-36).

True Christians are not of this world. Jesus tells Pilate that his kingdom is not of this world. Or at least not yet. This is why we pray for God's Kingdom to come and for His will to be done…

Because our citizenship belongs to the Kingdom of Yahweh, we must not get overly focused on loyalties to secular nations. We must obey Caesar, and give to him our required taxes. But we must never forget that we will never be back in our homeland until our Father's Kingdom comes.

October 7th True Christians Have Peace

"And he will certainly render judgment among the nations and set matters straight respecting many peoples. And they will have to beat their swords into plowshares and their spears into pruning shears. Nation will not lift up sword against nation; neither will they learn war anymore" (Isaiah 2:4).

True Christians are peaceful. They are different. You can see it, feel it. This is a small reflection of the peace that will come with our Father's Kingdom. How wonderful it will be when we can all beat our swords into plowshares and our spears into pruning shears.

Until our Father's Kingdom comes, may He give us an extra dose of patience, love, and peace so that we can endure these final times.

October 8th True Christians Have Fruit of the Spirit

"On the other hand, the fruitage of the spirit is love, joy, peace, long-suffering, kindness, goodness, faith, mildness, self-control. Against such things there is no law" (Galatians 5:22, 23).

True Christians demonstrate fruit of the spirit. Faker Christians look like everyone else in the world. True Christians demonstrate the fruit of the spirit. Faker Christians demonstrate "faker" fruit of the spirit on Sundays or if a lot of people are watching.

Please take a minute to memorize this scripture. These fruits of the spirit are such wonderful examples of what flows out of a person whose heart is filled with God's love.

October 9th True Christians are Yahweh's Witnesses

"YOU are my witnesses," is the utterance of YHWH, "even my servant whom I have chosen, in order that YOU may know and have faith in me, and that YOU may understand that I am the same One. Before me there was no God formed, and after me there continued to be none. I—I am YHWH, and besides me there is no savior." "I myself have told forth and have saved and have caused [it] to be heard, when there was among YOU no strange [god]. So YOU are my witnesses," is the utterance of YHWH, "and I am God"(Isaiah 43:10-12).

True Christians are witnesses of the love of Yahweh. During the times of Isaiah, the Hebrews were chosen to be witnesses for Yahweh. In modern times, Yahweh has chosen people from all nations to reflect His love and principles.

Being a Witness of God means that you shine for Him, that you make Him proud and happy. The commandments remind us never to blaspheme the name of God by being a bad witness. If you associate yourself with Yahweh you better live a righteous and holy life. We would not want to make Him look bad.

October 10th True Christians Live By The Golden Rule

"All things, therefore, that YOU want men to do to YOU, YOU also must likewise do to them; this, in fact, is what the Law and the Prophets mean" (Matthew 7:12).

True Christians do to others as they would have done to themselves.

In theory, we want people to be patient and loving with us so we must always be patient and loving with them.

In reality, people will be stupid and mean to us because we love Yahweh. Nonetheless, we must still be patient and loving with them.

Please take a minute to memorize the location of this scripture. We all know it, but not everyone is quick to remember where it comes from in the Bible.

October 11th True Christians Know That God's Name (Yahweh) is a Strong Tower

"The name of Yahweh is a strong tower. Into it the righteous runs and is given protection" (Proverbs 18:10).

True Christians use the name of Yahweh as a strong tower.

There is no doubt that the name of Yahweh is powerful. Otherwise, why would the Christendom have gone through so much effort to hide it, to translate it out of bible, to mispronounce it as Jehovah, or to confuse it with Jesus in a trinity. There is only one God and Yahweh is his name. There is no other.

Using the name of Yahweh is powerful. Pray to Yahweh. Say Yahweh. Seek Yahweh. Thank Yahweh. Worship Yahweh.

October 12th True Christians Have Bright Eyes

"The orders from Yahweh are upright, causing the heart to rejoice; The commandment of Yahweh is clean, making the eyes shine" (Psalm 19:8).

True Christians are recognized by their joyful eyes.

Today's scripture reminds us that following the commandments of Yahweh keeps you clean, makes your heart rejoice, and causes your eyes to shine. Place two people side by side and you can tell who is the atheist and who is the lover of Yahweh. Living correctly and in accordance with biblical principles will fill you so full of love that people will see it running out of your eye balls.

October 13th True Christians Have Peace

"Do not be anxious over anything, but in everything by prayer and supplication along with thanksgiving let YOUR petitions be made known to God; and the peace of God that excels all thought will guard YOUR hearts and YOUR mental powers by means of Christ Jesus. Finally, brothers, whatever things are true, whatever things are of serious concern, whatever things are righteous, whatever things are chaste, whatever things are lovable, whatever things are well spoken of, whatever virtue there is and whatever praiseworthy thing there is, continue considering these things" (Philippians 4:6-8).

This is a wonderful scripture because it reminds us to give our worries over to God in prayer and to think about positive things.

If your loving father was the King of England and your oldest brother was loving and kind and generous, then you would have few real worries. Who cares if you didn't have a lot of money, your older brother would help you. Why worry about justice? Your father would help you. In reality, our loving Heavenly Father Yahweh is King of the Universe and Jesus will soon be His delegated loving, kind and generous King. We may have worries and injustice in this world but when our Father's kingdom comes, He will wipe away every tear.

The second part of this scripture reminds us to think positively. Please don't fill your mind with negative news, violent and immoral television, and the same worries as secular people.

True Christians have peace. What are you worried about?

October 14th True Christians Bring Yahweh Joy

"And he went on to say to them: "Go, eat the fatty things and drink the sweet things, and send portions to the one for whom nothing has been prepared; for this day is holy to our Lord, and do not feel hurt, for the joy of Yahweh is YOUR stronghold" (Nehemiah 8:10).

True Christians find a stronghold in the joy of Yahweh.

In today's scripture the Israelites are again honoring the commandment of Yahweh to celebrate a holy festival. They must relax, not work, feast, and be generous. Being obedient to Biblical principles is one way which Christians can honor Yahweh and make his heart rejoice.

Proverbs 27:11 **"Be wise, my son, and make my heart rejoice."**

October 15th True Christians Shine Brightly

"Likewise let YOUR light shine before men, that they may see YOUR fine works and give glory to

YOUR Father who is in the heavens" (Matthew 5:16).

True Christians shine. They don't go around trying to make spectacles of themselves to get attention and to glorify God. But by loving their neighbors and living in accordance with Biblical principles, they stand out. They shine. They glow.

Do you look like the secular people of this world or do you shine as a reflection of Yahweh's love?

October 16th True Christians are a Sweet Odor

"But thanks be to God who always leads us in a triumphal procession in company with the Christ and makes the odor of the knowledge of him perceptible through us in every place! For to God we are a sweet odor of Christ among those who are being saved and among those who are perishing; to the latter ones an odor issuing from death to death, to the former ones an odor issuing from life to life. And who is adequately qualified for these things?" (2 Corinthians 2:14-16)

True Christians are recognized by their pleasant aroma in this world.

As we discussed yesterday, true Christians stand out. They don't worry and look like the people of the world. They shine as if reflecting God's love here on earth. In a similar way, true Christians are a pleasant aroma.

When someone with bad odor walks by, you recognize it immediately. When someone who smells great walks by, your nose recognizes them immediately. As Christians, our loving attitudes and acts of kindness should make us instantly recognizable to the "neutral" or "bad odor" people of this world.

October 17th True Christians Know The Difference Between Clean and Unclean

"They should instruct my people about the difference between what is holy and what is common; and they will teach them the difference between what is unclean and what is clean" (Ezekiel 44:23).

If you drop a white silk scarf into the mud it takes one second for the whiteness to be made dirty. It may take hours of cleaning to make the scarf clean again. In some cases, the scarf will never be clean again.

Similarly, it is important to not become dirty or defiled by the things of this world. It only takes a second to get spiritually dirty. But it may take months or years to be made clean again.

True Christians know and teach the difference between what is holy and what is common, what is clean and unclean.

October 18th True Christians Keep Clean

"The form of worship that is clean and undefiled from the standpoint of our God and Father is this: to look after orphans and widows in their tribulation, and to keep oneself without spot from the world" (James 1:27).

True Christians are not stained by the world or traditions of men.

Please, if only you would stop accepting the hypocrisy and tradition based lies of your church. Do what the bible says. Yahweh is real. What He says is inspired and true. Begin studying the bible immediately so that you can honor Him with your life, decisions, thoughts, efforts, and heart, before it is too late.

I pray that you already have had your eyes opened to the fact that so many of the beliefs of your church come from the hypocritical traditions of men in clear violation of biblical truth.

Knowing and being obedient to Biblical truth is a matter of life and death, everlasting life and judgment. So please be more concerned with gaining the approval of Yahweh than your local minister or priest.

October 19th Sins Have Consequences

"Your own errors have prevented these things from coming; Your own sins have deprived you of what is good" (Jeremiah 5:25).

Obedience to Biblical truth is important because the consequences of your mistakes and sins may prevent you from receiving what is good.

If you sin, you will keep yourself from closeness with God. Of course, you can genuinely repent and restore a good relationship with God. But many times, you will still have to suffer the earthly consequences of your bad decisions.

A man who betrays his wife may repent and be restored to a good relationship with God. But his marriage may be ruined, he may have to live with a sexually transmitted disease, he will be financially responsible for his ex-wife, and he may have to father an unwanted child for the rest of his life.

There are consequences to sin and these consequences usually keep people from enjoying what is good.

October 20th You Reap What You Sow

"Do not be misled: God is not one to be mocked. For whatever a person is sowing, this he will also reap" (Galatians 6:7).

Biblical truth is important because you reap what you sow.

Whether or not you believe in God is unimportant. Yahweh is real and He believes in you. And whether or not you believe in the resurrection and judgement is also unimportant. The resurrection and judgement are real and will happen to everyone.

Jesus told us many times how Yahweh will judge. He will judge us based upon biblical standards. He will judge us the way we judge others. He will treat us the way we treat others. Whatever people did or didn't do the least of Jesus' brothers they did or didn't do to Jesus himself.

God is real and all knowing. The resurrection and judgement are real. We will be judged as we judge. We will reap what we sow. This is a warning to non-Christians but a source of peace for Believers. Justice is coming. May He be merciful.

October 21st Draw Close to God

"Draw close to God, and he will draw close to you" (James 4:8).

Draw close to Yahweh and He will draw close to you.

Remember, you are only as close to Yahweh as you want to be. He always wants to be close to us. He loves us. But He lets us decide how close we are to him.

If you want to be close to Him you will be. If you don't care for Him, then you will be far away.

October 22nd Hypocrisy or Truth

"Jesus replied, "And why do you, by your traditions, violate the direct commandments of God? (Matthew 15:3 - NLT)

People should follow Biblical truth, not the hypocrisy and traditions of their church.

We owe our life to the one true God. Lovingly, He has made Himself very known to us through His Scriptures. It is our duty and pleasure to read, study, and live our lives in accordance with the truths and principles of these scriptures.

Sadly, the ancient church ignored many Biblical truths and continues today to teach goodhearted people to follow their man-made traditions. What is worse is that so many of these man-made traditions are in direct violation of scripture.

Knowing and being obedient to Biblical truth is a matter of life and death, everlasting life or judgment. You should be more concerned with gaining the approval of God than pleasing your local minister or priest.

October 23rd Halloween is Evil

"There should not be found in you anyone who makes his son or his daughter pass through the fire, anyone who employs divination, anyone practicing magic, anyone who looks for omens, a sorcerer, anyone binding others with a spell, anyone who consults a spirit medium or a fortune-teller, or anyone who inquires of the dead. For whoever does these things is detestable to Jehovah, and on account of these detestable practices Yahweh your God is driving them away from before you. You should prove yourself blameless before Yahweh your God." (Deuteronomy 18:10-13)

As Halloween is quickly approaching I want to take two days to address how True Christians do not celebrate Halloween.

Christians celebrate the festivals that Yahweh commands. Halloween is not one of those festivals. Halloween is a pagan celebration. Its roots are pagan, dare we say evil, and do not honor Yahweh. There is nothing wrong with dressing up in a costume. But there is something wrong with dressing up in a costume if it is done while participating in a pagan tradition or if the costume itself honors what Yahweh detests.

Today's scripture reminds us that Yahweh forbids witchcraft, sorcery, omen reading, and spiritism. These are the hallmarks of Halloween. This is why true Christians can't celebrate Halloween.

Do you want Yahweh to detest you or do you want Yahweh to be proud of you?

Next week, simply don't celebrate Halloween. It is easy to not celebrate Halloween. If people are rude to you or mean to you then rejoice because you are doing it right (Matthew 5:11).

October 24th Hate what is Evil

"O YOU lovers of Yahweh, hate what is bad" (Psalm 97:10)

Halloween is evil. There is nothing Christian about celebrating a pagan holiday in honor of the dead.

Vampires, werewolves, witches, zombies and magic are so popular these days. They are the subjects of the most popular movies and bestselling books. People can't get enough. Let me clarify, pagan people can't get enough.

Those who love God hate what is bad. This means they hate Halloween because they hate what is evil. Yesterday's scripture reminds us that Yahweh detests anyone who **"employs divination, anyone practicing magic, anyone who looks for omens, a sorcerer, anyone binding others with a spell, anyone who consults a spirit medium or a fortune-teller, or anyone who inquires of the dead"** (Deuteronomy 18:10-13).

As Christians, we must love what is good and hate what is bad… even if everyone in our neighborhood or family is celebrating it.

October 25th Love God

"'You must love Yahweh your God with your whole heart and with your whole soul and with your whole mind.' This is the greatest and first commandment. The second, like it, is this: 'You must love your neighbor as yourself.' On these two commandments the whole Law hangs, and the Prophets" (Matthew 22: 37-40).

Loving Yahweh with our whole heart means that we completely love Him. We love what He loves and hates what He hates (see yesterday's Word of Wisdom).

Loving Yahweh with our soul means that we must honor him with our lives, with our energy. We must prioritize what He mandates and make Him and his ways our priority.

Loving Yahweh with our mind means that we must study, know, and use the word of God. Many people love God but they don't use their minds. They simply sit in church each week and do what their minister tells them to do. They blindly follow their church even if their church leads them away from God. This is unacceptable. Jesus tells us to use our minds and to love God with our minds. Doing so will reveal truth and help us to live our lives in accordance with Biblical truth.

Do you love Yahweh as priority one, with all your energy, and in accordance with Biblical truth?

October 26th Love Your Neighbor

"'You must love Yahweh your God with your whole heart and with your whole soul and with your whole mind.' This is the greatest and first commandment. The second, like it, is this: 'You must love your neighbor as yourself.' On these two commandments the whole Law hangs, and the Prophets" (Matthew 22: 37-40).

If you are a true Christians then your neighbors will know it and feel it. They will feel your generosity and love and experience your helpfulness. They will see that you are clean and keep yourself from being defiled by this world. They will be thankful for your help and charity.

If you love your neighbor the way you would want them to love you, then for sure they are going to notice.

Do you reflect God's love in how you love and care for your neighbor?

October 27th Completely Choked Out

"As for that which fell among the thorns, these are the ones who have heard, but by being carried away by anxieties, riches, and pleasures of this life, they are <u>completely choked</u> and bring nothing to maturity" (Luke 8:14).

The parable of the sower in Luke 8 is a story many of us know. The sower sows seed. Some seeds fall on rocks, some amongst thorns, and some in good soil. Today's scripture is the seed that falls amongst thorns. These are the people who hear the word of God but who are so worried about "anxieties, riches," and "pleasures" that the word of God never grows in their hearts. They are choked out by the influences of this world.

Let us focus today on riches. And I will use a personal example

I want this devotional to be a blessing to people. I want this devotional to point out hypocrisy and false traditions while opening eyes to biblical truth. Although it has taken over one year to write this devotional, I have decided to make this devotional available for free on our website. Get a daily email or download the entire devotional eBook for free. If you want a paperback then you will have to pay for it.

I struggled with charging for the book for a long time. But Jesus tells us the standard for Christian ministry. (Matthew 10: 8) **YOU received free, give free.**

We can't let worries about money prevent the word of God from taking root in our lives. Life is not about money. It is about loving and worshiping our amazing God, Yahweh.

Please worry less about making money and more about letting the "word of God" soak deep into your life.

October 28th Pay Attention to How you Listen

"Therefore, pay attention to how you listen, for whoever has will be given more, but whoever does not have, even what he imagines he has will be taken away from him" (Luke 8:18).

Jesus was such an amazing story teller. He said things which had two or three levels of meaning. He said simple agricultural stories, such as the "Parable of the Sower" which are still relevant and understandable today.

Jesus tells us in today's scripture to "pay attention to how we listen." Perhaps he is reminding us to deliberately and actively listen to what he says, what the bible says. Jesus had so much wisdom. It is our pleasure, and duty, to pay attention to what he says.

Jesus said frequently "for those with ears to hear listen" or "for those are willing to accept it" (Matthew 11:14). A great example of this is when he was talking about Elijah coming back to earth as John the Baptist and that he will again return before in the final days before God's Kingdom comes (Malachi 4:5-6). Many people won't accept this thinking. But Jesus reminds us to open our ears and minds to the truth.

Yahweh, as quoted in Isaiah, also reminds us to "pay attention." **"This is what Yahweh has said, your Repurchaser, the Holy One of Israel: "I, YHWH, am your God, the One teaching you to benefit [yourself], the One causing you to tread in the way in which you should walk. O if only you would actually pay attention to my commandments! Then your peace would become just like a river, and your righteousness like the waves of the sea."** (Isaiah 48:17-18)

October 29th Fight the Good Fight

"Fight the fine fight of the faith; get a firm hold on the everlasting life for which you were called and you offered the fine public declaration in front of many witnesses" (1 Timothy 6:12).

As Christians we are not supposed to fight. We are supposed to love. Jesus is not recorded as physically fighting anyone. There might be a reason for this.

We are, however, encouraged to fight the good fight of faith. We are encouraged to stand strong for Yahweh. We are encouraged to love in a time when selfishness is so prevalent.

If you love Yahweh and love your neighbors then the world is going to hate you. This is why Christians need to prepare themselves for a fight. Not a fight with fists, but a fight with truth and love.

We will spend the next few days discussing scriptures which remind us to fight the good fight of the faith.

October 30th Stand Firm

"Finally, go on acquiring power in [the] Lord and in the mightiness of his strength. Put on the complete suit of armor from God that YOU may be able to stand firm against the machinations of the Devil; because we have a wrestling, not against blood and flesh, but against the governments, against the authorities, against the world rulers of this darkness, against the wicked spirit forces in the heavenly places" (Ephesians 6:10-12).

Today's scripture reminds us that our fight is not against flesh and blood but against evil and against the leaders of this world. This is not a physical fight but a spiritual fight.

When the world tells you that it is authorized to violate the word of God then you must stand for the truth. When the world tells you that you must deny your God and His existence then you must stand for the truth. Evolution, homosexual marriages, wars, fornications, false doctrines, and atheism are just a few examples.

As Christians, we must reflect God's love and truth. We must resist evil and the unbiblical norms of this world.

October 31st No Fear

"Even though I walk in the valley of deep shadow, I fear nothing bad, for you are with me" (Psalm 23:4).

Many people know Psalm 23. It is a poetical prayer which reminds us that Yahweh God is always near to us and that He Protects us. This is partially true and partially false.

Yes, God is near to us. He is all knowing and ever present. He can and He does protect His people. However, God doesn't protect us from all suffering.

Not until God's Kingdom comes will we have peace on earth. Until then, we will have to suffer the consequences of this evil world. We know that there is suffering in this world. And while we know that suffering is caused by sin, evil, and chance or unforeseen circumstances, we also know for sure that God doesn't cause suffering.

Sin has consequences. Evil makes people suffer. And sometimes accidents happen. But this isn't caused by God and soon He will stop it all together.

November 1st Fear Disappointing God

"And do not become fearful of those who kill the body but cannot kill the soul; but rather be in fear of him that can destroy both soul and body in Ge·hen′na" (Matthew 10:28).

Man may hurt and kill you. But if you were righteous, God will resurrect you when His Kingdom comes and give you everlasting life. Regardless of what happens to you physically, in the end, a righteous Christian will ultimately be victorious. But the key word is "righteous."

We must not fear men. We must fear disappointing God to the point that we disqualify ourselves from everlasting life.

November 2nd Resist Sin

"In carrying on YOUR contest against that sin YOU have never yet resisted as far as blood" (Hebrews 12:4).

Today's scripture reminds us that we must resist sin to the point of bleeding. But before someone can resist a sin he must be able to identify a sin. Too often these days people do things without even knowing that they are sins. They smoke, they get tattoos, then fornicate. The world says this is authorized. The bible says this is prohibited.

Once you know something is a sin, it must be avoided. If you repeatedly sin then you love that sin more than you love God. And that makes you a faker. Sin must be avoided, fought, and conquered. We must love God more than we love sin.

November 3rd God Hears Prayers

"If we confess our sins, he is faithful and just to forgive us our sins, and to cleanse us from all unrighteousness" (1 John 1:9).

God forgives sin and answers prayers.

There are books, blogs, magazines and "so called" famous money-making ministers and preachers telling us reasons why God doesn't listen to our prayers and why God doesn't answer our prayers. To make things even worse, they have the audacity to mention 5, 7 or 10 reasons why. This is so sickening because our loving heavenly Father encourages us to turn to Him, confess our sins, and receive His forgiveness and mercy. We can see this truth in multiple scriptures and through multiple examples of our fellow sinners in the bible.

Who are they to say: "Hey you imperfect human, guess what? There are 5 reasons why God doesn't listen to your prayers."

Who are they to make such a shameful statement? How dare they say what God listens to and or answers?

Yahweh knows that we are imperfect humans, sinful, and that we sin in innumerable times and ways.

Don't listen to declarations from self-righteous people who think they know everything, to include what is in God's mind. This false line of reasoning can make us feel inferior, possibly even dragging us away from God, and cause us to be too ashamed to pray for forgiveness for the mistakes that we make or for repeated sins.

God is the listener of prayers. Period.

We need to confess, pray with honesty from the heart, and work on ourselves!

November 4th Friends must be Honest with Each Other

"Faithful are the wounds of a friend, but deceitful are the kisses of an enemy" (Proverbs 27:6).

To have a good friend, YOU must be one. Be a good friend and deepen friendships to make them last.

A family member, let's call her Martha, recently called me while waiting for her friend to "show up" at a local coffee shop. During the conversation, which lasted for over 30 minutes, Martha said: "who knows if my friend will show up at all. She is so flaky."

That made me think. Seriously, who wants to have a friend that you can't even rely on for a cup of coffee? What happens in a real emergency? The term "flaky" already says it all: a person you can't rely on or count on.

Martha isn't a young teenager, but is a wife and mother of two in her 40's. So sad, isn't it? The advice we gave Martha on the phone was to tell her friend that this behavior is disrespectful and that it is not nice to be flaky. Martha was afraid to hurt her friend's feelings so she decided not to bring up the "issue." Martha further said that she would simply stop being friends with such a "flaky" person.

How sad I thought. Rather than confronting the friend about being flaky, which may lead to her friend becoming a better, more responsible person, Martha simply decided to stop being her friend.

Friendships should always be built upon a foundation of honesty and love. If you want your friendships to last, then you should be able to address situations which affect your relationship with your friends, right?

November 5th Forgiveness

"Be kind to one another, tender-hearted, forgiving each other, just as God in Christ also has forgiven you" (Ephesians 4:32).

Forgiveness is an emotional and spiritual healing process that happens between you and God. Reconciliation is a healing process that takes place between you and another person. Sometimes we are not able to have the reconciliation we would wish for, but we are always called to forgive.

Let's take one biblical example, Joseph. God elevated Joseph to a position second only to Pharaoh. It was to Joseph that his brothers eventually bowed and pled for mercy. Joseph forgave his brothers. (Genesis 50:19-21). What about us? Can we forgive family members who have done us wrong? Or are we craving family drama instead of peace and love with others?

Never forget God's abundant grace and the forgiveness He has granted us in spite of our own sins.

November 6th No Secular Country can Claim to Represent God

"That they may know that you alone, whose name is Yahweh, are the Most High over all the earth" (Psalm 83:18). WEB

Let us talk today about Patriotism. Yes, but patriotism as mentioned in the scriptures with regards to God's name.

The Bible is clear about the fact that God's name, YAHWEH, will be declared to ALL nations and peoples of the world.

We shout "America!" and talk about how much better we are than everyone else. But this is not biblical. We project Christianity on to the American flag and assume that God acts like an American. But this is not how it works.

If you are an American, feel free to celebrate American freedoms and realize how blessed you are to live there. But you must remember that at the end of the day a True Christian's citizenship is in the Kingdom of God. Wars, a million abortions a year, Hollywood's sinfulness, corruption… even the best country falls way short of the holiness of the God's coming Kingdom.

Think of "paradise" and how wonderful it will be when the earth is full of only loving people from all over the world. Be very cautious when it comes to political preferences, patriotism, and identity. Don't forget who the god of this current world is: **"We know we are from**

God, and the whole world lies in the power of the evil one" (1 John 5:19).

November 7th Christians Don't Gossip

"Let your conversation be always full of grace, seasoned with salt, so that you may know how to answer everyone" (Colossians 4:6).

Seriously, did you ever get involved in a case of gossip?

A close family member is a person that I will call a GOSSIP. She won't say a single nice word about anyone in the world. But after she bad talks and gossips someone's reputation into the dirt she always finishes her diatribe with "Bless her heart!"

I think that by adding "Bless her heart" to the end of her gossip attack she thinks she is being a nice and holy person. Perhaps she is giving herself absolution for sharing her poison and venom. It is as if she believes that "the situation is ok as long I wish a blessing on the heart of that poor, terrible, sinful person I just slandered with my words." Obviously, this is not loving and not biblical.

I used to be guilty of listening to this slander, which made me a part of the gossip process. But now I simply walk away from the table or kindly asked her to change subjects. I let her know that we don't want to be part of her STORIES.

Let us remember what our grandparents taught us: "If you can't say something nice, then don't say anything at all."

We should not have a judgmental attitude towards the sins, problems or mistakes of other people. Rather, we should ask how can we can be a blessing to them in word and deed.

Sure, it's nice to escape our own issues by talking about someone else's for a while. But let's try to remember to speak with grace because our sins are just as sinful as anyone else's.

November 8th God is Good

"Taste and See that Yahweh is good" (Psalm 34:8).

This is such a nice scripture with so many applications. I like Psalms 34:8 because it reminds us of tastes and the enjoyment we get from food. YHWH lovingly designed us with the ability to differentiate so many flavors and to enjoy the vast spectrum of herbs and spices and fruits and vegies and… My wife and I frequently include this scripture on thank you cards or invitations to dine at our house.

I also love this scripture because YHWH is good. Actually, He is amazing and wonderful and loving and merciful….but for the sake of further analyzing this scripture, let's summarize Him as "good." If you never tasted YHWH or life in accordance with His principles or commandments, then you are really missing out on the yummy life, the good life. Just like an unknown food, so many people refuse to eat or try living a Christian life. But those who do get a taste of the love and peace associated with living an obedient life which honors Yahweh instantly know that it is good. May you, too, taste and see that a life in accordance with Yahweh's ways is, in fact, good.

November 9th Bad Associations

"Do not be misled. Bad associations spoil useful habits" (1 Corinthians 15:33)

Today's scripture is short but powerful. It reminds us that if we are friends with the world we will spoil the good habits of holiness. If we are friends with atheists at work, then we will spoil the good habits of righteousness. If we are friends with our evil neighbors, then we will spoil the good habits of truth.

As Christians, we are supposed to love our neighbors, not be friends with them. If your neighbors, colleagues, family, or friends are not actively seeking God and trying to live their lives in accordance with biblical principles, then please be careful before they pull you away from our loving Heavenly Father, Yahweh.

Novemeber 10th Jesus's Baptism Was Predicted and Written Down 500 Years Before His Birth

"You should know and understand that from the issuing of the word to restore and to rebuild Jerusalem until Messiah the Leader there will be 7 weeks, also 62 weeks…" (Daniel 9:25).

Did you ever think about how time was split in half by the birth of Jesus? Every date in the world is either Before the Common Era (BCE) or Common Era (CE),

Before Christ (BC) or After Christ (AC). Jesus split time in half

Today's scripture comes from a prophecy given to Daniel about 500 years before Jesus was born. It says that the from the time that Nehamiah and the Jews are given permission to rebuild the temple which the Babylonian's destroyed, it would be 69 (7+62) weeks of years. A week is 7 days. So 7 days x 69 weeks equals 483. Change 483 into years and we now know when Jesus would be start his ministry.

King Artaxerxesv gave Nehemiah permission to rebuild the temple in the 20th year of his reign, or 455BCE. 455BCE plus 483 years is 29CE.

Simple math then tells us the exact time of the Messiah. It points to 29CE. This was when Jesus was baptized and started his 3.5-year ministry. This is why Herod was waiting for the Messiah so he could kill him. This is why the disciples we waiting for a messiah. This is why Simeon was waiting to see the Anointed one before dying.

November 11th Hearing "Well Done" from Yahweh is the only Recognition we Need

"His master said to him: 'Well done, good and faithful slave! You were faithful…" (Matthew 25:23).

Many people these days are hungry for reassurance, approval, or recognition. This could be the employee who works too hard to get his Boss's approval or it could be a teenage girl who only feels loved if she is in a relationship. Some young men join gangs to get recognition and approval while others find their identities within their online videogame community. But this should not be so. The only approval we should ever seek is the approval of our loving Father, Yahweh.

Jesus reminds us in Matthew 25 that our goal is to hear our master say to us at the end of our lives "well done good and faithful servant." Yahweh has blessed us with so many talents and abilities and gifts. And so we must use them for His glory and invest them in His service. The only recognition we truly need comes from Him. If we allow ourselves to accept glory or recognition from others, especially those who do not know or love Yahweh, then our priorities are wrong.

We must only seek Yahweh's approval.

November 12th Prophecy is Wonderful yet Scary

"So my word that goes forth from my mouth will prove to be. It will not return to me without results, but it will certainly do that in which I have delighted, and it will have certain success in that for which I have sent it. (Isaiah 55:11)

If Yahweh says something will happen, it will happen. This is why Prophecy is so wonderful and yet also scary.

Prophecy is wonderful because when Yahweh says it is going to happen, it is going to happen. This helps us strengthen our faith in Yahweh. This helps us to put our trust and belief in Him. It is so wonderful to see something prophesied years or centuries earlier come true.

But prophecy is also scary because once it is written, it will be so. For example, we know that in the end times the great and fear inspiring day of Yahweh is coming (Revelation 16:14). This is going to be a wonderful, yet scary day. We know that in the end times people will not be able to buy or sell without having the "Mark of the Beast" on their hands or heads (Revelation 13). And if you have the "Mark of the Beast" then you will not make it into the Kingdom of God. So how will those who love Yahweh buy and sell food?

We who love and honor Yahweh can trust that He will provide for our safety. Nonetheless, we know through prophecy that we will see some exceptionally wonderful and scary events in the years to come.

November 13th Joyfulness, Anxiety, Prayer, and Peace.

"Always rejoice in [the] Lord. Once more I will say, Rejoice! Let YOUR reasonableness become known to all men. The Lord is near. Do not be anxious over anything, but in everything by prayer and supplication along with thanksgiving let YOUR petitions be made known to God; and the peace of God that excels all thought will guard YOUR hearts and YOUR mental powers by means of Christ Jesus." (Philippians 4:4-7).

This brilliant scripture gives us great advice about Joyfulness, Anxiety, Prayer, and Peace.

Joyfulness: Philippians 4:4 is a wonderful reminder to get over ourselves and to rejoice, regardless of our circumstances. Yes, life can get very hard. But the blessings of life always outweigh the temporary pain of our circumstances. So regardless of what is going on around us we need to rejoice and be joyful to God for the privilege of life.

Anxiety: We are told not to be anxious about anything. This means we are not supposed to be overwhelmed by circumstances or fears. Of course, we all get anxious. But the solution is prayer, not dwelling on our worries.

Prayer: God hears our prayers. So when we need something, we should ask Him in prayer. When praying, we also are encouraged to let God know we are thankful for all His blessings. Prayer also helps us become closer to our loving God, Yahweh.

Peace: Admitting that we need God's help is an effective way to take some of the stress off of our shoulders. Being thankful for what we have, perhaps even giving thanks in prayer for some of these blessings, is a way to focus on positive things, not on our worries. When we pray, God gives us peace which will help us to endure any day, any situation.

November 14th Think Positive be Positive

"Finally, brothers, whatever things are true, whatever things are of serious concern, whatever things

are righteous, whatever things are chaste, whatever things are lovable, whatever things are well spoken of, whatever virtue there is and whatever praiseworthy thing there is, continue considering these things" (Philippians 4:8).

Today's "Word of Wisdom," a continuation of yesterday's scripture, encourages us to think positively. If we think positively, we will be positive. If we think negatively, we will be negative.

Your thoughts effect your disposition. Have you ever noticed that positive people are always positive, even in bad circumstances, while negative people are always "downers," even in the best of circumstances?

Being positive not only brightens your mood, it affects so many other aspects of your life to include performance, relationships, and of course your health.

Because there is a lot of sadness and evil in the world it is easy to be focused on negative things. But when your glass is always half empty, rather than half full, your negative perspective influences your health, your relationships, and your conduct. So choose not to be negative, but instead focus on things which are positive.

God doesn't want us to be naïve / dumb or to ignore the problems of the world. But He does want to focus more on positive things like love and truth and righteousness.

Todays scripture is a simple recipe for a happy life. Think positive be positive.

November 15th Be Careful not to Associate with Bad People

"I have not sat with men of untruth; And with those who hide what they are I do not come in. I have hated the congregation of evildoers, And with the wicked ones I do not sit" (Psalm 26:4-5).

The bible gives us plenty of good advice concerning friendships, partnerships and with whom we should or shouldn't spend time. Today's scripture gives us a good example set by King David who did not become friends with "men of untruth," men who "hide what they are," "evildoers," and "wicked ones." For obvious reasons these men are not the kind of associates we want for ourselves. And we can be assured that our loving Father Yahweh would not want us to waste our time with these types of people.

If you want to be wise and live in accordance with biblical principles then you can follow King David's example in this scripture by not associating with evil or wicked people. You should spend time with those who love God and want to encourage you to be more like His son, Jesus.

November 16th God is an Environmental Activist

"… and your own wrath came, and the appointed time for the dead to be judged, and to give [their] reward to your slaves the prophets and to the holy ones and to those fearing your name, the small and the great, and to bring to ruin those ruining the earth." (Revelations 11:18).

Although we like to think of Yahweh Almighty as a loving God we can't forget that he is a God of justice. And when He renders His justice in the future, He will clearly pay back those who are ruining the earth. Although it will be just, it will be sad for those who value making money more than protecting the environment.

What this scripture tells us is that we all need to continue to take care of our Father's magnificent creation. What a blessing this earth is. May we all do our share to keep it healthy.

November 17th Biblical Fashion Advice (part 1of 7)
God is the Best Fashion Designer

"Accordingly, as God's chosen ones, holy and loved, clothe yourselves with the tender affections of compassion, kindness, humility, mildness, and patience" (Colossians 3:12).

Today is the first of a six part series entitles "Biblical Fashion Advice." Our loving Father doesn't care if we wear Gucci, Prada, or Louis Vuitton as long as we also clothe ourselves with the tender affections of compassion, kindness, humility, mildness, and patience.

Far too often these days we see people who dress like misfits. In accordance with modern fashion trends, they wear worn and torn clothes, skull heads, spikes, piercings, and tattoos. Sadly, their eyes and their character are similar to their dark and selfishly tough outfits.

On the other side of the spectrum are fashionistas or the ultra-rich who wear designer clothes and tailored suits.

Sadly, their eyes and their character are similarly dark and selfish. They just hide behind a nicer ensemble.

Regardless of being posh / elegant or grungy / edgy, Yahweh cares about your heart. He wants you to be compassionate, kind, humble, mild, patient. If you have these qualities in your heart it will reflect in your eyes, your character, and in the way people see you. And nothing could be more beautiful.

November 18th Biblical Fashion Advice (part 2 of 7) Strip off your old Personality

"…Strip off the old personality with its practices, and clothe yourselves with the new personality, which through accurate knowledge is being made new according to the image of the One who created it" (Colossians 3:9-10).

Too often good fashion advice is about what to wear. But today, the second day of fashion week at Apply Wisdom.com, we are going to focus on what not to wear.

God tells us through His scriptures that we are supposed to "strip off our old personality" so we can cloth ourselves with the new personality. Characteristics of the old personality are found in Ephesians 4: 22-30 and include corruption, deceptive desires, falsehood, stealing, trash talking, malicious bitterness, anger, wrath, screaming and abusive speech.

If you have been changed by Yahweh's loving kindness then you must strip off these unsightly characteristics and put on the beautiful and fashionable new personality of love.

November 19th Biblical Fashion Advice (part 3 of 7) Clothe yourselves with Love

"But besides all these things, clothe yourselves with LOVE, for it is a perfect bond of union" (Colossians 3:14).

If you have been changed by Yahweh's LOVE then you show it by clothing yourself with LOVE.

How much LOVE should you wear? All of it….all you've got. When you are wearing LOVE you are never overdressed.

LOVE transcends all things. Whenever you are in an ambiguous situation, LOVE is the answer. LOVE is the "default setting." Jesus' favorite tactic was LOVE. God was motivated by LOVE. Jesus gave Himself for us out of LOVE. The commandments are summarized by LOVE. Everything we do should be the result of LOVE. Every blessing we have is a result of Yahweh's LOVE.

So when you get dressed today (or any day) don't forget to put on your most important fashion accessory: LOVE.

November 20th Biblical Fashion Advice (part 4 of 7)
Wear your Body Armor

"Stand firm, therefore, with YOUR loins girded about with truth, and having on the breastplate of righteousness, and with YOUR feet shod with the equipment of the good news of peace. Above all things, take up the large shield of faith, with which YOU will be able to quench all the wicked one's burning missiles. Also, accept the helmet of salvation, and the sword of the spirit, that is, God's word (Ephesians 6:14-17).

Living each day in a way which honors our heavenly Father and mirrors His love to those around us is not an easy assignment. Today's scriptures was written by Paul while he was imprisoned in Rome. No doubt Paul was inspired by his circumstances (imprisoned and guarded by a Roman soldier) to think of the struggle to be a good Christian as a war, one in which we need to dress ourselves like a soldier, prepared for daily battle with the world.

Ephesians 6 reminds us to have all of our clothes secured by the belt of truth, to wear righteousness over our hearts, to have our feet firmly planted on a solid foundation of peace. We must accessorize by carrying a protective shield of faith, putting on the helmet of salvation, and brandishing the sword of the spirit of the word of God. Note that all our clothing is defensive, passive, and protecting, except for the sword, which is the word of God. We can swing and slash our way through the battle of life by using heartfelt, but true, loving words of wisdom from the scriptures.

Today, rather than putting on your favorite jeans and hoodie, dress like a soldier and get ready to lovingly win the war for your soul.

November 21st Biblical Fashion Advice (part 5 of 7) Yahweh Forbids Tattoos and Cuttings

"And YOU must not make cuts in YOUR flesh for a deceased soul, and YOU must not put tattoo marking upon yourselves. I am Yahweh" (Leviticus 19:28)

God's standard for our beauty and health forbids us to get tattoos and to cut ourselves. The bible is very clear about this point and so there is nothing to debate.

True Christians should not have a tattoo, think about getting a tattoo, or even think that tattoos are cool. When God forbids something then it is obviously something bad. So we shouldn't covet that which is bad (Psalm 97:10)[22] and think Tattoos are cool.

If you knew this scripture and still got a tattoo, then shame on you. You are not smarter than God. If you have a tattoo, but just learned this scripture, then seek forgiveness and prayerfully consider what you should do next.

As children of God we are supposed to be recognized by our love (John 13:35)[23]. We are not supposed to be recognized by our tattoo artwork or cuttings.

---

[22] Psalm 97:10 "O you who love Jehovah, hate what is bad"
[23] John 13:35 "By this all will know that YOU are my disciples, if YOU have love among yourselves."

Stop trying to look like the people of this world (who are nothing more than passengers on a sinking ship) and start living and dressing in accordance with biblical standards, Yahweh's standards.

November 22nd Biblical Fashion Advice (part 6 of 7) Men Dress like Men and Women Dress Respectably

"No garb of an able-bodied man should be put upon a woman, neither should an able-bodied man wear the mantle of a woman; for anybody doing these things is something detestable to Yahweh your God" (Deuteronomy 22:5)

Men should dress like men and women like women. This is the biblical standard for apparel and fashion. Modern day unisex fashion is not what God prescribed or condones. Perhaps one reason Yahweh is so adamant about men dressing like men and women dressing like women is that God wants people to accept their roles in the family. For example, He doesn't want a man to be complacent and let his role as "head of the household" be transferred to his emancipated wife.

God further reminds us that **"women should adorn themselves in respectable apparel, with modesty and self-control..."** (Colossians 3:13). Christian women are supposed to dress in respectable apparel, with modesty.

We cannot and should not dress like the shameless people of this world. God is not against looking our best, but spending too much time and too much money on our appearance is silly.

God sees our hearts and we should spend all our time and money and efforts making sure that our hearts, not our cloths or hair, are our most beautiful feature.

November 23rd Biblical Fashion Advice (part 7 of 7) Don't worry about It

"Also, on the matter of clothing, why are YOU anxious? Take a lesson from the lilies of the field, how they are growing; they do not toil, nor do they spin; but I say to YOU that not even Sol′o·mon in all his glory was arrayed as one of these. If, now, God thus clothes the vegetation of the field, which is here today and tomorrow is thrown into the oven, will he not much rather clothe YOU, YOU with little faith? So never be anxious and say, 'What are we to eat?' or, 'What are we to drink?' or, 'What are we to put on?' For all these are the things the nations are eagerly pursuing. For YOUR heavenly Father knows YOU need all these things" (Matthew 6:28-32).

The above wisdom comes from Jesus during his famous Sermon on the mount. The three biggest takeaways here are (1) don't worry about it, (2) God will provide, and (3) perhaps what you are already wearing is exponentially more beautiful than any designer outfit.

(1) Don't worry about it: If you worry about fashion then you are rich and chances are that you have more clothing and shoes and jackets than 90% of the rest of

the world. Poor people worry about not freezing tonight or having one complete pair of shoes. Rich people worry about what shoes go with a specific outfit. Clothes and fashion styles come and go. But wearing the new personality and dressing yourself with love will never go out of style. So don't worry about it.

(2) God will provide: Even Jesus, who had no earthly riches, wore a seamless tunic, one which the Roman guards fought over and one which must have taken someone 6 months of loving care to stitch for him. If you have more than one pair of shoes and two hoodies then God already has provided for you. You are warmer and more stylish than 7 billion other people alive today. That is a blessing.

(3) Perhaps what you are already wearing is exponentially more beautiful than any designer outfit: Prada, Louis Vuitton, Channel, and Alberta Ferretti make lovely clothing. But nothing is more beautiful than seeing someone who loves God and has a pure heart.

November 24th Thank God

"Thank Yahweh, proclaim his name, make known among the peoples his deeds; Sing for him, make music for him, review all his wonders, Boast of his holy name, let the hearts of those who seek Yahweh be glad. Look to Yahweh and his strength; always be looking for his face. Remember his wonders that he has done, his miracles and the judgments of his mouth," (1st Chronicles 16:8-12).

This is the season of Thanksgiving in the United States and so we must take a few minutes to reflect on the magnificence of our heavenly Father, Yahweh, and give Him thanks and praise for all His many blessings and loving kindnesses.

We all have so much for which we can be thankful. And yes, we can and should be thankful to our earthly fathers, husbands, and caretakers who work hard to provide for our well-being. But we must ultimately be thankful to the One who gives us life, teaches us to love, and provides for our eternal well-being.

Today scripture is a song that the Israelites sang in thanksgiving to Yahweh once they had returned the Arc to the Tent of David. We, too, can sing these same words, even today, because we want to proclaim and glorify His name (Yahweh), sing and make music for Him, think about His wonders and the magnificence of creation and life, and ponder His strength, miracles and judgements.

Yes, Yahweh is the One to whom we must always be thankful… today, this season, and forever.

November 25th Destroy Sinful Desires

"Deaden, therefore, your body members that are on the earth as respects sexual immorality, uncleanness, uncontrolled sexual passion, hurtful desire, and greediness, which is idolatry. On account of those things the wrath of God is coming…" (Colossians 3:5-6).

God wants us to be holy, righteous and clean, and tells us to deaden ourselves to sin in its different forms. What this means is that we must kill off every aspect of our lives which could potentially support sin.

Deaden yourself to potential sources of sexual immorality. Root out and destroy all sources of materialism.

What it comes down to is do you love God more than sin? If you love yourself more than God and think sin will make you happy, then you will always find a way to let sin in. But if you hate sin and love God, then you will kill off every potential sin and deaden yourself to sin's influence.

In order to have Yahweh's approval we must **"hate what is evil and love what is good"** (Amos 5:15).

November 26th Put up with Annoying People

"Continue putting up with one another and forgiving one another freely even if anyone has a cause for complaint against another. Just as Yahweh freely forgave you, you must also do the same" (Colossians 3:13).

Put up with one another: This is sometimes hard because people can be so annoying and selfish. Putting up with someone doesn't mean that you have to "like" them, but it means that you have to "love" them. "Liking" them might mean spending time with them. And the bible tells us that we should only spent time with fellow believers. But "loving" them means always being kind and watching for opportunities to witness to them (through our conduct or through what we say).

Forgive Freely: When Jesus tells us to forgive someone "**seven time seventy times**" (Matthew 18:22), he is reminding us to forgive over and over. Even if someone is hard to put up with, we are required to forgive them. This doesn't mean that we allow them to walk all over us. Perhaps you should simply avoid that person. But when you do meet them and they are silly or dumb or mean, then forgive them, show them love and respect, and perhaps one day win them over.

As Yahweh has forgiven us, we must forgive others: YHWH's invitation for forgiveness is always extended to us. Some take it and others don't. In similar fashion, our forgiveness must also always be extended to our neighbors.

November 27th Be Understanding and Forgiving

"Stop judging that YOU may not be judged; for with what judgment YOU are judging, YOU will be judged; and with the measure that YOU are measuring out, they will measure out to YOU" (Matthew 7:1-2).

Yahweh will forgive you in the same way you forgive others. If you are spiteful, mean and unforgiving, then it is not going to go well for you on Judgment day because Yahweh will judge you in a spiteful, mean and unforgiving way. And we don't want that. However, if we are loving, understanding, and forgiving then Yahweh will be loving, understanding, and forgiving to us as well. This concept is easy to understand and remarkably consequential when put into practice.

So be as loving, kind, understanding, and forgiving as possible today and always because that is how we want our all powerful, heavenly Father to be towards us.

November 28th Don't Waste your Time

"Do not give what is holy to dogs, neither throw YOUR pearls before swine, that they may never trample them under their feet and turn around and rip YOU open." (Matthew 7:6).

Yes, Jesus said that we are supposed to make disciples of all nations (Matthew 28:19)[24]... but he also gave us some shrewd advice in the scripture above about not wasting our time.

Jesus reminds us that some people are such "dogs" that we don't need to waste our timing talking to them about what is holy. Some people are such "pigs" that we shouldn't waste our time giving them our pearls of wisdom.

The world is full of dogs and pigs, so don't waste your time ministering to them. Don't waste your time being friends with them. And for sure, please, don't waste

---

[24] Matthew 28:19 "Go therefore and make disciples of people of all the nations, baptizing them in the name of the Father and of the Son and of the holy spirit."

your time being yoked together with them in business or in marriage.

Like all animals, we also love pigs and dogs. So love them, but don't waste your time or wisdom on them.

November 29th Yahweh is One

"Listen, O Israel: Yahweh our God is one Yahweh. And you must love Yahweh your God with all your heart and all your soul and all your vital force" (Deuteronomy 6:4-5).

Yahweh is one. What does that mean? For sure it means two things. (1) Yahweh is the only God, (2) Yahweh is not half god or partly god or part of a group or team (trinity).

(1) Yahweh is the only God. There is no other god. There are no other gods. Allah and Buddha are false and powerless gods. Period. Only Yahweh made the heavens and the earth, created life, and deserves our worship.

(2) Yahweh is not half god or partly god or part of a group or team (trinity). Yahweh isn't Jesus. Yahweh made Jesus. Jesus is the 1st born of all creation. Yes, Jesus has been delegated many powers and authorities. But Yahweh is the only God and Jesus is His son. There is no trinity.[25]

---

[25] If you have any questions with this please do your research and find that the evil and false doctrine of the

In order to acceptably love Yahweh our God with all our heart, soul, and strength, we must know and recognize that He alone is God.

November 30th God's Wisdom is so much better than Human logic

"Happy [or blessed] are those conscious of their spiritual need, since the kingdom of the heavens belongs to them. Happy are those who mourn, since they will be comforted. Happy are the mild-tempered ones, since they will inherit the earth. Happy are those hungering and thirsting for righteousness, since they will be filled. Happy are the merciful, since they will be shown mercy. Happy are the pure in heart, since they will see God. Happy are the peaceable, since they will be called 'sons of God'" (Matthew 5:3-9).

This is the beginning discourse of Jesus's famous "Sermon on the Mount" which reminds us that God's wisdom is so much better than human logic.

Human logic says that "Happy" or "Blessed" are you when you "know it all" and are accomplished and self-righteous. But Yahweh's wisdom tells us that those who worry about their spirituality are the blessed ones, they will be allowed to live in the Kingdom of God.

Human logic says that "Happy" or "Blessed" are you when you are rich and can safeguard yourself with

---

trinity was invented by the catholic church. The word "trinity" is not even in the bible.

riches and big walls and locked doors. But Yahweh's wisdom tells us that He will comfort those who are vulnerable and mourn.

Human logic says that "Happy" or "Blessed" are you when you are strong, confident, assertive, and sassy. But Yahweh's wisdom tells us that the mild-tempered ones will live forever on earth in the Kingdom of God.

Human logic says that "Happy" or "Blessed" are you if you party and have fun and fill your life with entertainment and happiness. But Yahweh's wisdom tells us that those hungering and thirsting for righteousness will find what they are looking for.

Human logic says that "Happy" or "Blessed" are you if you are strong and powerful. But Yahweh's wisdom tells us that those who show mercy will receive mercy.

Human logic says that "Happy" or "Blessed" are you when you are cosmopolitan and tolerate all beliefs and ideas. But Yahweh's wisdom tells us that only those who are pure of heart will see God.

Human logic says that "Happy" or "Blessed" are you when you fight for what is yours and win. But Yahweh's wisdom tells us that only those who are peaceable will be associated with God's family.

God's wisdom is so much better than human logic. May we follow His directions, not ours, His wisdom, not ours.

December 1st   Expect Unrighteous People to be Dumb to You

"**Happy are those who have been persecuted for righteousness' sake, since the kingdom of the heavens belongs to them. Happy are YOU when people reproach YOU and persecute YOU and lyingly say every sort of wicked thing against YOU for my sake. Rejoice and leap for joy, since YOUR reward is great in the heavens; for in that way they persecuted the prophets prior to YOU**" (Matthew 5:10-12).

If you love God and actually put into practice the life changing wisdom He gives us through the Bible then people are going to hate you. But this has always been the case… before Jesus, for Jesus, and now. As an example, think of how Jeremiah was punished for speaking the words of God. Yet, he was proved right because what he prophesied came true in his own lifetime and "**wisdom was proved righteous by its works**" (Matthew 11:19). Recall how the people "scornfully laughed" at Jesus when he said that the little girl was only sleeping? Yet Jesus raised her from the dead.[26] Remember how the religious leaders called Jesus a liar and heretic and manipulated the justice system so as to have him killed? I guess they weren't that righteous after all.

So don't be surprised when modern day self-righteous people look down on you for being obedient to the bible and then go off to practice their sins or false traditions. Don't be surprised if your family and former friends

---

[26] Matthew 9:24-25

hate you because you are applying a bit of wisdom to your life. Sadly, this persecution has many precedents and is quite normal. So rejoice when the world thinks you are crazy because you worship and follow Yahweh. For sure be loving, but quietly and confidently know that we are on the side of truth and that they, in fact, are the crazy ones.

December 2nd Salt and Light

"YOU are the salt of the earth; but if the salt loses its strength, how will its saltness be restored? It is no longer usable for anything but to be thrown outside to be trampled on by men. YOU are the light of the world. A city cannot be hid when situated upon a mountain. People light a lamp and set it, not under the measuring basket, but upon the lampstand, and it shines upon all those in the house. Likewise let YOUR light shine before men, that they may see YOUR fine works and give glory to YOUR Father who is in the heavens." (Matthew 5:13-14).

Salt. Let's take a minute to think of salt as an illustration of "holiness and purity." As Christians, we are supposed to be salty (holy and pure). Sadly, it only takes a second to ruin something holy or pure. And once it is ruined, dirty, and no longer salty (holy and pure), it takes so much more work to make it clean again. Jesus even says that the unsalty salt is good for nothing and is thrown outside. So please be careful to remain uncorrupted by this dirty world and to maintain your Christian saltiness (purity and holiness).

Light: Jesus further says that his disciples should let their love shine so brightly that when people see it, they will give glory to our heavenly Father. So now you must ask yourself: Does the light of my love shine at all? Can others see, feel, experience the light of my love? And does my love shine so brightly that it brings Yahweh Glory?

December 3rd Jesus didn't destroy the Law but Followed and Fulfilled It

"Do not think I came to destroy the Law or the Prophets. I came, not to destroy, but to fulfill; for truly I say to YOU that sooner would heaven and earth pass away than for one smallest letter or one particle of a letter to pass away from the Law by any means and not all things take place. Whoever, therefore, breaks one of these least commandments and teaches mankind to that effect, he will be called 'least' in relation to the kingdom of the heavens. As for anyone who does them and teaches them, this one will be called 'great' in relation to the kingdom of the heavens." (Matthew 5:17-19).

Jesus did not come to destroy the law but to fulfill it. Jesus further says that every single word of the law will come true and that those who teach others to break the law will be called "least" in relationship with the kingdom of the heavens.

Since Jesus was the last sacrifice for sins, there is no longer a need for worshipers of Yahweh to make animal sacrifices. As a Christian you are supposed to offer yourself as a living and pleasing sacrifice to God.[27] Since God's people no longer live in the Sinai desert we are no longer under the purity laws of the camp. However, normal food and hygiene rules still apply because they were given for our benefit. Since there is no longer a tribe of Levites who minister at the Temple of God in Jerusalem, we no longer need to give 10% of our produce and money to the Levites. Nevertheless, Yahweh does want us to be generous and loving with our talents and possessions. Jesus showed us that we can and should be loving and helping on the Sabbath, but he still honored the Sabbath, and he did so on Saturday, not Sunday.

December 4th You better Be more Righteous than your Minister or Priest

"For I say to YOU that if YOUR righteousness does not abound more than that of the scribes and Pharisees, YOU will by no means enter into the kingdom of the heavens." (Matthew 5:20).

It is easy to presume that religious leaders are more righteous and holy than "normal" people. But occupation has very little to do with righteousness, and sadly most Christian Ministers and Priests are less concerned with righteousness and truth and more concerned with teaching the traditions of their denomination and seminary instructors. (And of course, their second priority is keeping the pews full of people who donate tithes and offerings.)

---

[27] Romans 12:1

Modern religious leaders so obviously love themselves and the attention they get being on stage, writing the latest book, delivering a "charming" but watered-down sermon… They are no more righteous than the Pharisees of Jesus's day. Please make sure that you are more righteous than they are. In fact, the only person you should measure yourself against is Jesus. He, not a faker modern day religious leader, should be your measuring stick for righteousness.

December 5th Only Get Appropriately Angry

"YOU heard that it was said to those of ancient times, 'You must not murder; but whoever commits a murder will be accountable to the court of justice.' However, I say to YOU that everyone who continues wrathful with his brother will be accountable to the court of justice; but whoever addresses his brother with an unspeakable word of contempt will be accountable to the Supreme Court; whereas whoever says, 'You despicable fool!' will be liable to the fiery Ge·hen′na" (Matthew 5:21-22).

God lovingly gave us a full range of human emotions. Although we are supposed to be known for our love, sometimes it may be appropriate to express your anger. Jesus expresses his anger several times in the bible. Most people easily remember when Jesus overthrows the money changers at the temple. But when Jesus rebukes the religious leaders to their face he clearly is angry at their unrighteousness and hypocrisy. It is very insightful that Jesus is only angry in the bible when confronting the hypocrisy of the faker religious leaders. Modern religious leaders are just as hypocritical as the

Pharisees of Jesus's day. Today's scripture reminds us that although there may be appropriate times to be angry, we are not to remain angry. So don't be afraid of anger, but keep it in check. Make sure it is caused because of injustice or unrighteousness, not because of selfish reasons. And then get over it, quickly, and go back to being ruled by the law of love.

December 6th Always be Good to Others

"Do not withhold good from those to whom you should give it if it is within your power to help" (Prov. 3:27).

Paying attention to the needs of others is a great way to put others first and to reflect the love of God. Too often people are only focused on themselves and are never able to notice others, let alone notice their needs. If you see someone who needs some encouragement, give it. If someone needs a few dollars for groceries, then help them out. If someone needs a job and you can get them one or give them one, then take a risk and invest in them. Loving our neighbor is a commandment, so we must always look for ways to show Gods love to those around us.

December 7th Don't put religious ceremonies ahead of reflecting God's love to your family.

"If, then, you are bringing your gift to the altar and you there remember that your brother has something against you, leave your gift there in front of the altar, and go away; first make your peace with

your brother, and then, when you have come back, offer up your gift." (Matthew 5:23-24).

God's wisdom reminds us of the importance of being at peace with your family. A person might be doing something important for God… in this example a man is giving a gift at the altar. But even if he is doing something important for God, he must stop it immediately, go reconcile himself and be at peace with his brother.

Of course, we are to place our love to Yahweh as the first and foremost priority of our lives. But if we are not reflecting God's love and forgiveness to our own family then what is the point of our religion, what is the effectiveness of our religion? Don't put religious ceremonies ahead of reflecting God's love to your family.

December 8th Justice is a Rare Occurrence these Days.

"Be about settling matters quickly with the one complaining against you at law, while you are with him on the way there, that somehow the complainant may not turn you over to the judge, and the judge to the court attendant, and you get thrown into prison. I say to you for a fact, You will certainly not come out from there until you have paid over the last coin of very little value" (Matthew 5:25-27).

Criminals go free because of a procedural technicality. The innocent victim is counter-sued by the larger company. Not the one who was right but the one with the best lawyer wins. People lie and judges have favorites.

These are flaws in the systems and until God's Kingdom brings justice we will only have a poor shadow of it.

If you have a legal issue with someone it is very probable that you are not going to get justice. In today's illustration, a complaint is lodged against a person. Perhaps it is founded. Perhaps it is unfounded. Nonetheless, Jesus suggests that he should settle matters quickly before going to court. If he does go to court it is possible that he will be much worse off than before. Today's scripture reminds us that justice is a rare occurrence these days. So let us all ask Yahweh to help us be patient and wise as we wait for His kingdom to come.

December 9th Mind Your Own Business

"YOU heard that it was said, 'You must not commit adultery.' But I say to YOU that everyone that keeps on looking at a woman so as to have a passion for her has already committed adultery with her in his heart." (Matthew 5:27-28).

Jesus' words definitively tell us that a man should only have one wife and that he must remain absolutely loyal to her.

The expressions "so as to have passion for her" obviously means not to lust or covet, but it also touches upon the truth that the eyes see, then the heart wants.

Jesus is telling men to stop looking at any woman (on the street, in the car beside you, on TV, on the advertisement, or in a magazine) because it will entice your heart to sin.

Polygamy is officially declared immoral and outside the will of Yahweh. Jesus tells you to not even look at woman who is not your wife. This is because you are supposed to honor your wife and keep love pure. If you have a second wife it would be impossible to not look at her. So Jesus is mandating that men are to only have one wife.

Women, aren't you happy that Jesus commands men to be loyal to their wives, outlaws polygamy, and demands purity within marriage?

December 10th Masturbation is a Sin so Don't do it.

"If, now, that right eye of yours is making you stumble, tear it out and throw it away from you. For it is more beneficial to you for one of your members to be lost to you than for your whole body to be pitched into Ge·hen′na. Also, if your right hand is making you stumble, cut it off and throw it away from you. For it is more beneficial to you for one of your members to be lost than for your whole body to land in Ge·hen′na." (Matthew 5:29-30).

Sexual sin and lust will prevent you from entering the Kingdom of God. When Jesus says in Matthew 5:29 that it would be better to have one eye then have both and be thrown into Gehenna (which means total destruction) it is obvious that Yahweh doesn't tolerate sexual sin and lust.

Masturbation is immoral. Don't do it. Jesus' reference to the right hand in Matthew 5:30 is a discreet way of saying don't masturbate. Control your sexual urges, wait until you are married, and make a lot of wonderful love with your equally yoked, obedient, loving, real Christian spouse.

December 11th Only Marry Someone who Loves Yahweh

"Moreover it was said, 'Whoever divorces his wife, let him give her a certificate of divorce.' However, I say to YOU that everyone divorcing his wife, except on account of fornication, makes her a subject for adultery, and whoever marries a divorced woman commits adultery" (Matthew 5:31-32).

The difficulty of living a life with someone stupid is why our loving Father reminds women to only marry a man who lives all his life in accordance with biblical truth. The bible warns us not to be unequally yoked with nonbelievers. (2 Corinthians 6:14) **do not become unevenly yoked with unbelievers. For what fellowship do righteousness and lawlessness have? Or what sharing does light have with darkness?**

In the sad case that you are married to someone stupid or you violated biblical guidance and did not marry someone who lives their life in accordance with biblical principles, you must love them so well that they come into the truth. (Peter 3:1-2) **In like manner, YOU wives, be in subjection to YOUR own husbands, in order that, if any are not obedient to the word, they may be won without a word through the conduct of [their] wives, because of having been eyewitnesses of YOUR chaste conduct together with deep respect.**

No marriage is divorce proof. But if you marry a pagan then you can't expect them to love you as a reflection of their love for Yahweh. You can't end a marriage for any old reason. Jesus makes it clear in today's scripture that the only acceptable reason to get divorced is when someone sexually betrays the marriage. So please make sure that you marry someone who loves God and loves you.

December 12th Let you Words be a Reflection of Your Integrity

"Again YOU heard that it was said to those of ancient times, 'You must not swear without performing, but you must pay your vows to Yahweh.' However, I say to YOU: Do not swear at all, neither by heaven, because it is God's throne; nor by earth, because it is the footstool of his feet; nor by Jerusalem, because it is the city of the great King. Nor by your head must you swear, because you cannot turn one hair white or black. Just let YOUR word Yes mean Yes, YOUR No, No; for what is in excess of these is from the wicked one" (Matthew 5: 33-37).

Jesus reminds us to be men (or women) of our words. If we say so then it is so. If we say no, then it is no.

We are not supposed to talk trash or be ambiguous or renege on our obligations.

Many people today need to qualify what they say: "This is a true story," or "I promise on my mother's health," or "I swear to God," or "Trust me."

We shouldn't have to say things like this because we live our lives so honestly and honorably that everybody sees that when we say something we do it. People should be impressed with our righteousness and always trust that our no is no and our yes is yes. Are you a person who follows through with what you say?

December 13th How Pure is Your Heart?

"For the eyes of Yahweh God run back and forth throughout the whole earth, to show himself strong in the behalf of them whose heart is perfect toward him" (2 Chronicles 16:9).

Yahweh God can see things about you that no one else can see. Nice things, bad things, hidden things, the inner thoughts and desires that your family and friends have no idea are even floating around in your heart and mind. God sees them all.

Because our heavenly Father searches the entire earth to find those whose heart is perfect toward him, we should do our best every day to please him.

Consider that the text does not say "who are perfect." None of us are perfect. We are all sinners. Yahweh God knows this. But He does look for true perfection in the heart. He sees the way we are deep in our heart and not just the person we display for others.

Are you doing nice things for others, making charity, or donating a lot of money to cover up the mean-spirited person you really are? Are you the example of all the six things Yahweh God hates, or the seven things that He detests mentioned in Proverbs 6:16-19? What motivates you to do certain things? Is it to see and be seen? Is it because people expect you to do nice things because you claim to be a Christian? Do you do nice things because you are obligated to do them or because you want to do them?

Working on your heart is the most important aspect of being a true Christian. We can hide our true heart from others but not from God's eyes. Think about your heart and how God sees it.

December 14th   Don't Get Even. Don't Win. Be Generous

"YOU heard that it was said, 'Eye for eye and tooth for tooth.' However, I say to YOU: Do not resist him that is wicked; but whoever slaps you on your right cheek, turn the other also to him. And if a person wants to go to court with you and get possession of your inner garment, let your outer garment also go to him; and if someone under authority impresses you into service for a mile, go with him two miles. Give to the one asking you, and do not turn away from one that wants to borrow from you [without interest]" (Matthew 5:38-42).

Because God's ways are so much bigger and better than our ways, it is no wonder that today's scripture goes against everything that the world teaches.

The world says that if you are slapped you better fight back and win. Yahweh's wisdom tells us to love our neighbors and to turn the other cheek.

The world says that if you go to court you should pay for the better lawyer and win. Yahweh's wisdom tells us to love our neighbors and to give the complainant what he wants.

The world says that you should make lots of money and buy expensive things. Yahweh's wisdom tells us to love our neighbors and to be generous.

Please don't listen to the wisdom of this failing world. Instead, Apply Wisdom from Yahweh.

December 15th Love your Enemy

"YOU heard that it was said, 'You must love your neighbor and hate your enemy.' However, I say to YOU: Continue to love YOUR enemies and to pray for those persecuting YOU; that YOU may prove yourselves sons of YOUR Father who is in the heavens, since he makes his sun rise upon wicked people and good and makes it rain upon righteous people and unrighteous. For if YOU love those loving YOU, what reward do YOU have? Are not also the tax collectors doing the same thing? And if YOU greet YOUR brothers only, what extraordinary thing are

YOU doing? Are not also the people of the nations doing the same thing" (Matthew 5: 43-47)?

What an amazing scripture…a game changing paradigm shift from justice and selfishness to love. It says that a true Christian is so full of God's love that he even loves his enemies. Do you do that? You better. Yahweh expects you to.

Think of the person or people you consider your enemy? Who is that? Who are they? What have you done recently to love them? Have you been nice to them? Have you been generous to them? Do you pray for them? Have you talked to them about Yahweh or tried to share how they can apply Yahweh's wisdom? Doing so may change them from an enemy into a brother or sister….it might just save their lives.

December 16th   The Bible Forbids Eating or Drinking Blood

"However, by no means eat the blood, for the blood is LIFE itself--you must not eat the life with the meat" (Deuteronomy 12:23)

The Bible forbids us to eat or drink blood. Period. This scripture is crystal clear and there is no room for misinterpretations, right?

Watching a commercial the other day I realized how "common and normal" it is getting to eat blood. In many cultures and countries, it is on the food list. For example, the Germans commonly eat Blood Sausage or

"Blutwurst" and the British frequently eat the same but call it "Black Pudding."

A true Christian wants to be obedient to God and to live with a clean conscious. Right? A few years ago I addressed this subject in a bible group and some students justified their disobedience by referencing Mark 7: 18-19 where Jesus declares all foods as "clean."

"Right," I told them, "all foods." I reminded them that food is clean, blood is forbidden! God precisely makes a distinction between what He gave us humans for food and what is forbidden.

God clearly considers blood as "life itself," not as a food substitute like an apple, a slice of meat or a piece of bread. Let us be obedient Christians and enjoy the great multitude of wonderfully good food which God provides for us. To eat blood shows disrespect for life and for our God who gives it. Eating blood is a sin against Him!

December 17th Are You Trying Hard Enough?

"YOU must accordingly be perfect, as YOUR heavenly Father is perfect" (Matthew 5:48).

Yahweh God knows that humans are weak and prone to sin. He further knows that the "world is lying in the hands of the evil one" (1 John 5:19) and that it is particularly hard to live an obedient life based on the biblical principle of love.

But just because Yahweh forgives us doesn't mean that He should have to forgive us. We should try to be like Jesus, to be sinless, so we don't need His forgiveness. Remember, Adam and Eve were sinless until they ate the forbidden fruit. Jesus was sinless for 33 years. It is possible to live and be sinless. But to do so you are going to have to prioritize Yahweh over yourself, truth over lies, and obedience over selfishness. It is possible to be sinless and so we must try to be perfect like Jesus, our example.

December 18th It Doesn't Matter who is President or King

"The king's heart is in Yahweh's hand like the watercourses. He turns it wherever he desires" (Proverbs 21:1).

The 2016 U.S. Presidential Election was particularly nasty and divisive. Dirty, undignified, and embarrassing accusations between candidates were presented on a silver platter to the rest of the world. What a shame. Donald Trump, Hillary Clinton, their two vice presidential nominees, Mike Pence and Tim Kaine, and the other 2016 presidential candidates were all guilty.

Many of you have probably wondered "how should a true Christians have voted in 2016?" The thoughts running through my mind were never "if a Christian should vote in this corrupt system" or "for whom should a true Christian vote." No, I do not address these questions because a true Christian should know the right answer in his heart.

Today's scripture reminds us that God holds the heart of a king in His hand and that He can turn the king wherever He desires. Yes, God can control all kings. But not all kings represent Yahweh. Don't forget that Yahweh only anointed Kings to rule over his people in ancient Israel. The next King which Yahweh has appointed to rule in the soon to come Kingdom of God is the best King ever - his beloved son Jesus Christ.

Don't forget that when Jesus himself was asked about a political matter he answered "my kingdom is not of this world." So think about this dear readers… and don't forget that the WORLD is lying in the hands of the Wicked ONE! It doesn't matter who is king or president. Our hope is in the Kingdom of God and we must pray for an extra dose of love and endurance as we wait for it to arrive.

December 19th Yahweh is always as Near to you as you want Him to Be

"Keep on asking, and it will be given YOU; keep on seeking, and YOU will find; keep on knocking, and it will be opened to YOU. For everyone asking receives, and everyone seeking finds, and to everyone knocking it will be opened. Indeed, who is the man among YOU whom his son asks for bread—he will not hand him a stone, will he? Or, perhaps, he will ask for a fish—he will not hand him a serpent, will he? Therefore, if YOU, although being wicked, know how to give good gifts to YOUR children, how much more so will YOUR Father who is in the heavens give good things to those asking him" (Matthew 7:7-11).

Yahweh is always as near to you as you want Him to be. If you keep Him at an arms distance, He will stay at arms distance. Keep Him in a box and He will stay in the box. Keep Him at church and He will stay at church. If you want Him as priority one in your heart then, He will be priority one in your heart. If you ask for wisdom, you will receive Yahweh's wisdom. If you seek God, you will find Yahweh. If you knock at the door of life changing truth enough, it will eventually open up for you.

Yahweh loves you and wants the best for you. In turn, you must love yourself enough to know that you require Yahweh in your life. And once you know that you require Him in your life, you can ask for Him, and receive, seek Him, and find. Yahweh is always as near to you as you want Him to be.

December 20th The Golden Rule

"All things, therefore, that YOU want men to do to YOU, YOU also must likewise do to them; this, in fact, is what the Law and the Prophets mean" (Matthew 7:12).

Many people know the "Golden Rule" but they don't know that Jesus said the Golden Rule and that it is recorded in the Bible.

The Golden Rule doesn't say that if you are nice to others then others will be nice to you. It doesn't say that if you are loving to others and generous then others will be nice and generous back to you. It would be awesome if it worked this way. But it doesn't. Sadly, in today's selfish world, it is more likely that if you are nice and loving and generous to others, they will take advantage of you.

We can't control how others act or behave or believe. But we can control how we act and behave and believe. So regardless of the consequences, we should be nice, loving and generous. Yahweh wants us to reflect His love to others. So do to others what they will likely not do back to you….but what you hope that they would do back to you.

December 21st The Road Leading to Destruction is Huge

"Go in through the narrow gate; because broad and spacious is the road leading off into destruction, and many are the ones going in through it; whereas narrow is the gate and cramped the road leading off into life, and few are the ones finding it" (Matthew 7:13-14).

Sadly, 23% of the people of the world follow the false religion of Islam, 16% are unaffiliated, 15% are Hindu and believe in myriads of false gods, and 7% worship the false and powerless god, buddah[28]. This makes 61% of all people or about 4.25 billion people. 31% of the world are Christians but of those Christians, most are fakers. They worship with their mouths but not with their hearts. They aren't obedient to the bible and are not known for their love. How many Christians out

---

[28] https://en.wikipedia.org/wiki/List_of_religious_populations

there actually know that God's name is Yahweh, that the Sabbath is Friday sunset until Saturday Sunset, that Jesus died during Passover, not Easter, or what the Kingdom of God is? Billions have the potential to enter the Kingdom of God but they are all driving down the super highway towards destruction. Only a few million live in accordance with biblical principles, love Yahweh with their all, love their neighbors as themselves, and will make it into the Kingdom of God. The super highway towards destruction or the small road to everlasting life….which road are you driving on?

December 22nd Beware of Ministers / Priests who are Wolves in Sheep's Clothing

"Be on the watch for the false prophets that come to YOU in sheep's covering, but inside they are ravenous wolves. By their fruits YOU will recognize them. Never do people gather grapes from thorns or figs from thistles, do they? Likewise every good tree produces fine fruit, but every rotten tree produces worthless fruit; a good tree cannot bear worthless fruit, neither can a rotten tree produce fine fruit. Every tree not producing fine fruit gets cut down and thrown into the fire. Really, then, by their fruits YOU will recognize those [men]" (Matthew 7:15-20).

Because a tree is known by its fruit, it is easy to see if a minister is a faker or a hypocrite or a liar. Simply look at his fruits. Who cares if he has a PHD in Theology or graduated from a fancy seminary or university. If his fruits are hypocritical or unbiblical then he is a wolf in sheep's clothing. Below are the 16 Easiest Ways to tell if your Minister / Priest is a wolf in sheep's clothing:

1. He doesn't know or use the name of God: God has a name. His name is YHWH (pronounced Yahweh). His name is not Allah, God, or "the LORD." Yahweh wants us to know, use, and glorify His name.

2. He teaches the unbiblical doctrine of the trinity: The word "trinity" is not found in the bible. The trinity is a terrible lie and a false tradition made up by the catholic church. The truth is that YHWH is the only, true God, Jesus is His son, and holy spirit is another way to describe YHWH's power.

3. He celebrates Easter: Only an idiot teaches a lie about Easter being Jesus' resurrection even though Jesus was clearly killed during Passover (Nissan or Abib the 14th) and not during a pagan holiday to honor a false fertility god.

4. He celebrates Christmas: A hypocritical minister / priest teaches a lie about Christmas being Jesus' birthday even though it is an adopted pagan holiday to celebrate the winter solstice.

5. He doesn't honor the Sabbath on Saturday. Yahweh commands that we honor the Sabbath on Saturday. Yahweh never gave the horribly corrupt and hypocritical Catholic church permission to abolish the Saturday Sabbath in order to create a sacrilegious tradition for a "Lord's day" on Sunday.

6. He doesn't understand suffering and says stupid things like "God gives you a trial to make you stronger." God is love. God doesn't not cause pain and suffering. Suffering is the result of (1) Satan, (2) Human Sin, and or (3) Chance / Unforeseen circumstances.

7. He worthlessly baptizes babies, kids, and adults who don't understand or live lives in accordance with biblical principles. Baptism is for those who understand biblical principles, are obedient to them, and who want to dedicate their lives to Honoring YHWH.

8. He has a cross in his church or around his neck. YHWH clearly tells us in Exodus 20 and Deuteronomy 5 not to make images and statues of things and worship them. Yet, the faker protestant and catholic churches love to make images of a suffering and or dead and powerless Jesus on a cross and worship it. They pray to the cross. They pray at the cross. They finish prayers by making the sign of a cross. The instrument of Jesus death is not something to celebrate. If your son was innocent yet put to death in the electric chair or via lethal injection would you walk around with a gold electric chair or medical syringe hanging proudly around your next? Of course not!

9. He prays to Mary, saints, or to Jesus. The bible shows us that we are only supposed to pray to Yahweh. Mary and old catholic saints are dead and powerless. Praying to them is a waste of time and is called "Spiritism," which is strictly forbidden in the bible. Faker Christians all over the world pray to Jesus. Yes, we are to give thanks and ask for things in Jesus' name. But YHWH

is the hearer of prayers. Yahweh is the giver of power and blessings. Yahweh, alone, is God.

10. He promotes celibacy: Celibacy is a very rare selection / gift made my someone so he can fully dedicate himself to serving Yahweh. Many faker religions and their leaders violate the biblical requirements to "be fruitful and multiply" by mandating celibacy for clergy, monks, and nuns. Satan leads those denominations and is effectively killing off the blood line of anyone whose heart is inclined to worship Yahweh.

11. He teaches that communion is literally the body and blood of Jesus. Please know that eating the actual body and drinking the actual blood of Jesus is impossible, weird, super creepy, and a violation of biblical laws and principles. Communion is symbolic. Think of Jesus' life and sacrifice when you have bread and drink wine. But better yet, honor Jesus' sacrifice by living a life consistent with the living word of God.

12. He teaches that the bible is a wise story, relative and applicable only 2000 years ago. The bible is not a fun story to read but is the living and active word of God. It is not to be played with or interpreted. It is to be obeyed.

13. He is a woman: YHWH loves women and wants them to be empowered, loved, and led by Godly men. But men, not women, were designed by YHWH to lead the church and family.

14. He is Catholic: The Catholic Church violates so many Biblical truths. Its priests are doubly hypocritical

because they know that they work for such a corrupt and worldly organization yet they keep teaching hypocrisy, false traditions, and lies instead of Biblical truth.

15. He is a Chaplain: Chaplains serve Satan and his delegated representatives in the nations in contrast to the will of YHWH and in violation of biblical principles. A chaplain prays for soldiers who go off to war in support of that nation's objectives. But to maintain his job he never has the courage to say that his government, the war, or his commanders are immoral. This faker Christian supports his nation at the cost of watering down the truth of the scriptures. Just think of Lutheran chaplains in Germany praying for God to bless their soldiers as they went off to kill Americans during WW1. Or just think of Lutheran chaplains in the USA praying for God to bless their soldiers as they went off to kill Germans. Who decides which side has God's blessing? It certainly isn't the Pope.

16. He uses the word "journey" as in we are all on a "journey" or we are at different places in our "journey." Only faker Christians use the word Journey. We are not all on a journey to the common goal of everlasting life in heaven where we joyfully live as reincarnated fat baby angels. You are either on the side of truth and Yahweh… or you are not on the side of truth and Yahweh. Life is not a journey but is a gift from our Father who deserves and demands worship, love, and obedience.

Likely, your Minister / Priest is, in fact, a Wolf in Sheep's clothing. And so we recommend that you leave your church / cathedral / denomination immediately and live a life in accordance with biblical principles. A true Christian doesn't need a denomination but needs to be close to YHWH.

December 23rd Not all Self-Claimed "Christians" are making it into the Kingdom of God

"Not everyone saying to me, 'Lord, Lord,' will enter into the kingdom of the heavens, but the one doing the will of my Father who is in the heavens will. Many will say to me in that day, 'Lord, Lord, did we not prophesy in your name, and expel demons in your name, and perform many powerful works in your name?' And yet then I will confess to them: I never knew YOU! Get away from me, YOU workers of lawlessness" (Matthew 7:21-23).

This is an essential scripture for understanding obedience. We see that Jesus, the fair judge, will say he never knew people in verse 22 who call Jesus "Lord, Lord" and who did amazing works in his name. Back in the time of Jesus, to say someone's name twice was to imply intimacy with them. This means they loved Jesus. To call Jesus LORD (all capital letters) would mean that they confused him (Jesus) with Yahweh. So to call him Lord (Only the L in capital letters) means their doctrine was correct and they knew Jesus to be their master, leader, and the son of God. And wow, these people did great works like prophecy and expel demons. Yet, Jesus never knew them. Simply loving Jesus is not enough. And having correct doctrine is not enough. And doing great works is not enough. Obedience to Yahweh is perhaps what makes the difference.

December 24th Obedience Helps you Weather the Storm

"Therefore everyone that hears these sayings of mine and does them will be likened to a discreet man, who built his house upon the rock-mass. And the rain poured down and the floods came and the winds blew and lashed against that house, but it did not cave in, for it had been founded upon the rock-mass. Furthermore, everyone hearing these sayings of mine and not doing them will be likened to a foolish man, who built his house upon the sand. And the rain poured down and the floods came and the winds blew and struck against that house and it caved in, and its collapse was great" (Matthew 7:24-27).

A house made in the USA which passes code may still be made of 2x4 inch beams, particle board, paper insulation, and drywall. Sadly, we see that these houses blow away the second a strong wind blows though.

In contrast, a house made in Switzerland is required to be made of brick, has a concrete foundation, and will never blow away. The walls of a Swiss friend's lower budget apartment are 30cm or 12inches thick concrete brick. That is why many houses in Europe are a thousand years old and most houses in the USA fall apart after 20 years.

The bottom line is that if you build something to last forever it lasts forever. If you build something to look nice, it blows away with the first storm.

Our lives are very similar in that if we are obedient to what Jesus says and modeled, then we will build a family (house) that has a strong foundation and will last forever, literally. But if we only care about looking good and we are not obedient to the bible, then the first storm of life will blow us away.

Please reassess your life and build it upon a solid foundation of belief and obedience. We don't want to be blown around by the changing winds of popular ideas, but want to last forever and make it into the soon coming Kingdom of God.

December 25th Jesus has Astonishing Wisdom and Authority

"Now when Jesus finished these sayings, the effect was that the crowds were astounded at his way of teaching; for he was teaching them as a person having authority, and not as their scribes" (Matthew 7:28-29).

Astonishing Wisdom: When was the last time you were astonished? Jesus wisdom is astonishing and we would all be happier and more at peace if we followed his life changing wisdom. Let us commit to listening to and obeying what Jesus says.

Teaches with Authority: It is always impressive to listen to someone who is an absolute subject matter expert, knowing every single facet and detail of His subject. Jesus was that way about life. His father created life and as the first born of creation, Jesus taught with astonishing wisdom and authority. In contrast to the scribes of ancient Israel who merely echoed and parroted the traditions of their Jewish leaders, Jesus spoke the very words and principles of our sovereign God, Yahweh. Instead of following the false traditions of your modern catholic or evangelical church leaders, perhaps you should follow and apply the authoritative wisdom of Biblical truth.

December 26<u>th</u> God's Time is Not Our Time

"For a thousand years are in your eyes but as yesterday when it is past, And as a watch during the night" (Psalm 90:4).

Time is the word that men use to describe the power that makes thing change.

How wonderful it will be to see Yahweh's Kingdom come. Yet, according to the bible, it has been almost six thousand years since the fall of Adam and Eve. But what are six thousand years to Yahweh, our eternal and timeless Father? They are like 6 days. Soon the suffering and sin of this world will come to an end and we can enjoy everlasting life in the Kingdom of God.

If Yahweh's Kingdom would have come yesterday or last year then there would have been no hope for many. But He continues to be patient. Perhaps one of the many reasons He is so patient is so you can have your eyes opened to see biblical truth and to apply some wisdom to your life.

December 27th   Yahweh Reveals Big Things Through His Prophets Before Hand

"For the Sovereign Lord Yahweh will not do a thing unless he has revealed his confidential matter to his servants the prophets" (Amos 3:7).

Yahweh God likes to tell people what He is going to do before He does it. This allows Him to (1) be loving and warn people and (2) receive glory for holding the future in His hand.

Loving and Warning People: A perfect example of this is the great flood. Yahweh warned everyone. Yet no one listened. Only Noah and his immediate family were saved. Another example was when the prophets warned the Hebrews to honor Yahweh or else they would be conquered. Sadly, the Hebrews did not honor Yahweh and so Yahweh had to punished them by the hands of the Babylonians.

Receiving Glory: Only the one true God fully knows the future and can receive glory from predicating what will happen. A great example is when Yahweh revealed to Daniel (chapter 9:25), hundreds of years before Jesus was born, the exact year Jesus' ministry would begin and end. Yahweh used Micah to tell where Jesus would be born (Micah 5:2). The bible records hundreds of prophecies which came true many years later. All of this should bring even more Glory to our loving and amazing, all-powerful, living God, Yahweh.

There are relatively few prophecies which still must be fulfilled before the coming of the Kingdom of God. Do you know what they are? Are you prepared?

December 28th Don't Rejoice when your Enemy Suffers

"When your enemy falls, do not rejoice; and when he is caused to stumble, may your heart not be joyful" (Proverbs 24:17).

As true Christians we are supposed to be known by our love. Our conduct should come from the overflow of our pure and loving hearts. This loving conduct must be towards the good and the bad, the ones we love and those who are more challenging. Don't forget, Jesus tells us to love our enemies.

Today's scripture reminds us that we are not supposed to be happy when our enemy stumbles or falls. Because we are supposed to be loving to all, we cannot laugh and be happy when someone suffers. A great example is when the famous Muslim terrorist, Osama bin Laden, was killed. There was rejoicing in the streets of the so called Christian nation of America. This was the wrong conduct because we are supposed to be sad when someone dies, even if that person is our enemy.

So the next time you see your enemy fall on his face, don't rejoice, but be there to pick him up. Maybe you can win him over into the Kingdom of God through your unexpected loving conduct.

December 29th Don't Envy Wicked People

"**Do not become envious of wicked people**" (Proverbs 24:19).

The heroes of this world are not going to make it into the Kingdom of God. The heroes of Hollywood, the political leaders of this world, the Pope, and other wicked people might have power and money and success in this world, but they are not going to enter the kingdom of God. The inspired Bible reveals a truth which most people seem to ignore: **the unrighteous will not inherit the kingdom of God** (1 Corinthians 6:9). This concept is repeated so many times throughout the bible that it is impossible to dismiss.

So don't envy wicked people and don't make them your heroes. This world is quickly passing away and those who are first in the world will be last in the next.

December 30th Don't be Lazy

"**I passed along by the field of the lazy individual, and by the vineyard of the man in need of heart. And, look! all of it produced weeds. Nettles covered its very surface, and its stone wall itself had been torn down. So I proceeded to behold, I myself; I began taking [it] to heart; I saw, I took the discipline: A little sleeping, a little slumbering, a little folding of the hands to lie down, and as a highwayman your poverty will certainly come and your neediness as an armed man**" (Proverbs 24:30-34).

God's wisdom is so wonderfully simple in today's scripture: If you are lazy, your fields will be full of weeds and you will soon be living in poverty. Not many of us are farmers, but we all can understand the principles at work in today's proverb.

Although life is a huge gift and meant to be enjoyed, there are always things to do. Clean your house, clean your neighbor's house, refine your budget, love your neighbor, do more bible study, cook for a friend, write a card, visit someone sick… If you spend too much time in front of the television or playing video games or announcing how awesome you are on Facebook then you are going to neglect the way more important matters and will soon be in spiritual, if not literal, poverty.

December 31st Apply Wisdom

"The proverbs of… the son of David, the king of Israel, for one to know wisdom and discipline, to discern the sayings of understanding, to receive the discipline that gives insight, righteousness and judgment and uprightness, to give to the inexperienced ones shrewdness, to a young man knowledge and thinking ability." (Proverbs 1:1-4).

The purpose of the book of Proverbs, as written in today's scripture, is to help others know and apply wisdom. This is the same purpose of Apply Wisdom.com. We hope that the "Words of Wisdom"© series, and our books and articles also have helped you to apply wisdom, get disciplined and be disciplined, discern the more important spiritual matters of the world, gain understanding, insight, righteousness, shrewdness, knowledge, and the ability to think for yourself.

The bible is the ultimate source of wisdom and we hope that you read it, study it, and live in accordance with it. Our goal is that someday soon you will stop reading what we at ApplyWisdom.com have to say and only seek wisdom directly from the bible. But until then, we are happy to keep pointing you towards Yahweh and to help you to apply His loving and life-changing wisdom.

Conclusion

If you are looking for a recommendation as to what to do with your new found biblical knowledge….then I recommend you

1. Don't be a hypocrite. Stop follow man made traditions which violate biblical truth. This is going to hurt a bit but will be worth the effort. It is more important to please Yahweh than to please your local minister and friends.

2. Be strong. Self-righteous people are going to be angry at you because you want to stand up for what the bible says and no longer want to blindly follow traditions.

3. Rely on Yahweh through prayer and enjoy the peace that He gives you as a result of being obedient to His rules for life.

4. And most importantly….. let your life be governed by love. Lovingly answer people who ask you why

you are different? Love Yahweh your God and love your neighbor. (Matthew 22: 37-40) **'You must love YHWH your God with your whole heart and with your whole soul and with your whole mind.' This is the greatest and first commandment. The second, like it, is this: 'You must love your neighbor as yourself.' On these two commandments the whole Law hangs, and the Prophets.**

Apply Wisdom.com is modern theological consulting and an online Christian ministry dedicated to providing biblical, insightful, and pragmatic concepts to make your life better.

www.ingramcontent.com/pod-product-compliance
Lightning Source LLC
Chambersburg PA
CBHW071556080526
44588CB00010B/925